I0796707
STEREO
LONDON
45r.p.m.
TOP-1558
何かいいことないか子猫チャン
WHAT'S NEW PUSSYCAT ?
TOM JONES
ローズ

The Transplantable Roots of Catharine Huws Nagashima

Susan Karen Burton was born in Scotland, raised in New Zealand and has spent most of her working life in Japan. She began her career as a Japan Exchange and Teaching (JET) Programme assistant language teacher (ALT) in Hamamatsu, Shizuoka prefecture. She was later a Ministry of Education, Culture, Sports, Science and Technology scholar at Tsuda Juku University in Tōkyō. After gaining her doctorate in history from the University of Sussex, she lectured in Japanese universities for ten years before returning to the UK to complete a second doctorate, in creative nonfiction, at the University of Anglia. Her research interests include the recording of oral history, especially of the migrant experience in Japan.

FLAMEBASTER

The Transplantable Roots of Catharine Huws Nagashima

Encounters with the Welsh in Japan

Susan Karen Burton

Foreword by
Lord Gregory Mostyn

PARTHIAN

Parthian, Cardigan SA43 1ED
www.parthianbooks.com

Print ISBN 978-1-917140-43-0
Ebook ISBN 978-1-917140-44-7
Editor: Gwen Davies
Cover design and typesetting by Syncopated Pandemonium
Printed by 4edge
Published with the financial support of
the Books Council of Wales
British Library Cataloguing in Publication Data
A cataloguing record for this book is available from the British Library.
Printed on FSC accredited paper

This book was written with the support of the Daiwa Anglo–Japanese Foundation.

Contents

In memory of Sue Harvey, Rose Iwata and Kōichi Nagashima

Foreword

Lord Gregory Mostyn

One day in 2015, we were tidying up the library in Mostyn Hall when I was astounded to come across an old, dusty photo album. It looked as if it had been almost hidden, and yet by some luck we found it and began to flick through it. It is dated 1908, and chronicles my great-great-grandfather's journey through Canada and Japan with his wife and two children. It is filled with black and white photos, postcards and drawings of famous sights in Japan, including the Golden Temple in Kyōto, the beautiful castle at Nagoya and the red Shinkyō Bridge in Nikkō. Alongside all these fantastic and rare photographs is a diary, a daily update of what the family had done during their time thousands of miles away in far east Asia. They had ridden rickshaws, visited many shops and drunk tea with locals. Intriguingly, the album is almost a mirror into my own experiences of Japan.

In 2006, I had been celebrating finishing my university exams with my Japanese girlfriend at the time, and a very good friend of mine. We had time to burn as we waited for our results, and it was time to let off some steam. As morning approached, I wondered out loud what I was going to do: maybe get a job back down in London or go to some careers fairs. My friend said his path had already been decided: he was going to teach English in Japan. This was the spark that made me think: why not move to Tōkyō? I was clueless about the city, the country and the people, apart from that they liked sushi and had some fast trains. But it all made sense: I could stay with my girlfriend who was moving back to her homeland, I could join up with my friend who was going out there, and I could learn a new language and culture. Waking up the next day with a hangover, I told my parents that I was moving to Japan. They thought I had gone mad.

I applied online and went to a job interview in London. I was nervous as hell but got the job. I remember being sent in the post a CD and information pack titled *So You Are Going to Japan!* I threw it in the bin – I thought everything will be fine – I will arrive in Tōkyō, meet up with my girlfriend and friend, settle down, and it will be great! As I landed in Tōkyō in November 2006, I remember going to see my girlfriend, who told me to meet her at Shibuya station. We broke up instantly. Meanwhile, my good friend had relocated to Ōsaka. Maybe this wasn't such a good idea after all! I rang Mum and Dad the next day and said I wanted to go back to London, but they said, 'No no, stay in Japan, you've come this far and if it really doesn't work out, you can fly back whenever you want.' So I stayed, found a flat to move into in Tōkyō, and tried to find my bearings. This was back in the day with no Google Translate, no Google Maps, no online meeting websites or whatever. I soon found out that, boy, did I need to learn some Japanese! Ordering food, finding out where the toilets were – even which seat I could sit down on in the train – were all confusing.

It was very difficult in the beginning: Tōkyō can be a claustrophobic city, with tall skyscrapers hemming you in, masses of people walking all around you, shop signs leering down at you in a complex mess of characters. But with time, I learned to embrace it, and, as I met new people and got better at the language, I felt so at home. The people are kind and welcoming, and they are extremely helpful and polite, too. One day, I remember, after my Japanese had improved, I had dinner with an entire Japanese group, explaining to them in Japanese why my football team couldn't win a game. I thought, wow what is happening here? Then with the language came an improvement in an understanding of local customs. Don't cross the road when the light is red. Don't tip in restaurants. Apologise when you do something wrong. Some of my friends tell me that when I speak in Japanese, my entire body language changes to being more demure and shy. I have too many special memories to record them all here. The year I lived in Japan was simply the best year in my life. Japan is my favourite country in the world, and since 2007, I have been back there every year.

Which is why I was so surprised to see that album, showing that my family had made the trip before me, over one hundred years ago. After I found it, I decided to take my own photos of the same Japanese places the album explores: from Kyōto to Nikkō, from Nagoya to Yokohama. It took me three weeks, and involved many funny episodes. I made an album out of the 2015 photos, and that photo album currently lies side by side with the 1908 family album. Then in 2019, a producer from *Sekai Fushigi Hakken* heard about the old album and he wanted, as I had done, to find out why my family had gone to Japan in 1908. I appeared on TV and it was a great honour to show the volume;

even now, I can't believe the programme was actually viewed all across Japan.

The 2019 broadcast coincided with a dream that I have been pursuing in recent years: I love Wales and Japan a lot, and I would like to bring the two countries closer together. Since 2018, I have been attending events in Japan to promote Wales and Welsh tourism, and have been on Japanese television a few times while making speeches about my experiences in the country, the background of my family and their connection to it. I have also been giving Japanese-language tours, since 2019, for tourists who come to visit Wales. I think if anyone told me, in mid 2006, that this was what I would be doing now, I would have laughed straight back at them!

In any case, it was at one of these events in 2023, at a St David's Day dinner, that I met Susan Karen Burton, and spoke to her about her work developing *The Transplantable Roots of Catharine Huws Nagashima.* While I have written down here just a little snippet of my own story about my experiences in Japan, there are many more stories of Welsh people having their own adventures there. I think it is wonderful to see published such a wide range of encounters connecting Wales and Japan, and I'm sure you will enjoy reading the book as much as I have.

First Impressions 'It was a stupid, clichéd western–eastern culture clash'

Joe Cairnes: I still remember the feeling when the airplane door opened and that hot, humid blast of air hit me. I thought it was the effect of the jet engines, but no. I'm Welsh, I'm twenty-two years old and I was wearing T-shirts in the winter. So when I got to Japan, the heat was just debilitating.

Eddy Jones: It was all about how strange it was in terms of your physical feeling, and how your body responds to the place. And then the strangeness of the sounds, smells, the feeling of being completely lost. It was a complete misconnection of senses. You hear these stories of people who have got some kind of synaesthesia, somehow their senses get their wires crossed. I think there's that same feeling when you come here for the first time.

Eluned Gramich: Oh my goodness, I can't tell you what a shock it was. I remember the first night we arrived, obviously all jetlagged, and we had a surreal experience in a pizzeria in a metro station. We were given chopsticks and I remember us all looking at the chopsticks and poking at the pizza and wondering what we were supposed to do with it. It was a stupid, clichéd western-eastern culture clash. Then I went to my hotel room and I remember turning on the TV and seeing Japanese television, and just needing to turn it off because it was so overwhelming.

Clive Davies: As soon as I arrived, I felt more at ease than I've ever felt anywhere in my life. I don't know why but as soon as I landed in Narita there was something about the place. I felt instantly relaxed straight away. Of course, everything's very strange and alien and some things made me a bit nervous because you're out of your depth, especially language-wise. But for some reason I just felt that this is the place for me. And I still feel like that.

Abby Hall: I was never sure what I wanted to do in this life but for some reason Japan spoke to me. I'll be honest, it's not the country, it's not the people – while the country's lovely and the people are lovely.

I wouldn't say I'm a religious person. I wouldn't say I'm a spiritual person. But I have this feeling that this isn't the first time I've been here. It's such a strange thing to say. It's like I was returning to somewhere I've been before. Nothing here felt new to me. Yes, there are things that are really strange here. But it just doesn't feel foreign to me, it almost feels like home. For some reason, Japan speaks to me in a way that I cannot express even to this day.

Introduction

The First 'Welchman' in Japan

In the summer of 1619, three sailors lay chained in the hold of Dutch sailing ship, *The Angell*. Captured in a sea battle between the Dutch and the English off the coast of Java, they had been transported as prisoners to Japan. On the journey they were beaten, tortured and shackled beneath a waste pipe. The ship had dropped anchor in the middle of the bay of Hirado, a thriving trading post in the west of Japan, north of Nagasaki.

Observing *The Angell* from the shore was Richard Cocks, an employee of the East India Company and head of Hirado's English factory, a trading post housing the wares of the Honourable Company. Cocks had arrived in Japan in 1613 aboard *The Clove*, the first English ship to make landfall in the archipelago. When *The Clove* had departed six months later, Cocks and six merchants had been left behind to promote trading opportunities with the Japanese. A lack of subsequent ships, the poor quality of their cargoes, and Cocks' own preference for cultivating his vegetable garden over chasing sales opportunities, meant that the English factory's fortunes were suffering, especially compared to the Dutch factory nearby. Cocks made no attempt to rescue the sailors on *The Angell*. But someone else did.

The crew of *The Clove* were not the first Englishmen to set foot in Japan. Kent native, William Adams had arrived ten years earlier as the pilot of a Dutch vessel. Adams had narrowly escaped execution when the shogunate, the military leaders of Japan, realised his worth. Not only was he an expert pilot but he had previously trained as a ship builder. Now fluent in Japanese language and customs, Adams was also of great use to the men of the East India Company although they remained distrusting of his motives, suspecting he had gone native. But one sultry August night, Adams crept aboard *The Angell* and rescued two of the captured sailors.

The Dutch were incensed at the loss of their hostages. Such a daring feat could not be repeated. Yet the very next night, Adams climbed back aboard and freed the third man. Recounting this second rescue in a letter to the Company, Cocks noted that the third prisoner was a man called Hugh Williams. And he was 'a Welchman'.[1]

This is the first documented evidence of a Welsh native setting foot in Japan. But Williams probably wasn't the first Welsh sailor to step ashore in the archipelago. The early seventeenth century was a period of European exploration and expansion. The East India Company financed voyages in search of valuable and exotic cargoes: cotton, silk and tea from India, and pepper, cloves and nutmeg from the Spice Islands. Japan was viewed as a potential market for English products – calicoes, broadcloths, tools – which they could exchange for the country's rich deposits of silver. The 527-ton *Clove* had carried not only Richard Cocks but also a ship's company of sixty-three men, including a Thomas Jones, ship's baker, and a Christopher Evans, gunner's mate. We know something of them because their behaviour in Hirado was noted in letters and the ship's journals. Jones was caught trying to swim ashore at night to visit 'base baudye places' (brothels and drinking houses). Evans swam ashore repeatedly until he was dragged back and set in the 'bilbowes' (shackles).[2] He later absconded into the Japanese interior with six other crew members and was never seen again. It is possible that Jones and Evans were also Welsh, although we can't be sure because – with Wales having been unified with England under King Henry VIII – Welsh sailors were considered to be 'English' and listed as such on crew lists. But Wales is a seafaring nation and there can be no doubt that Welsh sailors were involved in the East India Company's first forays into Japan.

Wales has a long and continual history of migration. Welsh settlers have established settlements throughout the world, including farming villages in Canada, mining communities in Ukraine, and Y Wladfa, the Welsh colony in Patagonia. It is therefore no surprise that, four hundred years after Hugh Williams, Welsh citizens are continuing to travel to Japan and many are choosing to remain, some for a short time, others for life. As an oral historian with an interest in migration studies, I have spent many years recording interviews with foreigners who live and work in Japan, discussing their lives, their experiences, and their feelings about home, wherever that may be. In 2015, I travelled to the seaside resort of Zushi to meet a lady called Catharine Huws Nagashima. Sitting on tatami (rush matting) and sipping green tea, Catharine talked about hiraeth and the importance, despite sixty years living in Japan, of her Welsh roots. My account of the visit, 'The Transplantable Roots of Catharine

Huws Nagashima' (reprinted here in Chapter One), won the New Welsh Writing Awards Rheidol Prize for Prose with a Welsh Theme or Setting in 2020, and I was commissioned by *New Welsh Review*'s book imprint New Welsh Rarebyte to seek out more Welsh residents in the archipelago.

Unfortunately, Britain had just gone into Covid pandemic lockdown, and Japan's national borders were closed. No travel was possible. But there is a Japanese proverb which advises anyone planning a course of action to, 'sit on a rock for three years' (ishi no ue (ni mo) san nen). It means 'to be patient'. Exactly three years later, with the requisite three vaccinations and the support of a Daiwa Foundation grant, I was able to return to Japan to further interview its Welsh residents, to visit their homes and businesses, and to hear and record their stories.

This book features fifteen chapters about Welsh men and women who have spent an extended time in Japan. Although many of them initially moved to the country to teach English, either on the Japanese government's Exchange and Teaching Programme (JET) or for eikaiwa (private English language conversation schools), I have concentrated on those who are following other interests, either full time or as a hobby. I have tried to cover a wide range of lifestyles and interests, using interviewees' lived experiences to highlight aspects of Japanese culture as well as the joys and frustrations of everyday life as a gaijin (foreigner). Naturally, I also questioned them about their Welsh roots, their feelings about the concept of home and of hiraeth. Whether by accident or design, the majority of my interviewees could speak Welsh as well as English on departing Wales, a feature which in itself gave rise to interesting themes of language, identity, cultural sensitivity and ease of assimilation. In between the chapters, I have included themed extracts from many more interviews, to give voice to all the Welsh people I met on my journey.

According to Japanese population statistics, there are 19,040 citizens of the UK currently living in Japan: 14,005 male and 5,035 female.[3] While there is still no record of the number of Welsh included in these figures, if we estimate a figure based on the percentage of the UK population who are Welsh (4.5 per cent) that figure comes to 857.[4] The majority of these will be English language teachers who are likely to remain in the country for little more than a year or two. I estimate that there are probably two to three hundred Welsh living long term in Japan. That number may be higher, however, because Wales and Japan share a more recent history, and one which may have encouraged a higher percentage of Welsh to feel close ties to Japan. In the early seventies, with the decline of the Welsh steel industry and the closing of the coal pits (and job losses estimated in the hundreds of thousands), the Welsh Development Agency sought to attract large scale Japanese manufacturing.[5]

The 1964 Tōkyō Olympics signalled Japan's recovery from almost total destruction in the Second World War. As it entered a period of high economic growth, Japanese companies sought to establish overseas factories to meet the global demand for Japanese goods. Takiron, which made PVC corrugated sheeting, was the first company to open a factory in Wales, in Bedwas, Gwent, in 1972. Hitachi (Hirwaun), Sony (Pencoed and Bridgend), Panasonic (Cardiff, Gwent and Port Talbot) and many others soon followed, their factories primarily manufacturing consumer electronics such as televisions and video cassette players, of which Japan was a pioneer at that time. By the eighties, at the height of Japan's manufacturing capacity, Wales hosted the largest concentration of Japanese electronics companies outside Japan and the United States.

Many of the interviewees in this book have strong childhood recollections of the Japanese presence in Wales. Interviewee Geraint M remembers growing up near the Sony television plant and seeing the Japanese expatriate families around town:

> There seemed to be a Japanese community that arrived in the eighties. In the Rhondda there was a Burberry factory where they would make those Mackintosh things. And there was a factory shop. So, of course, you would see the Japanese couples who were obviously buying gifts, stocking up on the omiyage (souvenirs) from Burberry in order to take them home.

Ursula Bartlett-Imadegawa recalls the impact of Japanese management practices on the Welsh workforce:

> I can remember as a young girl watching the television, and the fascination with the new Japanese companies that came in. I can remember the newscaster interviewing this [Welsh] guy and he said, 'They have lunch with us in the same canteen. None of this "tablecloth in another room and the bosses over there". No, they eat the same as us.' And [he also] said, 'We couldn't believe it, they were moving something in and we suddenly realised it was a couple of ping pong tables. And

> then the boss turned up and played ping pong with us.'

This lack of segregation proved popular, particularly with former miners, as it mirrored the close teamwork necessary to ensure safety in the pits. Lacking a class-based hierarchy, it was also standard procedure in Japanese companies for blue collar workers, with the right training and attitude, to be promoted into management. Welsh workers could also profit from in-house training, which showed Japanese companies' commitment to employing workers long term. Expertise in factory floor practices such as kaizen (continuous improvement) and 5S workplace organisation – sort, set in order, shine, standardise and sustain – made welcome in other industries those Welsh workers who had been trained by Japanese companies.

The Japanese presence in Wales in turn stimulated exchange programmes, which gave some interviewees their first encounter with the culture. Translator Gareth Jenkins began learning the language at secondary school when Ceredigion County Council employed a Japanese teacher. He later did a two-week homestay in Japan, funded by the Aberystwyth–Kaya Friendship Association, a group started with the support of Frank Evans who had been a prisoner of war in Kaya during the Second World War. Gareth went on to study business studies with Japanese at Cardiff University before joining the JET Programme in 2001.

Several Welsh universities offer Japanese language and/or business studies courses, and some interviewees took advantage of these. Like Gareth, public relations consultant Abby Hall also studied Japanese and business at Cardiff University, then stayed on for a master's degree in Japanese translation before moving to Japan and establishing a career in public relations.

The global popularity of Japanese consumer electronics was swiftly followed by a wider appreciation of its arts and entertainments, which also played a part in tempting its Welsh fans to move to Japan. St David's Society Japan's president, Ursula Bartlett-Imadegawa discovered ukiyo-e woodblock prints and kabuki classical theatre in her Cardiff fifth form class, which led her to accepting a teaching post at an international school in Tōkyō. Video game localiser Geraint Howells grew up playing Japanese video games and now works for Nintendo. As a child, JET Programme participant, Bethany Jo Cummings' love of Studio Ghibli movies led to her hiring a private teacher so that she could take 'A' Level

Japanese in Porthcawl. Film writer/director/producer John Williams moved to Japan because of his love of Japanese arthouse movies. Teacher Eddy Jones first met CW (Clive William) Nicol at the Kotatsu Anime Festival in Wales where the environmentalist was promoting an anime (animated film) inspired by Afan no Mori, his forest in Japan. Ex-Cardiff nightclub bouncer Jaime Morrish was pulled to Japan by his black belt in jiu jitsu. Teacher Gerald Gallivan and Abby Hall both sport Japan-inspired tattoos (which ironically cause them problems in Japan).

Cultural exchanges work both ways. This book also features interviews with three Japanese citizens who spent time in Wales and who, through the St David's Society Japan, keep the Welsh spirit alive in their homeland. President of the St David's Society Japan's Kansai branch, Chikako Hirono spent six months teaching Japanese language and culture at a primary school in Cardiff. Dr Takeshi Koike teaches Welsh at his Tōkyō university, a language he first encountered on a one-year exchange programme in Lampeter. Former radio disc jockey, Yūko Nakauchi took a summer Welsh language programme in Lampeter and returned to study for an undergraduate degree in media studies, in Welsh.

When Japan fell into recession in the early

nineties, some Japanese factories in Wales closed or moved their operations elsewhere. But there are still sixty Japanese-owned companies in Wales today, and Japan continues to exert a strong economic and cultural influence on Welsh people.[6] For many of the interviewees in this book, the seeds of interest in Japan were planted back home in Wales, and for them, that contact has been life changing.

I timed my research trip to Japan for spring so that I could be there on St David's Day and attend the annual dinner of the St David's Society Japan. I would like to thank the members of SDSJ for their help and contacts, particularly club president, Ursula Bartlett-Imadegawa and club historian, Catharine Huws Nagashima. I am also grateful to the Daiwa Foundation for their financial support which enabled me to undertake research in Japan, and to my editor Gwen Davies for her patience during those three years when I had to bide my time 'sitting on a rock'.

I would also like to thank the following people for their help, advice and support: Bet Davies, Richard Powell (himself an ex-Japan resident), Lisa Fairbrother, Yuri Kusuyama, Gwen Norris, Helen Smith, Ve-Yin Tee, Ian Thomson, and the Tanaka family: Marico, Towie and Naho. Also, Norman and Sheila, my parents and beta readers.

Most of all, I would like to express my deepest thanks to the interviewees in this book who opened their lives and homes to me, and who answered my constant and intrusive questions with infinite grace and patience.

Shortly after winning the New Welsh Writing Awards, I zoom-called Welsh freelance journalist, Lily Crossley-Baxter. It was during the Covid pandemic lockdown, and she was living in – and largely confined to – a shared house in the Tōkyō suburbs. 'Would enough Welsh people want to speak with me about their lives in Japan?' I wondered.

'I reckon they would,' she answered. 'What's that saying? There's no better Welshman than a Welshman outside of Wales? They bloody love talking about it.'

They did bloody love talking about it. And I am grateful to all of them.

Chapter One

The Transplantable Roots of Catharine Huws Nagashima

Catharine Huws Nagashima

'I believe that it is a person who has roots who is able to transplant themselves and create new roots,' remarks Catharine Huws Nagashima as we eat our vegan lunch in the café bar of Cinema Amigo. Interviewees often say the most interesting things when I am not recording. My digital recorder is still in my bag so I scribble a note on a paper napkin.

It is a fresh spring day in the seaside city of Zushi, Japan. Pale sunlight arcs through long glass windows, playing over an eclectic assortment of dusty velvet cinema seats rescued, it seems, from derelict theatres. We pay at the bar, leave by one door and walk around the back to a much older part of the building, to a sukiya, a single-storey structure of thick beams and solid columns supporting an ornately tiled roof. In the porch we remove our shoes, pushing our feet into indoor slippers. Ahead a long corridor stretches into the shadows with sliding fusuma (opaque sliding panels) opening to high-ceilinged rooms left and right. This is Catharine's home, where she put down her roots. She has lived here since 1965.

Catharine with her parents, Edrica Huws (née Tyrwhitt) and Richard Llywelyn Huws, 1940

Catharine was born in London in 1938 to an English mother, the artist and poet Edrica Huws (née

Tyrwhitt), and a Welsh father, Richard Llywelyn Huws, the naval architect known for a series of kinetic water fountains he designed in the 1950s and 1960s. Evacuated from London during the Second World War, the Huws family settled in the village of Talwrn on the Isle of Anglesey in a nineteenth-century house with no electricity or running water. Yet the family lived well. Catharine's mother would despatch her and her sister to local smallholdings to offer tea and sugar from their wartime rations. In return, they were allowed to watch the milking, and were sent home with butter and eggs. Catharine, fluent in Welsh, assimilated into the landscape: she knew the steepness of every hill, what grew in every hedge and the name of every neighbour. This is where she put down her first roots. 'I felt in my heart that I was Welsh,' she says.

Catharine took her love of the landscape to the University of Wales, where she studied geography and became a passionate Welsh-language campaigner. In the holidays, she travelled in Europe and, in the summer of 1958, she flew to Greece to visit her aunt. Catharine's aunt was the town planner Jaqueline Tyrwhitt, an important figure in the postwar modernist movement in architecture. Then a professor of urban design at Harvard University, she was planning to build a house in the Attica peninsula on her retirement. Most summers she worked as an adviser to Constantinos Apostolou Doxiadis, known as the father of Ekistics.

Ekistics is the science of all human settlements, from the simplicity of a single room to the theoretical concept of a planetwide city. Doxiadis believed that designing a sustainable habitat was not solely a practical matter of construction and layout – the domain of architects and town planners – but also of building a community, requiring the expertise of sociologists, anthropologists and ecologists. To ensure a healthy and happy society, he believed, one needed to create harmony between people and their environment. The word Ekistics, which Doxiadis invented, derives from Greek, and encapsulates the concept of establishing a habitat, connecting networks, and becoming settled. It is the study of where and how you put down roots.

As nations sought to rebuild after the Second World War, Doxiadis' ideas gained traction, and his urban planning company opened offices on five continents. To encourage a wider dialogue in Ekistics, Doxiadis regularly invited experts from other fields to sail around the Aegean with him. These included Canadian philosopher, Marshall McLuhan (who coined the term 'the medium is the message'), American architect and futurist Buckminster Fuller (who popularised the geodesic dome), American cultural anthropologist Margaret Mead, and French geographer Jean Gottmann. 'He was interdisciplinary before being interdisciplinary had become fashionable,' observes Catharine, who met several of these famous figures. Catharine thought Doxiadis Associates a fascinating place, and dreamed of working there. In 1963, she could wait no longer. She quit her job in London and motored all the way back to Athens on her Austrian Puch scooter, working freelance until the company required a geographer.

Catharine on her Puch scooter, Aberystwyth 1960

Aunt Jaqueline had bought a plot of land but had yet to build her house. She was sharing a flat with Catharine in Athens when a Japanese former student from Harvard arrived. Kōichi Nagashima had just completed his master's degree in urban design and came to spend a year's fellowship at the Athens Center of Ekistics. Kōichi and Catharine had a lot in common. Aside from a shared interest in the landscape, they were both Catholic. Kōichi was fourth-generation Catholic, which is rare in Japan. Indeed, for over two hundred years, it was illegal. In 1638, with the proselytising presence of the Portuguese Catholics threatening to destabilise the rule of the bakufu, the military government, Japan closed its borders to westerners (except the Protestant Dutch) and massacred its remaining believers. Known as sakoku, this period of extreme protectionism lasted until 1853. Today, most Japanese identify as Shintō or Buddhist but the Nagashimas were very westernised, and this included their religion. Catharine and Kōichi married in Athens. When it was time for Kōichi to return to his work in Japan, Catharine went with him.

Catharine's textbook image of Japan was of a largely agricultural country. She imagined rice paddies and farmers in coolie hats. But from her work with Doxiadis she was aware that Japan was undergoing an urban transformation. Cities were expanding at such a rate that they were gobbling up surrounding towns to form a vast metropolitan landscape. This was creating the Tōkaidō megalopolis, connecting Japan's three largest cities: Tōkyō, Ōsaka and Nagoya.

The nation was also experiencing breakneck economic and technological growth. The year before Catharine and her husband arrived, the 1964 Tōkyō Olympics had heralded Japan's postwar recovery. Ten days before the games opened on 10 October, the first line of the Shinkansen bullet train began operating between Tōkyō and Ōsaka. Families rushed to buy television sets to witness Japan come third in the medal tables, winning sixteen gold, five silver and eight bronze medals. Only the United States and the Soviet Union gained more.

If the Olympics signalled Japan's return to the global stage politically and economically, the arrival in 1966 of two idols of the western popular scene really set it swinging culturally. That summer, The Beatles played the Budōkan stadium, while Sean Connery – as James Bond – sped through the neon-lit streets of a modernised Tōkyō, filming *You Only Live Twice.* This was the country in which Catharine was to put down new roots.

Kōichi was not entitled to live-in housing provided by his company. According to Japanese tradition, the eldest son and his wife were expected to reside with his parents, caring for them in their old age and inheriting the family homestead on their deaths. But the newly-weds wanted a place of their own, and they inspected several modern city apartments. Unfortunately, on Kōichi's salary, all they could afford was a single room of six woven tatami (rush) mats with a small kitchen and no garden. 'It was just so dreary,' remembers Catharine. 'I couldn't bear the thought of the two of us in a six-mat room with a view of a concrete wall.' Then Catharine's father-in-law offered them the use of an old summer house, south of Tōkyō in a seaside city called Zushi.

During the period of sakoku, no westerner had been permitted to settle in Japan. Any 'southern barbarian' who landed on Japanese shores was put to death. This situation lasted until the 1850s when Japan was reopened – by threat of force from American gunships – to global trade. Westerners were once again allowed to enter Japan but were initially restricted to a number of small foreigner-only settlements where merchant companies built warehouses and shops, and traded primarily in silk and tea.

The largest of these grew out of a little fishing village called Yokohama. The harbourside district of Yamate was home to a few hundred western bankers and merchants (predominantly British and American) and several thousand Chinese who acted as their managers and go-betweens. As restrictions on travel were gradually relaxed, westerners began to explore the surrounding countryside. Zushi on the eastern rim of Sagami Bay, a wide crescent of shallow water, soon developed as a summer resort, a place for businessmen and their families to sail and swim, away from the heat and humidity of the city. In 1894, the Japanese imperial family established a villa further along the coast in Hayama, while the increasing presence of writers and artists gave the area a bohemian feel. Today it is a middle-class commuter town one hour away from Shinjuku station in central Tōkyō. At weekends it is popular with boaties tracking fresh coastal winds and surfers chasing gnarly waves.

Seeking to emulate the relaxed lifestyle of the foreigners and aristocrats, in 1900 Kōichi's grandfather, a lawyer named Washitarō Nagashima, bought a plot of land in Zushi and built a wooden bessō (summer house) on it. During the Great Kantō Earthquake of 1 September 1923, a catastrophic event which devastated Tōkyō and killed over 140,000 people, the back part of the house collapsed. The remaining structure was dragged to more open ground and, whether by accident or design, turned ninety degrees. Before it could be restored to its original location, Washitarō Nagashima died and the house has remained out of kilter ever since. Today the house sits in the middle of a sloping garden with the Tagoe River flowing along its eastern boundary and down to the bay.

In the autumn of 1965, Catharine and her husband travelled down to Zushi to inspect the summer house. They found it on a narrow road lined with pines known as yashiki-dōri (street of residences) because of the number of bessō positioned along it. And it was nailed shut. This was common practice to deter burglars and to provide protection from typhoons when the house was unoccupied during the winter months. Doors would be locked from the inside and amado (storm shutters) pulled across the windows. But a handy feature in Japanese summer homes was an outside door in the bathroom which allowed bathers to run up from the beach and towel off without treading sand through the house. This too had been sealed at the end of the summer season but an uncle who lived next door and was acting as caretaker came and pulled the nails out for the couple.

Catharine wandered around the dark interior, her stockinged feet sinking softly into the rush matting of the tatami floors. She pulled back the fusuma to reveal a series of interconnected rooms of tea-brown wood with sepia-tinted walls. Kōichi's younger brother had sent him a telegram in Greece saying that the Zushi house was uninhabitable. What he meant was that his American fiancée would not live in a house without a flush toilet. But for Catharine, having grown up in rural Wales, this was not such a hardship. Immediately she decided, 'Oh yes, I can live here.' And they moved in.

'I mean, you can see it's a lovely place, isn't it?' she says today, standing among a lifetime's collection of rustic pottery, lacquerware, oil paintings, scroll wall hangings and books. We are in the main room, a warm, cluttered bric-a-brac shop of a space at least sixteen tatami wide with a fifteen-foot ceiling. It is a fusion of Welsh and Japanese heritages. On numerous cupboards, sideboards and drawers, sit clusters of small frames containing faded photographs of family members from both nations. In a corner rest two musical instruments. One is a Japanese biwa, a short-necked lute. The other is a harp.

The room has a wide tokonoma, an alcove where scrolls and flowers are placed for guests to enjoy. Propped to one side, almost hiding a large hole in a paper-thin wall, hangs an inky black-and-white photograph of Washitarō's kimono-clad father, one of Japan's last samurai. At one time he lived in Tsukiji, a

Tōkyō district with a large foreign settlement, where he drove a horse and carriage. It was one of his regular customers, a French missionary priest, who converted him and his family to Catholicism. On the opposite wall hangs one of Catharine's mother Edrica's artworks, a patchwork picture crafted from scrap materials, called 'The Birthday Bouquet'. 'That's what she would have liked to have woken up on her birthday to find,' reminisces Catharine wistfully. She moves to a narrow kitchen to brew a pot of green tea, padding to and fro in knitted layers and extra socks, her smoke-white hair tucked into her knitted cap. There are several low tables in the room, each piled high with books, bills and supermarket coupon leaflets. Catharine sweeps balls of wool from one and places a teapot on it. We kneel and tuck our legs underneath us. I take out my notebook. Catharine's lyrical voice is clear but soft, and I push my digital recorder across to her side of the table to catch every word.

When Catharine and her husband moved into the 'out of kilter' house, it had running water and, with the flick of a Bakelite switch, electricity. But bath water had to be heated by lighting a fire under the goemonburo (a cauldron bath) and burning combustible household rubbish and garden rakings. Ecologically, Catharine thought this was a good idea.

Catharine bathes a child in the goemonburo 'cauldron' bathtub

'I can put up with this for the sake of the environment,' she decided.

The squat toilet was an elegant ceramic bowl set into the floor above a large urn. Although there was a lid, Catharine had to be careful not to let anything fall in. If she lost an indoor slipper down the hole, it was gone for good. But if she dropped her purse, someone had to reach in and dig it out.

When the urn was full, Catharine would walk to a public telephone box and call city hall to book a visit from the vacuum car. On arrival, the vacuum car operators would remove a small stone partition on the outer wall of the house below floor level. They would then feed a hose into the urn and the vacuum car would suck out the contents. (Catharine recalls that the Milk Marketing Board lorries had a similar machine for collecting the milk from farms on Anglesey.) The vacuum crew would measure the volume removed and Catharine paid with the requisite number of coupons from a book purchased from the council office. To Catharine's mind, this was a much more sophisticated system than that available to the houses in Zushi's back streets. Too narrow for the vacuum car, they had to rely on the services of a man pulling a cart with six wooden casks on the back. He had to reach in and draw out an urn's contents with a long bamboo scoop on a pole. 'And when you're pregnant and feeling slightly queasy and you bump into one of these, oh!' she laughs, holding her stomach.

Catharine quickly became pregnant. In three years she gave birth to a daughter, then twins and then a son. In the seventies, the Nagashimas had two more children. Needing to eat foods that were nutritious and affordable, Catharine bought *The Standard Tables of Food Composition in Japan*, a publication which listed the calorific and nutrient content of traditional Japanese foodstuffs such as tōfu, dried sea lettuce, toasted green lava and algae. In 1965, rice was still rationed, and households had to register with their local rice merchant, something Catharine, vainly

Catharine consults her nutrition handbooks

scouring the Japanese grocers and supermarkets, did not immediately realise. Catharine's husband registered himself but did not know how to enrol a foreigner, so they survived on his ration alone. Catharine tried to find genmai, unpolished brown rice, but it was not easy to come by, and her husband refused to eat it since it brought back childhood memories of the war. Instead they ate the Japanese staple, polished white rice, considered pure and tasty but which, lacking the nutritional husk, caused Japanese children to suffer from beriberi. To counter the lack of vitamin B, Catharine consulted the book and bought wheatgerm separately. Later she was able to buy haigamai, rice with the bran removed but the wheatgerm remaining. Struggling to understand the book and to comprehend all the grades and varieties of rice was one of the ways Catharine learned to read Japanese.

She also decided to acquire a taste for nattō, fermented soybeans with a slimy consistency and the pungent stink of rotting rubbish. 'I decided I'm going to have to learn to like this, and so I did,' she states, matter-of-factly. Pulsating with protein, iron, minerals and vitamins, it is a nutritious addition to the native diet, and many Japanese enjoy a spoonful on rice for breakfast.

Western food was prohibitively expensive. One hundred grams of the cheapest Australian cheddar was available only in the import shops of the smartest downtown Tōkyō stores like Takashimaya in Nihonbashi. At seventy yen, this was the same price as a taxi ride home from the train station or to post an airmail letter to Wales. For fifteen yen, you could have the same weight of fresh tōfu delivered to your door. Occasionally, Catharine's family sent food parcels from home but they took three months by sea, and arrived dented and battered. Once her sister sent a parcel of soft French cheeses but, by the time they arrived, they had all dried up.

Aerogrammes and rolled-up magazines were the primary means of contact with family back in Wales. International postage was such a huge expense that Christmas cards were sent by sea and had to be posted by October. It took a year to get a telephone line, and it could only be used for domestic calls. For important news, you sent telegrams.

Like most Japanese homes, the Nagashima's house was not insulated. There was neither heating nor air conditioning. When the Nagashimas moved in, the kitchen was a single gas burner in a dank sunless corner at the back of the house. They repositioned it to the sunnier front living room and later installed a large metal stove heater on which Catharine could boil kettles. In time, the Nagashimas bought an electric rice cooker and, when their first daughter was born, a twin-tub washing machine. They added an electric vacuum cleaner in time for ōsōji, the ritual house-cleaning exercise that is carried out just before the New Year. 'And my husband who never lifted a broom was suddenly doing the cleaning because it was an electric gadget,' recalls Catharine, rolling her eyes.

During the oil shock of 1973, when an oil embargo was placed on several countries including Japan, they also fitted a horigotatsu, an electric heater sunk into a recessed floor into which family members could dangle their legs. Above the recess sat a low table and a large padded blanket which extended from the table frame on all sides to cover the family's laps and hold in the warmth. In winter, it is Japanese tradition to sit like this with friends and family, peeling satsumas and shelling peanuts.

In the summer, the house was opened up. Translucent shōji panels were slid back and windows pulled wide to encourage the circulation of cooling sea breezes. In June, during breaks in the rainy season, snakes would emerge from the garden foliage to dry themselves in the sun before shedding their skins. Finding one coiled on the veranda one day, Catharine waited until it slithered onto a rug and then scooped the whole thing up with two brooms and flung it back into the garden.

Catharine brought to Zushi the same attitude of sociability and cooperation that she had grown up with in Wales. Every winter morning she turned out with neighbours to sweep the yashiki-dōri, raking pine needles from the dirt road while exchanging local gossip. The neighbours gave Catharine okazu, the small side dishes of fish, vegetables or tōfu that accompany the obligatory bowl of rice. In return, she boiled them marmalade from the fallen citrus in their gardens. As her six children grew, she joined the

Parent Teacher Association, circulating leaflets and manning school crossings. And she did her duties on the neighbourhood rota: collecting charitable donations and overseeing the weekly rubbish and recycling programme.

As passionate about her new land as she had been about her old, Catharine joined several environmental groups and became a citizen activist, lobbying to save a local nature reserve from the bulldozers of the United States Navy – a permanent and expanding postwar presence in Sagami Bay. She canvassed, fund-raised and marched, and got quite a local reputation. When their cause was lost, she redirected her activist skills and ecological knowledge to become a machizukuri (town planning) consultant, helping local communities to improve their living environment. And despite being well past retirement age, she taught – and still teaches – Ekistics at a university in nearby Yokohama, where she likes to focus on environmental issues, particularly at neighbourhood level. Growing up in one minority culture, she is aware of the importance of speaking out for local rights.

Catharine was not the only foreigner resident in the area. Along the coast in Hayama lived Dorothy Britton. Born in Yokohama in 1922, Dorothy had been the last baby baptised in the Anglican church before it collapsed in the Great Kantō Earthquake. As a child, she had played on the beach with children of the imperial household, and she remained friendly with Emperor Akihito and Empress Michiko throughout her life. As an adult, she had composed music and played the harp. It may well be that the empress' well-known love of Welsh harp music came from Dorothy. Dorothy had died the week before my visit to Zushi. The harp in the corner was originally hers.

Catharine also joined the Association of Foreign Wives of Japanese (AFWJ), which was started by her next-door neighbour's American daughter-in-law, Joan Itoh. The story goes that in 1969, Joan was travelling on a train when she met another American woman, the wife of a local doctor. Realising there must be more foreign women married to Japanese men out there, Joan enlisted the help of Jean Pearce, a columnist for the English language *Japan Times* newspaper, and booked a table for twenty at the American Club in Tōkyō. Sixty excited foreign women turned up. The group now has around five hundred members and is a hive mind for legal, culinary and cultural information about Japan, such as what one should give to a child's teacher as a midsummer gift (cold noodles, cooking oil or even washing powder, and always in presentation packs) or how much money should be offered at a funeral (5,000 yen for a friend, 10,000 yen for a relative, and always presented in a sealed envelope with a black border).

But some members, observes Catharine, use the AFWJ as 'a dumping ground' to voice complaints and rail at their isolation. She knows of foreign wives who have packed up and fled home, citing problems with in-laws and the loneliness of monotonous existences with husbands who, committed to their companies, are largely absent. The Japanese word for housewife – okusan – translates literally as 'Mrs Interior' and it is in the home, the domestic sphere, where wives have traditionally been expected to discover their eikyū shūshoku, their 'eternal employment'. Catharine remembers travelling back to Wales on holiday and dropping by to visit a friend. The friend's husband came to the door and said, 'Oh, tonight's her night out.' He was in the middle of bathing the children and putting them to bed. Catharine was amazed. In Japan you could never have anything like that, she admits. 'Some women can put up with it – the ones who are still here – and some can't. I don't say I didn't mind it. Of course I minded but I survived it, that's what I am saying.'

'But how *did* you survive it?' I ask as we sip our tea.

Catharine considers for a moment, and we return to the subject of roots. 'I think one of the reasons I've been able to adapt well to life in Japan is because I have this deep connection with my own community in Wales,' she says. In her student days, when Catharine was scootering around Europe, people often enquired where she was from. 'Je suis Galloise,' she would answer. 'Why are you so parochial? Why do you have to insist that you are Welsh?' her friends asked. But Catharine says she knew in her heart that she was more international than they were. Because of her Welsh roots. Having developed a strong national, cultural and linguistic identity at a young age enabled Catharine to understand who she was and where she belonged, no matter where in the world she travelled. 'Once I'd decided that I was Welsh then it didn't matter anymore, I could be anything. But you have to have that first initial identity.'

It is a lesson she has taught her own children. Until 1985, foreign mothers in Japan were unable to pass on their nationality so, legally, all the Nagashimas' children are Japanese. But growing up they looked different and, in Japan's homogeneous society, that made them easy targets in school. In spite of this, Catharine was adamant that their first identity must be Japanese. 'A child has to be one thing first, and then it can be anything it likes. I know that from my own experience.'

Zushi beach, 1966. Catharine pushes her pram (made in Wales but bought in a sale from the Takashimaya department store in Tōkyō)

In recent years, the term 'hāfu' in Japanese has come to identify a small but growing minority of people with one Japanese and one foreign parent. 'Hāfu' symbolises a person living half in one culture and half in another. Or in both at the same time. Until the age of twenty-two, a 'hāfu' can travel on two passports, that of either parent's nationality. But then they must choose a national identity and give up one passport. This makes no sense to Catharine. Catharine knew from her own upbringing that a child cannot be 'half and half' or 'both', and she was adamant that her children consolidate their Japanese identities first, 'and then they can be free to be British as well which I think on the whole has worked out for them.'

This is not to say that Catharine hasn't been altered by Japanese life. 'Everybody changes. I mean, I'm sure you're a different person in Japan. I am too,' she reasons. But having formed and consolidated that first Welsh identity meant she knew who she was and was consequently free to adapt herself to her new surroundings, to assimilate herself into her adopted culture, and to know where to draw a line. Only a plant with a strong root base can survive being transplanted elsewhere.

Transplanted roots must also be well nourished. Catharine now owns the family house in Anglesey and tries to get back there whenever she can. Although the council charge her for a second home, she regards it as her first. She doesn't nail it shut in the winter.

As the interview draws to a close, I excuse myself and wander into the long dark hallway, sliding back doors until I find the bathroom. It's a surprisingly large room, spacious enough for the three toilets it contains, lined up next to each other along the outer wall. At one end sits a futuristic Toto machine which at the press of a button offers the obligatory heated toilet seat and a blow-drying function. The toilet in the middle was installed in the seventies or eighties. It is a flush toilet but with no bells, whistles or sudden water jets. And next to it, set into the floor, is the original ceramic toilet bowl. Blue and white and delicate as a china teacup, it is filled today with an assortment of shells from the nearby beach. The three toilets are an odd sight and I laugh out loud. Yet together they symbolise three significant periods in Japan's history: the years of rapid technological transformation just after the opening of the country to those 'southern barbarians'; its postwar industrialisation and the rise of the eighties bubble economy; and Japan as it is today, a nation so technologically advanced that I can't figure out how the Toto toilet flushes.

The 'out of kilter' house has continued to evolve in other ways too. The wooden shutters have been replaced with strong aluminium frames and, judging by the bundles of cables snaking from light switches, it has been rewired several times. A later house, designed by Catharine's husband, was annexed to the original and this is now Cinema Amigo, the small café and bar run by their youngest son, Gen, who shows independent films on a roll-down projector screen to movie buffs and local bohemians. It is the only cinema in Zushi.

The 'out of kilter' house

The 'out of kilter' house is one-hundred-and-twenty-four years old, and Catharine Huws Nagashima and her husband have lived in it for sixty of those years. They are its longest residents. But it is Catharine who has spent the most time here, raising and educating six children, stoking the fire under the goemonburo bathtub, translating the nutrition handbook or, like today when I return to the living room, practising her harp. Both house and resident have been uprooted from their original sites and transplanted 'out of kilter' on alien ground. Yet both now sit perfectly, grounded in their community in this little seaside town one hour from Tōkyō by train.

Welcome Forgive and forget?

***Gareth Jenkins** works as a medical interpreter at a hospital in Fukuoka on the island of Kyūshū. He studied business with Japanese at Cardiff University, but his interest in the language began in high school:*

I was in secondary school in Aberystwyth. I don't know why but Ceredigion had employed a Japanese teacher, a woman called Kawaguchi-sensei who taught around the high schools. It sounded fun so I thought I'd try it. It was one lesson a week when I was fifteen or sixteen. I was learning hiragana, katakana, all the basic characters and the meanings and how they look like pictures. So I got the hook that way.

Then there's another story. I don't know if you've heard of a guy called Frank Evans.* He's from Aberystwyth too, and he was a prisoner of war of the Japanese back in the Second World War. He was captured in Hong Kong and he was taken to Japan to work in a nickel mine. When the war ended, he returned to Wales. And he never knew where he'd been held.

Forty years after the war, he heard about a veterans' trip going back to Asia. He took this trip and they went around Hong Kong seeing where they'd fought and where they'd been captured. On the plane back to Wales he sat next to a Japanese lady and he told her his story about being held in Japan but he didn't know where. She got on the case and she found out he'd been held in Kaya (near Kyōto). She told Frank Evans that she had found the place but she also got in contact with the mayor of Kaya. And the mayor of Kaya invited Frank to come over and visit the place again. He was welcomed back. That's how the Aberystwyth–Kaya Friendship Association was born and, through that association, I got a chance to visit Kaya in 1996 when I was sixteen.

I got to meet Frank Evans. It was just before I left. He was a very cheeky, fun-loving, friendly guy. And he forgave the people who held him, pretty much. If you read his book you'd understand. The way he was held there with no food, and him talking about having to catch frogs in the rice fields for a bit of extra nutrition. Hellish conditions. He survived. Barely. But he managed to go back and forgive the people and visited the places where he'd worked: forced work. Basically, down to his personality and his ability to forgive, the friendship association was born.

It was June going into July when I went to Kaya, so it was rainy season. The first thing was the heat. Second thing, the food was great. I remember really liking okonomiyaki. But above all, just Kaya. It's in the north of Kyōto prefecture. A beautiful area. I had my greetings that I had learned through those lessons. And I did a two-week homestay and was just blown away by the Japanese, who were very kind and welcoming. They created a fun-packed schedule. They took me to Hiroshima, Ōsaka, Kyōto, all the major places. And I didn't have to pay for a thing. I got the flight out there but I think the Japanese side funded everything else. And I remember getting gifts all the time. My host family had to find me another bag just to fit all the omiyage (souvenirs) to take home. It was like nothing I'd experienced before.

*Thomas David Frank Evans (1917–1996) of Llanwnnen was captured by the Japanese in the Battle of Hong Kong in December 1941. He was transported to the Oeyama POW camp in Kyōto prefecture where he and other prisoners of war were forced to work in a nickel mine. Evans published his memoirs, *Roll Call at Oeyama*, in Welsh in 1981, and in English in 1985.

***Geraint M** treats me to breakfast at the Tokyo American Club (TAC) in Azabudai. A native of the Rhondda Valley, he is a French and Spanish linguist by training and has worked in senior management roles in several countries. He met his Japanese husband in London and they married in New York. In 2016, when his husband was transferred to Japan, Geraint accompanied him as a 'trailing spouse'.*

Geraint's husband is the 'primary' member of TAC. Geraint is listed as 'spouse' and receives emails from the club addressed to 'Mrs M' even though they have his photograph on record. Consequently, our conversation centres around the continuing inequalities for couples in same-sex marriages in Japan:

Even though we are legally married in the US, our marriage is not recognised in Japan because he is a Japanese citizen. Same-sex marriage is not recognised by the Japanese government for its own citizens, whether they marry another Japanese citizen or whether they marry a foreign citizen. So, just to be clear, if two Americans came here in a same-sex marriage, their marriage would be recognised for immigration purposes. A foreigner who is here with a Japanese spouse in a same-sex marriage does not have immigrant status. And therefore, when we came to Japan, I had to come under my own aegis.

The options that were available to me were to come as a student or to find employment from outside Japan. The simplest and most effective way in the short term was for me to apply for a student visa. There are several types of visas available, some of which are called 'cultural activities'. That would be things like flower arranging. It's the one that's mentioned most often. It's ikebana. It's never kendō, let's put it this way. You come and do that for a certain amount of time. Alternatively, you come here as a student to learn Japanese. In my case, it seemed to make more sense to come here as a very mature student to learn Japanese. That visa is time limited. It's a maximum of two years, the assumption being that if you haven't learned it in two years, you never will.

The regulations are appropriately strict. It requires a minimum of twenty hours' study per week for approximately forty-eight weeks of the year. Your attendance and academic progress are monitored. It's not a stamp in your visa with no worry about any follow-up. You need to be a good and faithful student.

As a linguist by background, I was probably a bit smug before I got here thinking, 'Okay, I know how to learn a language. I've also been an ESL teacher. I know how it's taught. I understand the dynamics. This won't be easy but I know exactly what needs to be done.' Knowing what needs to be done and then having the motivation to do it are two separate things. It's very hard to find the motivation when you know you're there through obligation rather than true desire. And to find myself suddenly back in a classroom: 'Repeat after me, "I, you, he, she, they, cat, dog, house, car..."'. It was a tabula rasa moment. I was now exactly the same as everybody else. And everybody else was twenty to twenty-four years old. It was one of the most demotivating moments I've had in my life. And, having worked professionally in relatively senior roles in other countries, to suddenly find myself in a Japanese language school every day with people who were literally half my age – who could have been my children – was a shock to the system. I lost agency, which was troubling for me. Personally, because I lived in a country where I didn't speak the language, something which I had never experienced previously when living overseas. And also professionally, because I no longer had a job to define myself. There was that loss of prestige. I'd held senior roles in business, I had my own money. All those things that a normal, responsible adult might have mid-career. And I suppose the biggest challenge for me was the disconnect between who I thought I was professionally and who I became personally.

The drive for moving to Japan was actually a business decision which was made available to my husband, that he accepted, and I agreed that he accept. But the impact of the move was probably greater for me. Is this my sob story moment? In my opinion, the impact on me was far greater than any other corporate wife in the company. How many of the corporate wives – trailing spouses – had to go to school for twenty hours a week and learn a language and be good at it, in order for their husband to do a job that the company wanted them to do? How many women have to go to school in order for their husband's employer to benefit?

At the time we came, we didn't know how long we would be here, so a two-year visa seemed fine. In the interim, it became clear that we would be staying longer. I needed to find some form of employment, and the obvious place to find a job was at my husband's firm. That raises any number of conflicts of interest because he's a senior executive. I'm not a nepo baby, to quote the current parlance. I'm a nepo spouse.

I've said to co-workers, 'I'll fail on my own merits. If I'm not doing the job I'm supposed to be doing, please tell me.' I also realise from a cultural and political point of view that I have to be beyond reproach. I can't be seen to be anything other than a very good person. I'm always the person who's there on time. I'm always the person who's the most helpful. I may fail fairly frequently but I know that I have to perform a certain role.

When I changed my status from student to worker, I had to go and update our jūminhyō (residence certificate) at the local government office. But they said, 'You're not in this man's household.' And, of course, when you reply that you're married to this man, it does not compute. But then we moved house last year. We used to live in Minato. Now we live in Shibuya where we were able to register as a same-sex household. I couldn't tell you what the practical benefits are but it's a 'use it or lose it' kind of thing. So we registered to show that it does have a purpose. In some areas of Japanese life, we are considered a household, in others we're completely unrelated. Even if my husband were to fall ill or worse, I am not his next of kin.

I think people are shocked when they realise that my husband has fewer rights in Japan as a Japanese citizen than a foreign person does as an immigrant. Because if he was American married to an American, he could come and bring his partner on a spousal visa. But because he is Japanese, he was not able to do that. I really object to the fact that a Japanese person in their own country has fewer rights than a foreigner.

For myself, I fully respect every country's right to determine their own immigration rules. At the same time, it's hard to feel welcome here when you're clearly told that you are 'less than'. I'm not Japanese. And I'm not foreign and married to another foreigner. I'm foreign and in a same-sex marriage with a Japanese citizen, and that means I'm unmarried according to Japanese law.

I recently renewed my five-year working visa. When that expires, I will be able to apply for permanent residency. But before then, my hope is that Japan will allow same-sex marriage – and recognise our marriage – and finally confer the same rights on my husband as his fellow citizens.

Chapter Two

Springtime on the Old Hamada Farm: Simon Whalley's island life

'Is there anything good, little cat?' Simon Whalley with his Tom Jones record

It's a clear spring day and I am on a car ferry sailing across the Seto Inland Sea to one of the 14,000 plus islands that make up the Japanese archipelago.[7] Only around 430 of these are inhabited and, with the continuing decrease in the Japanese population, there are many on which animals outnumber humans. On Aoshima, one of eleven 'cat' islands, felines (originally imported to catch rodents on fishing boats) outnumber the dwindling human populace by forty to one. In Japan, redefining islands and other rural locations as tourist attractions is a way to financially rejuvenate an area.

From the ferry, I can see Ōkunoshima (shima and jima mean island) where in the 1920s the Japanese Imperial Army built a secret chemical weapons factory to manufacture mustard and tear gas (in contravention of the 1925 Geneva Protocol which they signed). The island has since been overrun by wild rabbits hence its nickname, Usagijima (Rabbit Island). The island is a popular tourist attraction. You can take a ferry to feed the rabbits and visit the poison gas museum.

Today I am heading to Ōsakikamijima, otherwise known as Education Island, where it is hoped that the opening of a high school, university and a fisheries college will attract students, tourists and money to the area. Waiting for me at the ferry port is Simon Whalley, a teacher at the high school. Amongst the farmers and fishing folk waiting on the quay, he is easy to spot. He is bearded, shaven-headed and the only foreigner. Revving the engine on his beat-up white van, we speed through the island's deserted town centre and follow a road winding steeply upwards.

Simon is from Aberdare in the Cynon Valley. In 2000, after graduating with a degree in tourism management and business from the University of Gloucestershire, he packed a rucksack and flew to Asia to dive, surf and teach the occasional English class. Arriving in Japan in 2003 (via the Philippines, Vietnam and Taiwan), he opened a bar in the town of Hakodate on the northern island of Hokkaidō. He met wife, Kaori, when she applied for a job there.

Hokkaidō is a cold, mountainous place, closer

to Vladivostok than to Tōkyō. The beaches are open for one month in August and – with five months of snow in winter – temperatures can fall to minus twenty degrees centigrade. After five years, Simon and Kaori decided to relocate somewhere warmer and, after gaining a master's degree in teaching English to speakers of other languages (TESOL) from Sheffield Hallam University, Simon switched from hospitality to education. For a time, they moved around Japan with a cat and a dog and, from 2011, a son named Indy (after Indiana Jones). But then an academic contact offered Simon a job on Ōsakikamijima teaching in a new type of high school.

The aim of the Hiroshima Global Academy is to foster peace through holistic learning. Opened in 2020, its intake comprises forty per cent overseas students (currently from Mexico, Ghana, Uganda and India) and sixty per cent Japanese, who study in English for the International Baccalaureate. Simon works in the language and literature department. We swing past the school but we do not go in. I am not here to visit Simon at work. I am here to see his home. Because moving to Ōsakikamijima enabled Simon and his wife to follow a long-cherished dream, to buy a farm and live a self-sufficient, vegan lifestyle.

Buying a farm in Japan is not difficult, even for

a foreigner. Due to a recession-led decline in local industries and an exodus to the cities, rural land is plentiful. Ōsakikamijima's population has fallen from 22,000 to 8,000 inhabitants, most of whom are over seventy years old. With a land area of 44km² there are millions of tsubo (1 square kilometre = 302,500 tsubo) available including farms which come with akiya thrown in. Akiya are empty homes. There are estimated to be around ten million in Japan.

You can find akiya all over Japan, boarded-up houses slowly collapsing in on themselves. Whole villages have been abandoned to the elements, beaten by typhoon winds and strangled by snaking vines. And not just houses. Visiting haikyo (ruins): deserted hotels, amusement parks, hospitals, factories and even zoos, is a popular pastime for the urban explorer in Japan. Even my old neighbourhood, in a western suburb of Tōkyō just twenty minutes from the central shopping hub of Shinjuku, was dotted with crumbling kominka (traditional wooden houses), with furniture and personal possessions foraged by local wildlife (both human and animal) and scattered on the wind. When homeowners pass on without families to inherit, their properties are left to decay. Even when a distant relative can be found, they may refuse to accept a free house, citing steep inheritance and property taxes. Besides, young Japanese don't want old houses. 'They want everything new,' says Simon. 'They don't like bugs.'

Whilst the Covid pandemic did prompt a temporary rethink, buying up rural real estate remains the preserve of a small number of eco-friendly Japanese and of foreigners who can't believe their luck. Although a resident visa is required to obtain a mortgage, some smallholdings are so inexpensive they can be bought outright. 'That's the beauty of Japan at the moment,' says Simon. 'If you're into living in the countryside and you want to get your hands dirty, it's paradise.'

With no estate agent on Ōsakikamijima, the Whalleys sought their farm via an akiya bank, a database of vacant and abandoned homes compiled by the local town hall. The property they chose is situated on the side of a steep mountain, Mt Kannomine, 453 metres above sea level. The old Hamada farm measures 2,117 tsubo, around 7,000 square metres or just over an acre and a half. When Simon climbed to the farm's highest point, he discovered a cluster of family graves whose inscriptions suggested that the Hamadas had been cultivating the land since the Edo period (1603–1868). Now it was for sale for 2.5 million yen (£12,219).

The akiya bank put the couple in contact with the

owner, a junior member of the Hamada family who had moved to Chiba, east of Tōkyō. The couple was surprised that he would sell land that had been in his family for generations – and to a foreigner – but as Simon recalls, 'He came down and basically gave us the keys and said, "Good luck"'. They moved in on St David's Day 2020.

When we pull into the driveway, two dogs, Odie and Lara, race out to greet me. There are also five semi-nomadic rescue cats who appear intermittently. Kaori welcomes me with a cup of English tea and we take a tour of the property while twelve-year-old Indy kicks a football around.

The house is a box-like two-storey structure with a flat roof. It is larger downstairs than upstairs, which allows for a wide terrace on the upper floor. With the help of his neighbours, Hamada senior had built the house in the seventies but for some reason had never finished it. When the Whalleys saw it, it had lain empty for over thirty years but, because it is made not of wood but of concrete, it was in surprisingly good condition. It needed no major structural work nor had suffered from the myriad problems that often thwart buyers of wooden akiya, namely rot, earthquake damage and infestations. Simon refers to it as 'the bunker'.

The bunker

Another problem traditional Japanese wooden houses can throw up is bugs, all kinds of burrowing, chewing, stinging insects including termites which can consume a wooden house's foundations. 'Are there any bug problems here?' I ask, and receive a stern look from Simon. 'As a vegan I wouldn't say bugs are a problem,' he chides. But the couple did raise the floor of the house three inches to allow for a through-draft in the summer, and they laid charcoal underneath to suck up moisture and deter the termites. 'But you wouldn't believe the size of the spiders and poisonous centipedes we've seen here,' adds Simon, happily. I hesitate while removing my shoes in the genkan (porch).

Inside, the couple took the house back to its breezeblock skeleton, ripping out false walls, dropped ceilings and excess doors, and opting – out of economic necessity – for a modern industrial look. It is simple but utilitarian, with a serene Japanese style. On the walls, you can still make out the calculations scribbled by Hamada and his neighbours as they designed the house.

From the entrance, stripped wooden floors lead through an open dining area to a large kitchen, and around to Indy's room. In a large main room they have kept the shōji (sliding panels) and, for the moment, the very spongy tatami matting. In daytime, this is their lounge where Indy plays video games. At night, it is where Simon and Kaori sleep.

High ceilings and large windows allow for the circulation of cool mountain air in the summer and negate the need for expensive air conditioning. In winter, the Whalleys use the traditional method of heating, kerosene. Insulation and central heating are not standard in Japanese homes. A sliding wooden panel between the bathroom and the kitchen also allows for some kind of heat exchange. Or maybe it supports the old adage that a Japanese husband at home needs only utter three words: 'Meshi! Furo! Neru!' ('Food! Bath! Bed!'). Hamada senior could have sat in the deep Japanese tub and been served his dinner through the hatch.

The Whalleys have recently renovated the upper floor and, as I carry my suitcase up the steep wooden stairs, I smell fresh paint. Simon's mother will be visiting soon. After that, the couple plan to join an international farmstay programme and offer the top floor as accommodation in exchange for labour.

Another reason why akiya are unpopular with many Japanese is that they tend to be filled with junk. The Whalleys spent weeks clearing out the Hamada house: ditching obsolete televisions, repurposing old furniture and emptying cupboards crammed with unused gifts, particularly presentation boxes of towels. 'The Japanese give gifts all the time,' notes Simon. 'And they just go straight in the cupboard.' But they have also discovered treasures such as an antique gramophone with a winding crank and a bulbous stylus. With it came a pile of sixties EPs priced at ten yen each, including the 1965 Tom Jones' hit, 'Nanika ii koto nai ka nekochan?' (is there anything good, little cat?, otherwise known as 'What's New Pussycat?'). 'You were obviously meant to buy this house,' I say, as Simon holds up the record.

Reaching up to a bookshelf, Simon pulls out a metre-and-a-half-long replica of *The Yamato*, the largest battleship in the world and the flagship of the Japanese fleet until it was sunk by the Americans in Okinawa in 1945. Hamada junior had carved it when he was a schoolboy. Although the Seto Inland Sea is a national park, it is also a heavily industrialised zone with clusters of shipyards dotted along the coast. *The Yamato* was built nearby at the Kure Naval Base so it is possible that his ancestors saw the real thing.

From the upper floor we step outside onto the terrace and gaze down at Yamajiri (literally 'bottom of the mountain'), a hamlet of houses clustered into a fold of the peak. The Whalley's house is the second highest property, on land so steep I can look down onto the roofs of all the others. I count around forty houses but Simon tells me that there are only about twenty families living here. Many of the houses are empty. Simon points to one nearby. 'That's free,' he says. 'And it's got a lovely garden.'

The Whalleys too have an attractive garden. From the terrace, we can inspect the twelve beds they have turned over (while trying not to kill any earthworms, notes Simon) ready for spring planting. Last year, they grew: tomatoes, kale, cucumbers, pumpkin, zucchini, beets, Japanese spinach, edamame beans, shiso (perilla mint) and daikon radish. Simon is also keen to grow some spicy chillies from which he can make hot sauce for his beloved vegan curries. His Habanero and Moruga were unsuccessful so this year he's going to try a variety called Peach. The farm also has stepped terraces on which they could cultivate rice but Simon is not keen on the mosquitoes that flooded paddy fields would attract. As their staple they have planted potatoes instead, both sweet and regular types.

Last year, hearing that cotton had once been grown on the island, Kaori planted some seeds she received from a local artist. Cotton needs a lot of water so Kaori was not hopeful but it grew well and, after she had separated the fluffy cotton from the pods, she handed it back to the artist to use in a handicraft project. A river runs through the Whalley property but it has recently run dry. Simon says he'll have to climb up the mountain to find the source of the problem. I'm surprised to hear that Yamajiri does not rely on local water. It is pumped over from the mainland.

Close to the house, cherry and plum trees are in early bloom and seem particularly attractive to bees. Simon would like to establish beehives on the property but, as we gaze down through a cloud of pink blossoms to the neighbouring farm, I see an old man wandering through his mikan (satsuma or mandarin orange) orchard waving a stick, which is emitting clouds of vapour. 'It's Roundup,' notes Simon sadly. And it's required by the Japanese Agricultural Association (JAA). The younger generation, who are more likely to farm organically, are internet savvy and can sell by mail order or at farmers' markets. But older smallholders still rely on the JAA to buy their produce, and the organisation demands that their fields and trees are sprayed monthly – though Simon has noticed that they never spray anywhere near the crops they grow for their own families' consumption. Simon is concerned about the clouds of pesticide drifting onto his property. When neighbouring farmers spray nearby mikan trees he insists that he be given time to call in his dogs and close all his windows. But you can't enclose bees and they are extremely susceptible to glyphosates, as are many other insects. There used to be fireflies on the mountain. Every June they would light up the trees like fairy grottos. Last year, Simon saw only one lonely light, a direct result, he says, of overzealous crop spraying.

Retrieving our boots from the genkan, we climb upwards to see the rest of the farm. When Ōsakikamijima was a rich farming island, the mountainside was covered in mikan trees and tobacco plants. But, when the farms fell into disuse, nature reclaimed the mountain, covering it in a vast secondary forest. After the Hamadas moved away it repossessed the farm too, burying it in a mass of vines as thick as human legs which strangled anything that grew in their path. When the Whalleys surveyed their new home from an upper floor window, all they saw was impenetrable green jungle. 'It looked like a fairy tale forest,' Simon remembers. And as the couple hacked through it they discovered sleeping beauties. In a clearing, we come upon a grove of mikan and hassaku (a cross between a grapefruit and an orange), dripping fruit onto the ground. The trees produce so much that the Whalleys give bags of fruit away to friends and neighbours.

Scaling a stout wire fence, we climb higher. Pheasants screech and dart away. Simon points to sturdy red and white oaks, cedar, cypress, pine, maples and Japanese camellia, also known as kubikiri ('throat-cut') trees because in times of drought they instantly drop their heart-shaped leaves. There are luminescent vines which, Simon tells me, glow white at night. There is even a tree which releases spores in such a vaporous cloud that it appears to be smoking and is sometimes mistaken – by tourists – for a forest fire. Stumbling through the undergrowth, we come upon stepped terraces delineated by low concrete walls and presumably constructed at the same time as the house.

Under piles of leaves, we find a date etched in the concrete, 1976. Nearby, winding vertically upwards and disappearing into the trees, is a metal track. It is the old 'mikan monorail' which ran freshly picked produce down from the mountain in carts.

Simon and the old Hamada tombs

On the way back down, we come across the Hamada graveyard. The more recent haka (stone tombs) are visible and possibly cared for by someone. Older tombs are buried deep in vegetation. As I scramble around taking photographs, my foot hits a small stone Buddha. I prop it up near a grave. We return to the house via a meandering path which takes us through a thicket of bamboo and past the old mikan storehouse where the family now keep their bicycles, and which Kaori would one day like to convert into a vegan café.

Before darkness falls, we all jump in the van and drive to the top of Mt Kannomine along a twisting road dotted with jizō statues in red crocheted hats and bibs, Buddhist spirits which protect the land and hopefully the road too. In some places it falls sharply away but shiny new barriers have recently been erected with, according to Simon, 'pork barrel money', government funds dished out in an attempt to revitalise the area. But there aren't enough visitors to justify the expense, he says, and when we reach the summit car park, it is deserted. As the sun sets, we wander around the viewing platforms, seeing no one.

The Whalley family at the summit of Mt Kannomine

It is said that, on a clear day, you can see 115 islands from the top of the mountain. But as we begin to count them, distant chimes echo up through the trees, summoning us home. Japan's public tannoy system is tested every day at 5pm, usually with a rendition of the folk song *Yūyake Koyake* (sunrise, sunset):

> The sunset is the end of the day,
> The bell from the mountain temple rings,
> Hand in hand, let's go back home together with
> the crows.

The tannoys are deployed in times of natural disasters: typhoons, tsunami, earthquakes. In rural areas, the tannoy also brings news of births, deaths and announcements about rubbish collections. Two weeks before my arrival, the tannoy announced the death of one of Yamajiri's residents, a young father called Matsumoto who had worked tirelessly to try to rejuvenate the island. When the police released Matsumoto's body, his father drove him home where Kaori and other neighbours were waiting to carry him into the house. The funeral was held in the evening and the body cremated the next day. After ninety days, the ashes will be placed in the family tomb which, like that of the Hamadas, is situated on the family's property.

No one in Yamajiri can understand why Matsumoto took his own life but there is speculation that he had become overworked and felt unable to ask for help. Many of the people who attended his funeral had been brought to the island by him. He had even driven the Whalleys around, showing them properties for sale. The reason he worked so hard to attract newcomers was because one of his own friends had also committed suicide, 'actually in that house there', says Simon as we arrive back in Yamajiri. 'Suicide houses,' he murmurs. 'There's quite a few here. And they're free.' Having seen no injuries on his body, Kaori does not know how the man died. But she heard that the common method in rural areas is to drink pesticide.

The delicious casserole that Kaori prepares for dinner appears to be topped with cheese and slices of sausage. It's actually vegan. Simon stopped eating meat ten years ago after watching a movie about cruelty in the food chain. He went vegan five years later. But it is a challenge to be vegan or vegetarian in Japan as neither option is widely available nor clearly signposted. And what constitutes meat sometimes differs from the western concept. For many Japanese, 'meat' equates to beef which is not part of the traditional Japanese diet. Consequently, pork, ham and chicken can sometimes be found in vegetarian dishes. Simon recalls asking for a meal with 'niku nashi' (no meat) in a restaurant and being served bacon. 'Oh!' responded the waitress, 'Bacon dame?' (is bacon no good?) Veganism is even less well known. Fish and meat stocks may still be used in soups labelled as vegan, while dairy products are added to sauces without a second thought. To be vegan or vegetarian in Japan, you must read the labels and interrogate your server.

Simon finds the lack of dietary knowledge baffling because traditional Japanese cooking is heavily influenced by Buddhist shōjin ryōri (devotion cuisine) which arrived with Zen Buddhism in the sixth century. Because of an abhorrence of violence against any living thing, shōjin ryōri is vegetarian with an emphasis on tōfu and vegetables, and on creating dishes that offer a variety of colourful foods known as the 'pattern of five': red, green, black, white and yellow. Meals should also offer the five tastes (sweet, sour, salty, bitter and umami), and provide a wide balance of nutrients without the need to add meat or fish. But outside of Buddhist temples, shōjin ryōri is not always easy to find. And it may not be vegan. Eggs are acceptable in shōjin ryōri, and sometimes fish.

The Japanese continue to enjoy the greatest longevity in the world, credited in part to the cancer-killing properties of green tea and maitake mushrooms, the prevalence of oily fish dishes and the lack of any sugary dessert options. (Other contributing factors include the late industrialisation of Japan and the low rate of smoking until the eighties.) But younger Japanese, heavily influenced by Hollywood and western trends, are more inclined to follow a western diet. There are McDonalds, Pizza Huts, Burger Kings, Subways and Mr Donut shops on every corner, and on Christmas day, Kentucky Fried Chicken hire security staff to control the queues which reach right down the street. (You can't easily find turkey in Japan so chicken is the next option.) 'Now you go into shopping malls and the queue for McDonalds is massive,' cries Simon. 'Whereas all the Japanese restaurants, there's no one in them. It's bizarre.'

In anticipation of a heavy influx of foreigners for the 2020 (which became the 2021) Olympic Games, several chain restaurants did begin offering non-meat options. But as no foreign spectators were allowed to enter the country and none of the foreign competitors or officials were allowed outside the Olympic quarantine bubble, there were few takers, and they have since disappeared from menus. Choice remains limited. When Simon makes one of his rare trips to the city of Hiroshima he opts for the vegan standby, the Indian restaurant. The nationwide chain, CoCo Ichibanya serves vegetarian curries in many (but not all) of its restaurants. So he mostly eats at home. Not only is Kaori an excellent cook but, Simon admits, she has done most of the planting in their kitchen garden. And she built her own greenhouse.

After dark, it is wise to stay indoors on Ōsakikamijima. Although wild boar are symbols of courage and prosperity in Japan, they are also aggressive. They roam all over the Japanese archipelago (they have particularly flourished in the depopulated areas around the Dai-ichi Nuclear Power Plant in Fukushima) but with so much overgrown land on Ōsakikamijima, they run free and breed rapidly. To keep the population under control, the town hall pays 10,000 yen (£48) per adult boar tail, encouraging locals to hunt them with dogs or trap them in cages loaded with juicy mikan. After the boar are shot, their meat is rendered at a little abattoir next to an old elementary school (now closed due to lack of students) and sold to restaurants in Hiroshima city where it is considered a delicacy. Locals can purchase wild boar insurance from the town hall which covers the medical costs of anyone injured by a boar before 6pm. If you are bitten or gored after that time it's your own fault. Which is ludicrous, says Simon, as boar are nocturnal. The entire Whalley property is contained inside a wire fence which keeps the dogs in and the wild boar out. If the family have to go out in the evening, they take the van.

Simon often goes running on the mountain. If he finds any boar caught in traps, he releases them, even as they try to bite off his toes. One day he came across hunters musing over two squealing babies in a cage. The town hall does not pay out for babies so, when Simon pleaded with the hunters, they shrugged and handed them over. Simon spent days building a sturdy fence for Rocky (named because he was bleeding under one eye having been bitten by one of the hunter's dogs) and Amber (because she was going to be an ambassador for change in attitudes to wild boar), who were initially timid but soon came to enjoy belly rubs. Simon was considering the purchase of an expensive enclosure and founding a boar sanctuary when the babies disappeared. He still doesn't know how they got out but is now looking to replace them with goats to help clear the land. I'd like to see a wild boar, I say. Simon says I will probably hear them tonight. 'They make a hell of a noise when they run through the bamboo grove.'

That night I sleep deeply. In Tōkyō you can't

escape the constant roar of traffic or the hum of the air conditioner. Here all is quiet. Then, just before dawn, I hear a hollow clattering noise, like someone playing a child's xylophone. Something is moving through the bamboo grove. I leap up and peer out the window but see nothing except a vertical wall of trees, liquid in the twilight, like a green tsunami about to engulf the house.

On my forty-minute voyage to Ōsakikamijima, I had noticed that many of the surrounding islands have been connected by giant suspension bridges. As we speed back to the ferry port, I ask Simon if he thinks his island will get one. He hopes not. Whenever a bridge is built, he says, residents island hop to the mainland and the local shops go out of business. Simon points out the town's surviving local stores: the *Yours* supermarket, a *Wants* drugstore and a hardware shop. 'Besides,' says Simon, 'You feel like you're going somewhere when you go on a ferry, right?' But the Whalleys rarely travel to the mainland and when they do, they miss their home, their pets and their garden. In summer, if they want to go somewhere, they jump into kayaks and paddle to nearby islands, trailed by sunameri porpoises.

In a neon-bright, highly industrialised country, Ōsakikamijima seems like a rural idyll. But Simon sounds a note of warning. Japan, he says, is in the eye of a storm of climate change, with increasingly severe landslides, floods and heatwaves. Owned and controlled by conglomerates, the Japanese media never links these natural disasters to humanmade climate change. 'The media doesn't talk about it at all,' he laments. 'And people don't realise how bad things are.' Compounding this misinformation are the foreign television shows which claim that the Japanese are in touch with nature and that their country is an unspoiled agrarian paradise. 'But it doesn't exist!' he wails in exasperation. 'I mean, look around, everything's been concreted over. There's only one river in the entire country that isn't concreted now.'[8] Simon is a supporter of Greenpeace and a founder of Extinction Rebellion Japan. He has self-published a book on the threat, *Dear Indy: A Father's Plea for Climate Action*. 'It's just this myth that everything here is wonderful,' says Simon, as he drops me back at the ferry port. But Simon and Kaori Whalley's farm *is* wonderful. It is a little vegan oasis on a remote island in the Seto Inland Sea. Just watch out for the wild boar.

Remembering CW Nicol The prop forward David Attenborough of Japan

Clive William Nicol MBE (1940–2020) was Japan's most famous Welshman. Born in Neath, he moved to Canada at age seventeen, and then to Japan at twenty-two to train in Shōtōkan karate. A passionate naturalist and environmentalist, in the 1980s he began buying neglected areas of forest in Kurohime, a highland area in Nagano prefecture, clearing it of dead trees and planting biodiverse varieties of flora to encourage wildlife. Naming it Afan no Mori, he founded the Afan Woodland Trust (a Japanese organisation despite its name) and twinned it with Afan Argoed (now Afan Forest Park) near his hometown. The trust currently owns thirty-four hectares, manages a further twenty-seven and plays host to school groups who visit the forest to learn about the importance of protecting their environment and encouraging wildlife. It was also involved with rebuilding the elementary school in Higashi Matsushima, a town flattened by the 2011 tsunami, as well as establishing wetlands in tsunami-flooded coastal areas.

A prolific writer of fiction and nonfiction in English and Japanese, Nic (as he was known to friends) had a long-running environmental column in the Japan Times *called 'Old Nic's Notebook'. He appeared on many television shows, including the BBC programme,* Japanese Language and People *(1991).*

Eddy Jones *was Nicol's best friend. Eddy had taught Nicol's daughter at the British School in Tōkyō but did not meet the man until he bumped into him at a film festival in Cardiff where Nicol was promoting an anime based on one of his short stories. In 2004, when Eddy returned to Japan as a coordinator for international relations (CIR) on the JET Programme, they met again*:

I'd heard about CW Nicol and the things he got up to and he became a kind of heroic figure for me, seeing him on the TV back in the nineties and thinking, 'Bloody hell, he's opening his mouth and Japanese is coming out. How does he do that?'

I was working in the kenchō (prefectural office) in

Nagano city. I was actually working in the governor's office as an adviser and interpreter. The phone went. I think Nic was calling Governor Tanaka. The governor wasn't in but the resident gaijin was, so the phone was passed to me. I reintroduced myself to him and he was very warm. He said, 'Why the bloody hell have you not been in touch? Get yourself up here as soon as you can.' So that Friday, I went up to Kurohime and he showed me round. That was the first of many, many visits. I used to visit him regularly and we'd stay up into the wee small hours drinking whisky and talking about all kinds of things. Nagano became my second furusato (hometown). The mountains and the greenness of Nagano made me think of Wales.

Nic looked like a big grizzly bear. He called himself the Red Devil, the Aka Oni. Not incredibly tall, but chunky; prop forward material. Initially, he was shy. I think you just had to break the ice. What was he like? Incredibly kind, gentle, funny, irreverent. He would have called himself ganko in Japanese. Pig-headed. He wasn't afraid to get into verbal fisticuffs or real fisticuffs, probably, if he was passionate about particular things. And he was passionate about lots of things. I mean, he butted against a lot of people, butted against a lot of heads. That was the joy of the man because he was prepared to stand up to Yakuza

(Japanese gangsters) who were illegally dumping in the forests.

***Richard Mort** was working in Japan as a translator when, in 2006, his father and stepmother decided to visit him*:

CW Nicol was the most famous Welshman in Japan. I'd seen the BBC show *Japanese Language and People* when I was sixteen. So CW Nicol was on my radar. I faxed a few people, and his agent got in touch. I explained that my dad was coming to Japan; he's from Wales and was born in the same city. I said I thought it would be amazing if he could meet a Welshman who knows Japan and get the horse's mouth version of Japan from a Welsh person. That'd be a great thing. It's intangible, you know. You can't buy that kind of experience, can you?

We took a bullet train, the Shinkansen, from Tōkyō to Nagano city, and then a regional train from Nagano city to Kurohime. His forest was about fifteen minutes' drive from the station. We had lunch and then he gave us a tour of his forest, Afan no Mori. He was a naturalist by training and would point out flora and fauna, things that we wouldn't know but his expert eyes would, like badger tracks. He would talk about what grows there, what you could pick, how you could use it, and why it's important. You could tell that he was happiest in a natural setting. He was very much at home in the forest. And he was obviously proud to show it off. It was a unique experience.

He explained the bigger picture of the forest. Ironically, Japan is not a good country at conserving its nature. It's seventy-five per cent forest but they build roads to nowhere. I've read that there are 500,000 construction companies in Japan, which is ludicrous, and the roads to nowhere are just because someone has to use up a budget. He detested that, and he cared about conservation. That came across. He seemed very concerned. He communicated his strong desire to protect the forest and transmit that to future generations. He wanted future generations of Japanese not to be frivolous about what they do with their natural resources. Because Japan has lots of plus points. But the amount of plastic they use is among the worst in the world.

He gave talks to schools. He invited schools to visit and he would take them around with his ranger. It was to show the Japanese people, especially kids, that this is important. We need to bequeath to future generations; you need to look after the country. I don't think that kind of experience is easy to have in

Japan. And certainly not with someone like him who embraces both cultures; a real bridge.

Obviously, he'd been to Afan Argoed in Wales and he knew it was very valuable. I think he felt a strong connection with that forest. It could be from his childhood, but he remembered it very well. So he made a conscious decision to name his piece of woodland Afan no Mori meaning Afan Forest.

Part of the pleasure of the trip was to be able to stay in this guest house called Tatsunoko. He was very good friends with the owner, so we had dinner there. The guest house was also on my radar because Michael Palin, when he did *Around the World in 80 Days;* one of his stops was Kurohime. And he stayed at Tatsunoko. There's a picture on the wall of him and the BBC crew.

I was a bit nervous. I'm very good with people, usually. But he was famous in Japan. He was the David Bellamy or even the David Attenborough of Japan, so he'd got some presence. And he was physically imposing. He was like a lumberjack, a rough at the edges tough guy, weather-beaten. No airs and graces but he knew his stuff. I felt like I had to be on point when I was talking to him. Obviously a great, great guy with a big heart. He put his efforts where his values were. I think he did Japan a great service.

Neil (and Annie) Mort: My uncle, William Vaughan, was appointed a forestry commissioner in 1948. As a member for Wales, he did much towards the ambitious planting scheme in which he saw great hope for the country. That's virtually the same as what CW Nicol did in Japan: deal with the growth of the trees and manage them so that they benefit people. I don't think CW Nicol knew about my uncle. But he was very interested. Because the patch of forest that my uncle monitored was called Afan. It's open as a tourist visiting place now and it's called Afan Argoed. And CW Nicol's place in Japan was called Afan, exactly the same name. So CW Nicol was delighted to hear about this.

Annie Mort: He had a hall full of Wellington boots, and we all had to pick a size and go marching through his forest and it was fascinating. He was such a lovely man. He was so generous and kind.

Neil: He said, 'We'll meet up again in the evening. I will organise a dinner for us.' When we met him for dinner, he said, 'If you pay for dinner, I'll pick up the bar tab.' And we thought, fair enough. He appeared to like his involvement with the bar because he introduced us to this Japanese liquor, shōchū. This was about eighty per cent proof. I mean, it was off the scale, nearly...

Annie: ...And when we got to the airport to come home, that's the first thing we looked for in the duty free.

Neil: He was certainly happy where he was but he didn't want to eliminate his Welsh connection. He still had his Welsh accent which is remarkable, given the time that had elapsed. We are very privileged to be able to say we've been there.

Eddy Jones: I think he was generally welcomed by the Japanese. He took Japanese citizenship several years ago. Certainly the story he told me, very proudly, was that he actually delayed his cancer treatment because the previous emperor was visiting the forest. He was so honoured that that should happen. Prince Charles [as he was then] had visited before that, in 2008. But before the emperor abdicated, he invited Nic and his wife to the Imperial Palace. This wasn't the first time but this was the most special. They were walking around the woodlands and forests inside the imperial enclosure, and the empress was making tea for them. And Nic said that at one point, the emperor put his hand over Nic's and said, 'Thank you for what you've done for Japan.'

He became gravely ill so fast. He'd been in the Red Cross Hospital in Tōkyō for months. I visited him two or three times, and we talked about three or four times a week on the phone. I think he always backed himself to beat it. He returned from the hospital to Kurohime the Monday before he died. I remember phoning him the last time we spoke and he said, 'You'll never guess where I am.' And he was very, very happy that he was there. But he didn't last a week.

His ashes are buried in the forest, underneath a beautiful stone with some of his poetry written on it. We had a gathering for his birthday. The staff was saying, 'Let's decorate the grave with wildflowers.' And then somebody suggested singing 'Happy Birthday', which seemed strange. He would have chuckled.

Learn more about the Afan Woodland Trust at: afan.org.jp

Chapter Three

Made in Japan (and Returned to Porthcawl): Bethany Cummings takes home a Japanese film crew

Bethany Cummings, her family and the Japanese film crew in her parents' house in Porthcawl

It's early evening in Tōkyō and I'm riding the Ōedo subway line. Around me, commuters are sleeping, reading manga or playing games on their smartphones. On my phone, I'm watching *Made in Japan*, a popular TBS (Tōkyō Broadcasting System) television show in which foreigners return to their home countries and present Japanese products as gifts to excited family members. As the foreigners showcase their culture and offer personal insights into their daily lives, a studio audience ooh and aah while a panel of tarentos (talents or celebrities) make perceptive comments. The episode I'm watching features twenty-three-year-old Bethany Jo Cummings. In the summer of 2019, Bethany flew home to Wales, taking with her a cast-iron cooking pot, some ame (boiled sweet) lollipops and a Japanese film crew. Here's what happens.

On an overcast afternoon, Bethany knocks on the front door of her parents' pebbledash semi and is reunited with her surprised family: mother Thomasina, stepfather Dean, her older brother and sister, and two younger brothers. Overjoyed at her unexpected arrival, they celebrate with a stereotypically traditional Welsh meal: a stew of lamb, leeks and carrots, with a side dish of Welsh rarebit. But there is a problem. Bethany's mother and stepfather are vegetarians. Uh oh.

This fact causes consternation back in the TBS studio. Vegetarianism is not well known in Japan. Meat or fish is a traditional staple of every meal, even breakfast. But Bethany's parents won't touch any meat, while her half-brothers hate boiled vegetables and refuse the stew. What to do? Thank heavens for the Japanese cast-iron cooking pot! In no time, Bethany has steamed a dish of tasty vegetables which the two boys greedily devour. Catastrophe averted. But then mother Thomasina opens a packet of Uncle Ben's microwavable rice and, back in the studio, the celebrity panellists make horrified faces. It looks so pasa pasa (dry), they complain. Luckily, Bethany has brought a bag of Japanese rice. Again, she stokes the pot and in a trice, the family are filling their bowls with pika pika (glistening), moist rice. It smells delicious, the family agrees.

'Japanese people eat this every day?' exclaims Bethany's stepfather as he accepts a second helping. 'I'm really jealous!'

We learn that teacher Thomasina raised Bethany and her two siblings alone. This prompts a wave of aah noises back in the studio. In Japan, ninety per cent of Japan's 1.5 million single parent families are headed by mothers, eighty per cent of whom carry the 'taint' of divorce and half of whom live below the poverty line (the highest rate in the developed world).[9] Single mothers and their children carry a social stigma, so it is no surprise to the studio audience that young Bethany, slight and blonde, was horribly bullied. On camera, she relates (in fluent Japanese) how she went to school wearing hand-me-downs, while former friends called her dasai (frumpy, uncool) and put drawing pins in her indoor shoes. 'But I never told my mother,' confesses Bethany to the film crew, her voice faint and trembling. In a dramatic scene, the bullying incidents are recreated with actors and, back in the studio, the tarentos express their shock at this turn of events. Ijime, bullying, is a global problem but one that is well understood in Japan. 'The nail that sticks up will be hammered down' (derukui wa utareru) is a Japanese proverb. In Japan's group society, those who look or act differently may be targeted. In 2022, suicides by school-age children stood at a record high of 514.[10]

Traumatised, as she tells the film crew, Bethany became withdrawn and, for fear of encountering her bullies, never went to the Porthcawl festival. In Japan, matsuri (festivals) are important events in the Japanese summer calendar and to the studio audience it is unthinkable that Bethany missed out. But this year, with a film crew in tow, she has agreed to attend. She has even brought Japanese festival costumes for the whole family: bright yukata (cotton kimono) with obi belts for herself and her mother, and jinbei (matching top and trousers) for her stepfather and little brothers.

On the day of the festival, the film crew accompanies Bethany through the streets. 'She's obviously nervous,' notes the show's concerned host, and the studio audience worry for her. Mother Thomasina pulls Bethany aside and gives her a pep talk. Reassured by her mother's wise words, Bethany replies (according to the Japanese subtitles), 'I will go with a smile.' And she does just that. At the festival, she watches the merry-go-round and eats a stick of candy floss. Later that evening in the family's back garden, she twirls sparklers in the moonlight. Back in the TBS studios, the tarentos breathe sighs of relief.

The afternoon before Bethany returns to Japan, she sits down with her mother for a heart to heart. She reads out a letter she has composed. 'Mother, to me you are like the sun,' she begins. Mother Thomasina begins to cry. 'I was weak but you were always strong,' Bethany continues. The camera zooms in on the studio tarentos, tears glistening in their eyes. 'Mother, can you believe it? Now in my job in Japan I help foreigners in distress.'

The show ends with Bethany, now seated with the host and tarentos in the TBS studio, assuring them that she has made good friends in Tōkyō. And she says that by moving to Japan she has learned important lessons.

I wonder what these important lessons could be. So I alight at Azabu Jūban and head over to Ueshima Coffee, a traditional Japanese café chain that seems to be making a comeback. Azabu Jūban is an upscale residential neighbourhood which, due to the number of embassies in the area, has a noticeable non-Japanese (generally short-term expatriate) population. Bethany has recently moved to this area with her Japanese boyfriend. Despite the presence of numerous foreigners in the street, I recognise her immediately. She is still a slight blonde figure with a whispery voice but she now carries herself with confidence. We order cups of Ueshima's signature 'flannel drip' coffee and I begin by asking her why a 'bullied schoolgirl' from Porthcawl chooses to live six thousand miles away.

Bethany's introduction to Japan came early. In the early 2000s, Japanese anime were finding global cult fanbases and Bethany enjoyed watching them with her mother and sister. Studio Ghibli's *Laputa: Castle in the Sky* (1986) was Bethany's favourite but, too young to read the English subtitles, she dreamed of learning Japanese so she could follow the stories in their original language. As a secondary school student, she searched the internet for Japanese 'trendy dramas', stylish television shows for young people where she could pick up Japanese words such as sugoi (amazing) and kakkoii (cool). Unfortunately, the Japanese language was not taught at Porthcawl Comprehensive and there was only one 'teach yourself' book at the local library. Saving up her pocket money, she hired a private tutor, sat – and passed – her Japanese GCSE and 'A' Level in the same year. 'I may have overstudied,' she admits.

Bethany flew to Japan for the first time in 2014, during the rainy season when airline tickets were cheapest. By this time, she was in her first year studying Japanese at the University of Edinburgh. I point out that she took a big risk committing to a four-year degree without having previously visited the country. But she says that, having loved and studied the country since childhood, it was like coming home. 'I loved it,' she says. 'I left Japan feeling really positive about my degree and hopefully moving here afterwards.' Indeed, on her return to Edinburgh after her study year abroad in the central city of Okayama, she suffered such severe reverse culture shock that she used up the last of her savings to fly back twice before graduation. 'I felt this weird longing to be back in Japan, back to where things were kind of normal,' she explains.

It is therefore no surprise that upon graduation in 2018, she moved straight back to Japan on the JET Programme. As a coordinator for international relations (CIR) based at the local government office in Ōta city (one of twenty-three ku or wards within the Tōkyō metropolis), Bethany worked in the international section, translating documents and interpreting at international events. Telephone enquiries from foreigners were also routed to her desk, from where she attempted to solve their legal and personal problems such as how to register your bicycle, pay your city tax, and how to stop your spouse from forging your hanko (your official stamp or seal) on a notification of divorce and gaining full custody of your children without your knowledge. (It can be countered by lodging a Petition for Non-Acceptance of Notification of Divorce in advance.)

Whilst there are many CIRs in Japan, Bethany was the only one in Tōkyō. And, as the only foreign employee among five thousand Japanese staff, she was sometimes lonely. Few of her colleagues spoke English and none understood her jokes. 'Because my humour is so British it doesn't translate well,' she admits. There were also occasions when Japanese colleagues spoke to Bethany in a condescending manner, refusing to believe she could understand them. It was therefore important to her to make good friends outside the office. And that's when she applied to appear on *Made in Japan*.

So, I ask, was the programme a true depiction of events? Did her family really not know she was coming? And, if not, why was there bunting hanging over the front door? They did know, she admits. They knew the day but not the specific time. And they hadn't seen her for a year, so their delight was genuine, if not their surprise.

Made in Japan follows a set format. The foreign returnee must go on an emotional journey, and the three Japanese members of the film crew had a clear idea of how they wanted Bethany's visit to play out.

'They wanted it to seem real but they actually came up with a storyline to follow,' explains Bethany. All the gift products featured were chosen by the show's producers. They had originally wanted Bethany to take back a heated toilet seat but she had to point out to them that British bathrooms are not fitted with plug sockets. Instead, they decided on the Vermicular cast-iron multicooker pot. But for this piece of Japanese high technology to fit the show's narrative, it had to transform the family's life. Bethany's half-brothers actually like vegetables but were bribed with chocolate to make disgusted faces and say they didn't. Bethany's mother and stepfather are in fact vegan, not vegetarian, but the producers felt Japanese viewers would not understand the concept.

Stepfather Dean did enjoy the Japanese rice. Just not as much as the show makes out. Indeed, as I watched this scene, I detected some blatant overacting. Bethany recalls that every time her mother said something positive about the food, the film crew would urge, 'Ah, just a bit more! Just a bit more!' In vain, Bethany tried to explain that British people aren't so demonstrative. 'My mum was saying, "How enthusiastic can you *be* about rice?"' The family gave it all they had, 'taking the piss,' Bethany agrees. 'And the Japanese crew were like, "Oh that's brilliant".'

Receiving a pep talk from her mother on the way to the Porthcawl festival was also part of the show's narrative. Overcoming adversity is a core belief in Japanese culture, and to ganbaru (do your best) and taeru (bear it) are words Japanese readily understand. In reality, Bethany thinks her mother would simply have told her to 'suck it up'.

I point out to her that, if she really was scared of attracting the attention of her childhood bullies, she and her mother probably shouldn't have gone out wearing colourful Japanese clothes. But Bethany emphasises that the bullying was pushed as part of the storyline. A lot of people dress up for the Porthcawl festival and they were actually following festival floats (not shown) which featured people singing and dancing in all sorts of crazy costumes. 'I was a little nervous about wearing yukata to the festival but loads of people dress up so I got over it,' she assures me. 'Plus, I figured it would be a funny experience if I ran into people I knew from school.'

Also not shown were Bethany's birthday celebrations. This was on the day the crew filmed the family waving sparklers in the back garden at night (supposedly after the festival). Bethany's older brother and sister had arrived to help her celebrate but the filming took so long, they got stonking drunk and had to be kept out of shot. 'Are sparklers a summer festival thing in Porthcawl then?' I ask. Bethany shakes her head. 'They were trying to bring it closer to Japanese culture and make it relatable.' In Japan, evening fireworks are a summer matsuri staple, and the crew wanted to recreate that in Porthcawl for their Japanese audience. But they had such a hard time sourcing sparklers in Wales in summer that they had to order them online.

The reading out loud of a letter is a regular feature of *Made in Japan*. In Japan, letters of gratitude are read on special occasions. A sobbing bride will read out a letter to her parents at her wedding reception, thanking them for their sacrifices and presenting them with extravagant bouquets. It is meant to be an emotional moment and tears are obligatory. And indeed, when Bethany read out her letter, Bethany's mother managed to cry real tears, at least during the first take. 'You better have pressed record on that,' she joked with the film crew afterwards.

But Bethany did not write the letter. It was composed by the show's producers and left to Bethany and the Japanese interpreter to translate into English. 'She actually helped me a lot with it because the letter was *so* typically Japanese, none of it would be something I would personally write,' Bethany points out. 'Mother, to me you are like the sun' was the producer's idea. Nevertheless, it is a genuinely heart-warming scene.

Another highly emotional moment was the revelation that Bethany had suffered years of bullying, a 'daily hell' the show called it. I am hesitant to broach this subject with Bethany for fear of retraumatising her. But this too, Bethany confesses, 'was very much swayed in a way that matched their storyline.' In Japan, students exchange outdoor shoes for plimsolls or plastic slippers as soon as they enter their school building. Welsh students don't wear indoor shoes so boobytrapping the soles with drawing pins would not work. But the crew wanted to make it 'relatable to Japanese experiences of bullying' and the scene stayed in. Bethany's bullies never put drawing pins in her shoes and Bethany says she was never actively bullied, just teased and sometimes picked on. 'There were definitely kids who were picked on a lot more,' she says. Did the teasing she suffered encourage her to seek the comforts of a foreign culture? Did Bethany, as the television show suggests, 'escape' to Japan? (The actual word they use is nigedasu, to run away.) Yes, she admits, those early Studio Ghibli movies were definitely a distraction from her problems. And her interest in Japanese culture helped her to find an alternative group of fast friends – both in person and online – which allowed her to disregard those who picked on her at school. But no, she was never trying to escape. That was down to the show's narrative. 'The producers wanted an emotional storyline so they asked me to act that character.'

On the evening *Made in Japan* was broadcast, Bethany's smartphone began to vibrate with calls and messages from people she hadn't spoken to in years. 'Do you remember me?' they asked and reminisced about those difficult teenage years. One even sent a photograph of a letter Bethany had written in kanji (a Japanese script of Chinese origin) when she was fourteen. 'It brought back why I wanted to be in Japan in the first place,' she remembers. Those bullies did her a favour. She even attracted an overzealous fan, a man in his sixties who turned up at the Ōta ward office and informed her that his grandson was single.

All reality shows manipulate the narrative to entertain their audience. Bethany knew beforehand that the aim of the show is to take the foreign participant's homecoming experiences and filter them through the *Made in Japan* lens. Her return to the danran (warmth) of her family's home, her efforts to overcome childhood trauma and her letter of gratitude to her mother all express global themes with which a Japanese audience can readily identify. Simultaneously, the focus on superlative Japanese products, transformative for the lives of the families who receive them, is a way of affirming comforting notions of Japanese superiority. 'An emotional wall is broken down,' explains Bethany, 'and everything is made better, thanks to Japan.' After the broadcast, her social media accounts blew up with message requests from people saying how moved they had been by the show and how it had inspired them to try harder. 'Even if it is fabricated slightly, I'm very glad I did it,' declares Bethany. 'It's good that it has made someone happy.'

But perhaps not the Welsh Tourist Board. *Made in Japan* is part product endorsement, part travelogue, and Bethany's homecoming was also meant to showcase Wales. Yet the show announces it as a visit to igirisu (England) and the flag that appears on the screen is not the Red Dragon but the Union Jack. The studio audience aah over rural scenes of grazing sheep, and ooh when the announcer states that with a population of ten million, they heavily outnumber Wales' three million human residents. But when the family are enthusing over Japanese rice and adding various Japanese toppings including nori, did it not occur to Bethany to mention that the

Welsh eat laverbread? She did mention it, she says. She told them a lot of information about Wales that never made the final cut. Did the show do enough to introduce Wales to Japanese people? 'I think it could have done more,' she concedes. She diplomatically suggests that the crew were trying to keep the show 'understandable' to Japanese audiences, and that the producers wanted to introduce the whole of the UK, not just Wales. In fact, when filming wrapped in Porthcawl the crew (without Bethany) returned to London and filmed a segment on English tea. That did annoy her. 'Why didn't they bother to introduce Welsh tea? Such a shame.'

Nevertheless, the audience did get to meet a real Welsh family. Although the segment ran to forty-five minutes, the crew was filming in the Cummings' home for a week. Bethany's folks come across as good sports, wearing Japanese clothes to their local festival and enduring take after take while being force-fed rice and told to act 'a bit more'. Even *Made in Japan*'s host observes their good humour, commenting, 'They're a friendly family, aren't they?' Bethany says that her clan found the whole thing hilarious and enjoyed watching a video of the show after broadcast. 'Obviously they don't understand the Japanese, so they couldn't really understand how it had been changed slightly,' she says.

'But watching it and remembering the actual moment of filming was amusing.'

The Cummings family got to keep the gifts, too, including the cast-iron multicooker pot which retails at 90,000 yen (£439) in Japan. It doesn't get much use, Bethany confesses. 'I told them they should sell it if they're not going to use it.'

'And what about those ame sweets?' I ask. One of the gifts that Bethany presents to her family are depictions of each family member in hand-crafted lollipops. On camera, her mother says that they can never eat them but Bethany says they recently tried to do just that. Unfortunately, the sweets had melted. 'They said it was very weird to be eating their own faces.'

Bethany's 'ame' candy family

Bethany too was a good sport. She has fond memories of taking part in the show. And she still gets recognised at the gym. After four years as a CIR, Bethany moved to ByteDance where she is a content quality assurance analyst for TikTok, overseeing the moderation of uploaded Japanese videos, making sure they are safe and appropriate, and removing those which promote racism or bullying or nudity or sexual language. Now she gets to direct the narrative.

The JET Programme How to operate your new gaijin

Founded in 1987, the Japanese government's Exchange and Teaching (JET) Programme is an initiative which places native speakers (predominantly recent university graduates) in Japanese schools as assistant language teachers (ALTs) or in local government offices as coordinators for international relations (CIRs). At any one time there are over five thousand participants from fifty countries on the programme, and around seven hundred of them are British.[11] *Several Welsh interviewees originally relocated to Japan on the programme. Although all had been hired to teach the English language, they also found opportunities to introduce Wales and Welsh culture to their students.*

The following are just a sample of the many JET stories out there. For those who wish to learn more about the JET Programme, I recommend Getting Both Feet Wet: Experiences inside the JET Program *by Chandler and Kootnikoff (JPGS Press) or* Importing Diversity: Inside Japan's JET Program *by McConnell (University of California Press).*

Pred Evans (ALT in Miyagi prefecture from 1997 to 2000): I started off in a very low-level school in Sendai with things I saw which really surprised me. There were lots of bad children from disadvantaged backgrounds which didn't fit my image of a sedate, civilised school. There was a knife incident one day with one of the kids, one of the 'yankees' ('delinquent' teens). I thought in general the way the teachers handled discipline was incredibly patient, and something I'd never seen before. You'd see these yankee guys come in and sit in the deputy principal's chair and the deputy principal just hanging around until they decided to move. Whereas in the UK they'd have been chucked out. However, one day that concept was completely turned on its head when I saw a teacher beat the living daylights out of a kid. There was bullying as well. There was a 'chubby' kid, Otomo – I remember his name. He used to come up to my desk and have a chat with me because he didn't have many friends. He was a lovely guy but he was picked on a lot.

From my third year I was in a very good school. That was a different experience. I was given more responsibility. I was made football coach early on. There was no rugby at the school unfortunately, so the next thing they could think of for a 'Brit' was football. It was a very full day. I was there between seven in the morning and four in the afternoon. I had my own desk. Staffrooms in Japan are designed differently from the UK. Everybody's together in an office environment with the deputy head in the front, facing all the teachers at their individual desks.

Out on the streets, I was always considered by small kids as an American. 'Americajin' (jin means person) would be a common refrain. That used to grate on me. At school, I was also asked to pronounce some things differently and to repeat phrases from the textbook, like 'for here or to go' instead of 'eat in or takeaway'. I'd just go with the flow. But I found that there's a high respect for Britain and its history. I was often hearing the word 'gentleman' for the British, their sense of fair play and manners.

I was allowed to talk about Wales as well. I remember quite a few really fun classes where I was teaching them Welsh and the kids loved it. Especially words like shwmae for 'hello, how are you?' which is 'dumplings' in Japanese. They all remembered that, and all I would hear was hundreds of kids shouting 'shwmae' in the morning as I arrived at school. I would introduce them to Welsh culture and famous people as much as I could because I felt that was a part of what we were there to do as well, to teach them about the different parts of the UK. I tried to focus on the fun things because they were young in junior high school. So the longest place name in north Wales was always a good one. I would joke with things like 'Dw i'n dy garu di' (I love you). All the sounds of Welsh – rrrr, hhhh, ergh – and getting them to practise together. What else did I do? I'd sing my favourite song. It's a popular folk song about springtime coming ('Moliannwn'), and they'd all join in on the 'ffw la la' chorus because it's easy to sing. I'd try to keep it lively.

I think it's a great programme though there are lots of questions around its efficacy. Has it created much change in the education system in terms of the confidence of the Japanese in speaking English? It's been more successful on the internationalisation side, maybe the 'exchange' part of JET more than the teaching. I think it is of benefit to schools to have native speakers in the classroom influencing how English is taught, making it more communicative, interactive, student centred. But I think the biggest success of the programme is making friends with Japan for life. Not everybody goes into influential positions but certainly many leaders have. Some of the top guys in UK government have been on the JET Programme. Like Jeremy Hunt, for example. He keeps that quiet, as if he's a bit ashamed of it.

Andy Moore (ALT in Wakayama prefecture from 1998 to 2000): The board of education I worked for was pretty strict because I was the first ALT that they were in charge of. At the time, I imagined they had got a manual, 'How to operate your new gaijin', and they were looking at page one and following the guidebook to the letter, whereas any of the more experienced boards of education had thrown the manual away. So they wouldn't let me go in a car because they thought, if there was an accident, I would sue them. When they met for teachers' meetings in the area, everyone else went by car and I had to go by train.

During the school holidays, basically I was an office employee. My duty was to go to the office. My friends were going on skiing trips and I was sitting in my office, staring at my desk with nothing to do. I'm not sure if it was a form of punishment but they'd actually put a map of the world underneath the clear sheet on my desk, to make me think where I could be right then.

***Eddy Jones** had taught in international schools in Japan before returning to the UK to do a master's degree. He then joined the JET Programme as a CIR. (Nagano prefecture from 2004 to 2007)*: The JET Programme age limit was forty, so I got back into Japan with ten minutes to spare. That was a fantastic experience, especially as an older guy, because my impression of JET in the past was of young kids out of university just having a bit of a well-paid gap year. Okay, it often is. But I loved working in Nagano. I got to work in the kenchō (prefectural office). It was at the time of Governor Yasuo Tanaka who was a bit of a maverick, an interesting guy. He had a glass office on the first floor of the kenchō. To me it looked like a zoo cage. And it was always interesting if I was working in there and everybody else was out, because tourists would come into the kenchō. They wanted to see Governor Tanaka's famous glass office and they'd just see me, the big gaijin in the corner. I always felt like whipping a banana from my pocket and doing a few gorilla circuits of the cage.

Dan Bradley (ALT in Miyagi prefecture from 2006 to 2009): It was a pretty intense experience. Like a lot of people, I applied to big cities, and instead I ended up in the last village in Miyagi prefecture in Tōhoku. It was called Ōhira. It had about five to six thousand people and lots of rice fields. I split my time between elementary and junior high schools. Lots of the kids were brothers and sisters and cousins so I was definitely part of the community there.

I had a great lifestyle. The job was really fulfilling. The kids and the teachers were very hands on, and very happy to get engaged in the classes. And I had some great friends from the States and Canada and the UK and Australia. So it was really an amazing, surreal experience.

As much fun as it was, being an ALT is not a career. It's very fun and rewarding in short spells but there's no real progression. And it's very easy to feel like a constant novelty, which isn't good for your mental health. And the thing with the JET Programme is that it's a real bubble.

Joe Cairnes (ALT in Niigata prefecture from 2002 to 2004): I got sent to Shibata, a rural town of eighty thousand people surrounded by rice fields, lots of onsen (hot springs) and a ski resort within sight in the hills. My job there was partially to motivate the students: having a native speaker there gave opportunities to communicate. I think the job of an ALT is whatever the person can make it and, if you're an experienced teacher and you speak Japanese, then you could probably do a lot more than I did in terms of educational achievement. But I hope I left the kids actually wanting to study a foreign language.

We ALTs made our decision whether to stay or to leave in February of each year. And in February in Niigata, the land is covered with deep powder snow, and every weekend I would be driving off with the skis and snowboard for two-and-a-half days. But by the second year, I was thinking that I needed to get back to the real world. Now I look back, it seems a bit unfair, calling other people's livelihoods 'not the real world', but at the time we were saying, 'Yeah, we should get back to the real world.' But I never did. I realised I didn't want to be a teacher but I did want to be in Japan.

Chapter Four

'If I Ever Come Back, It Means I've Failed': Andrew Beak's big decision

Andrew Beak

Andrew Beak has made a momentous decision. He has asked himself the question that all foreigners in Japan must eventually ponder. Do I stay or do I go home? Andrew has chosen to stay. He has just been granted his permanent resident visa. He is paying into the pension scheme. He wants to buy a house. And he is starting his own business. As an English language teacher, it is the only way he can survive.

Many of the people featured in this book moved to Japan to be English teachers, either assistant language teachers for JET or to work for eikaiwa. Most did so soon after graduation, with the idea of spending a year or two exploring Asia while paying off their student loans. They have stayed on either because they have married a local and/or because they see a long-term future in the country. Some remain in teaching, perhaps studying for an MA or a PhD to enable them to obtain posts in tertiary education. Others move into new fields, retraining or utilising their Japanese-language skills. Andrew has remained in the eikaiwa industry for over a decade. Now he wants to work for himself and make some serious money.

We meet at Ōsaka train station on St David's Day. He is easy to spot. A gangly six foot two, he towers over the other commuters. We adjourn to a tonkatsu restaurant under the station concourse and, over breaded pork cutlets, shredded cabbage, miso soup and pickles, he tells me his story.

As a child Andrew was, he freely concedes, 'an extremely arrogant human being'. Born in Swansea and raised in Cardiff ('a difficult combination' he points out), he ranked among the top students for mathematics in Wales three years running. Considering himself a genius, he decided to study for a degree in astrophysics at Cardiff University, with an elective module in Japanese on the side because, he says, it was known to have the highest dropout rate. 'Younger me was a little bit odd, I'm going to be honest with you,' he admits. Andrew knew nothing about Japan and viewed the class as 'just a bit of fun' but he immediately fell in love with the Japanese language and ditched astrophysics. One year later, he moved to Leeds University and studied for an undergraduate degree in Japanese, following it up with a master's degree in Chinese.

Another reason to prefer Japanese over science is that it is not 'ninety-nine per cent strange men'. While at Leeds, Andrew met and married his first Japanese wife, although he now admits he was way too immature for such a commitment. After graduation in 2010, Andrew and his wife moved to a house in Yokohama which they shared with his wife's mother. Within the year the marriage was breaking down and, the day after the Tōhoku Earthquake in March 2011, Andrew found himself boarding a train to Kōbe, the city where he had done his study abroad year. 'Everybody thought I was running away from the quake,' he recalls.

Seeking work, Andrew fell into a series of jobs. First, he became an extra on Japanese television. During his study year, he had lived with a host family whose mother ran a finishing school, The Queen's, which offered courses in British afternoon tea, English table settings, housekeeping and butler service. Moving back in, 'Professor Andrew' sometimes provided assistance. His host mother also appeared on an NHK (Japanese Broadcasting Corporation) television show called *Bi no Tsubo* (the urn of beauty). One morning

Andrew came downstairs to discover the film crew setting up cameras, and was drafted in to help recreate a Georgian era afternoon tea with scones. Afterwards, the crew handed him a business card and Andrew found work as a foreign extra on advertisements and morning dramas. This was not his first foray into the gaijin talent business. While still married, he and his wife had walked into a jewellery shop and Andrew, to his wife's chagrin, had walked out with a contract to model women's jewellery. 'I have very feminine hands,' he says, waving long elegant fingers. With waxed arms and false nails, he found further 'hand' publicity work holding electronics.

In Kōbe, he also helped out in the kitchen of a patisserie. He had to roll and divide two kilogramme blocks of frozen cookie dough into five gramme balls, a cinch for Wales' mathematics genius. 'I was very good at calculating it,' he assures me.

Another gig involved dressing up as an animal to dance and sing with toddlers. He remembers it as, 'mostly children crying because they're terrified of foreign people dancing around them.' Then Andrew did what many English-speaking foreigners in Japan do when they run out of money. He took a job as an eikaiwa teacher.

Eikaiwa sprang up in the late twentieth century

to cater to a growing Japanese interest in travelling abroad for business and pleasure. During the eighties economic boom, taking English language lessons was both a useful pursuit and a form of conspicuous consumption. While schools drilled classes of up to forty-five students in English grammar and translation for highly competitive university entrance examinations, eikaiwa offered private, one-to-one or small group lessons with actual native English speakers and without high pressure tests. With offices situated near train stations, eikaiwa dangled the fantasy of a lucrative, jet-setting future in a convenient Japanese location. Japan's biggest current and recent chain eikaiwa are Aeon, Berlitz, Coco Juku, ECC, Gaba, GEOS, NOVA and Shane, but there are myriad others, such as those specialising in English classes for pre-schoolers (with singing and dancing in animal costumes), and lone-teacher businesses run out of front rooms.

During the bubble years, eikaiwa gained a reputation as places where the savvy foreign backpacker could pick up ready cash with minimal effort. Since foreigners were not yet a common sight, those who were lured to the country to teach English tell stories of astronomical salaries and cavernous apartments. Andrew knows a man who arrived in Japan in the sixties and was paid one million yen (£4,887) a month to teach at a university three days a week. But since Japan tipped into recession in the nineties, there has been less disposable income to spend on international travel or English lessons. Now a glut of eikaiwa are competing to attract students with ever cheaper and more convenient options. They have been forced to restructure their operations and cut salaries. Several (Coco Juku, GEOS and NOVA) have gone bankrupt. Yet collectively, eikaiwa conversation schools remain a multibillion-yen industry and the largest employers of English-speaking foreigners in Japan. As they actively recruit in campus newspapers and online employment sites, many young western graduates look to Japanese eikaiwa for a first job out of university and possibly beyond.

Since I imagine some Welsh students may pick up this book seeking information about English teaching opportunities in Japan, I want to pick Andrew's brains about the good and bad points of the eikaiwa industry. I won't name any of the eikaiwa where Andrew has worked. Neither he nor I wish to be sued. But the first point to note is that there are two types of eikaiwa: the good and the appallingly bad. The first school that hired Andrew was one of the better ones, he says. It was a non-Japanese language school with branches all over the world.

Andrew's employment began with a one-week unpaid training course. At the start of each month, Andrew would notify the company of his availability, and every evening they would email him his schedule for the following day. To accommodate office workers (such as salarymen and OL: office ladies), eikaiwa teachers often work 'donut days', early mornings and late nights with a long break during the middle of the day. For six years, Andrew worked twelve-hour donut days, six days a week with no holidays. 'When I was younger and I had the energy, it was fine,' he explains. 'But these days, I couldn't do it.'

Like many eikaiwa, Andrew's global school has its own teaching method. Students must purchase textbooks to take the classes. (In some eikaiwa, teachers receive a bonus for selling extra books to students.) Teachers can therefore walk into any classroom, open the approved textbook and teach to any level of student. 'They talk about the lessons being tailored to the students' needs,' says Andrew. 'It's not true. It's a conveyor belt of lessons. You always do the same thing.' It also means that language schools do not have to pay teachers for preparation time. And they can book a teacher up with a series of forty-five-minute lessons with breaks of only five minutes in between.

This can cause problems, as many eikaiwa branches are small and don't have their own toilets. When Andrew worked at the Sannomiya branch of his eikaiwa, the nearest toilet was a seven-minute walk away in a large office block. 'If you ran you could get there, use the toilet and come back just in time,' he recalls. If he taught six lessons in a row, he got a forty-minute break when he could rush out and eat lunch.

Sannomiya is the business district of Kōbe city. There, Andrew taught office workers with lessons paid for by their companies. Later he was transferred to nearby Ashiya city where the students were bored housewives. With their husbands working long days and their children in school, they had a lot of free time and they came to the eikaiwa, Andrew says, to have a chat. They didn't like the textbooks and they weren't particularly interested in improving their language skills. They just wanted to meet foreigners. This highlights a potential problem for foreign teachers, both male and female. Lessons were held in small private rooms, and many of these women, remembers Andrew – wincing – were very sexual. One even turned up for class naked. 'She was sitting down in a big trench coat in the middle of summer. It's very hot in the summertime so I said, "Do you want to hang your coat up?" She stood up. Opened it. Nothing on. Absolutely nothing.'

Women comprise the majority of students at eikaiwa. Although Japanese companies are increasingly realising the need for all its employees to attain English proficiency, it is male workers who are more likely to be offered in-house lessons. Working women have to make their own arrangements. In the traditional belief that they have housekeeping or childcare duties at home, female office workers are not generally expected to remain late in the office, giving them the opportunity to attend an evening class. Persisting gender inequalities in the workplace also mean that ambitious women may view English proficiency as an escape route to more fulfilling careers, either abroad or with Japan-based foreign firms which are more open to promoting women.

Eikaiwa also attract married women seeking to fill their days. And a young white male (a commodified symbol in Asia) embodies the western ideal of 'ladies first'. Eikaiwa are for-profit businesses. They know their customer base. It is no accident that their advertising often features a smiling white man sitting in close proximity to a Japanese woman. Given the suggestive nature of eikaiwa advertising, and the fact that students can select with which teacher they wish to spend time in a private room, harassment can – and does – occur. 'You're paid to have a happy face,' explains

Andrew. 'But they misunderstand the attention and it causes odd behaviour.' As paying customers, students are never admonished. Whenever a complaint is made, it is the teacher who is transferred to a distant branch. Or fired.

I ask Andrew if he recalls many foreign women suffering harassment, but he can't remember any he has worked with long term. Most female teachers at the global eikaiwa lasted two to three months at most. These days many conversation schools have converted to glass cubicles so managers can observe the teachers (and hopefully also the students) at all times.

As competition for students became intense, Andrew's global eikaiwa rearranged its salary structure, increasing lesson pay but removing all bonuses (Sunday pay, overtime and a higher pay grade for long-term employees). Andrew's work increased by twenty per cent but his salary fell by forty per cent. In 2016, after six happy years, he quit, which in hindsight was a terrible move, as his divorce was finalised the same week and he found himself without a visa.

On the rebound, he joined a 'freelance' eikaiwa, a working situation he describes as 'the worst I've ever experienced in my life'. Teachers at this school are not classed as employees but as outsourced contract workers. His job began with two weeks of mandatory unpaid training. Then every month, Andrew would inform the school of his availability and he would have to sit in the office during that time, whether he had a lesson booked or not. The eikaiwa is known for offering walk-in lessons, so teachers have to make themselves available. But if no walk-ins materialised or if a student failed to turn up for a booked lesson, he was paid nothing.

This school uses open booths, so teachers and students can hear the lessons going on around them, as can office managers. Teachers are expected to clean the booths before every lesson but, Andrew recalls, no one did, which led to schools closing during the Covid pandemic as the virus spread between staff and students. The staff room, where the drinks machines were located, was reserved for Japanese staff, and the toilets were too far away to reach on a five-minute break.

In rare cases, as long as teachers maintain a certain number of working hours (164 lessons per month but teachers are pushed to teach 220) and are available between 7am and 10pm (potentially fifteen-hour days), four days a week, this freelance company will sponsor working visas for highly qualified candidates and for those, like Andrew, who suddenly find themselves divorced. 'They will sponsor your visa for the price of your soul,' he says.

To work in Japan you must hold either a working visa or, if you are married to a local, a spouse visa. To qualify for a working visa, you must be working full time (a minimum of thirty hours per week) and earning at least three million yen a year. With a reputable company, this is possible.

The average salary for a full-time eikaiwa teacher is around 250,000 yen (£1,220) per month. That's three million yen a year (£14,645), less than the UK's national living wage of £11.44 per hour or £22,010 a year (2024 figures). Deductions of around ten per cent each for income tax, health insurance, city tax and pension contributions will take forty per cent of that. Unless you become an office manager, that figure will never increase. And the more unscrupulous eikaiwa don't pay even that. They cap weekly working hours at twenty-nine and salaries at 2.9 million yen to avoid sponsoring visas or having to pay health insurance or pension contributions. 'It's abysmal how low the salaries are,' says Andrew.

In recent years, there has been pushback from eikaiwa teachers who have formed unions and taken strike action. The Japanese government has begun looking into 'black' eikaiwa, which operate illegally and cheat unsuspecting foreign teachers out of payments and benefits. But in 2007, when teachers at Berlitz went on strike, the company attempted to sue them, claiming that the strike was illegal.[12] Although the teachers won, litigation dragged on for five years. Faced with a lengthy and expensive legal process to address grievances, many eikaiwa teachers simply pack up and go home.

Unsurprisingly, eikaiwa have a high turnover of teachers. For many, the job is a year or two of freedom and adventure after graduation. Ninety-seven per cent of eikaiwa teachers leave Japan within three years.[13] 'Everybody leaves,' states Andrew. 'Everyone is a temporary friend.' Andrew has friends all over the world, ex-colleagues he met in the eikaiwa business. But he'll probably never see any of them again. 'I remember the good experiences and move on,' he says.

Many of Andrew's British ex-eikaiwa friends have moved to Germany to work as translators for Nintendo. Andrew unsuccessfully applied there once, which is a pity as he was a pro-gamer in his youth. In 2000, at age fourteen, he played in the first national Nintendo Pokémon Championship at the Millennium Dome, losing in the semi-finals. 'I got so angry at losing, I never stayed for my awards,' he says, ruefully. I venture that an early interest in Pokémon may have disposed him to pursue the Japanese language but he replies that at the time he had no idea Pokémon was Japanese.

Despite constant staffing upheavals, eikaiwa can count on resident foreigners who are unwilling or unable to leave. These include the foreign spouses of Japanese nationals, often highly trained abroad but unqualified to do anything in Japan but teach English. Andrew, who has worked with lawyers- and doctors-turned-English-teachers, is adamant. 'Japan is not a place to come for success.' Other foreign teachers may be divorced from Japanese spouses but wish to maintain a relationship with their children. Japanese law does not recognise joint custody in divorce and, if a foreign parent returns to their home country, they may lose all contact. At the global eikaiwa, Andrew worked with eight other teachers and everyone, including Andrew, was divorced. 'There are a lot of divorced foreign men in Japan,' he says, 'just drifting through, doing nothing.'

But working at an eikaiwa does earn you a valuable asset: 'kone' or connections. 'The key to survival for any English teacher,' Andrew says, 'is private students.' For Japanese learners of English the price of a single lesson at an eikaiwa can be prohibitively expensive, anything from 7,000-15,000 yen. Students who pay out of their own or their parents' pockets, are keen to save money and – since teachers on low salaries are eager to find extra sources of income – it makes sense that they take on students as private clients. Called fishing, it's the secret to an eikaiwa teacher's survival. 'It's against the contract but it's what a lot of teachers do,' Andrew admits. 'A lot of students join these companies to find private teachers as well, so it works.' If a forty-minute eikaiwa lesson costs a student 10,000 yen and the teacher is paid 1,500 yen, then even if the teacher charges 5,000 yen for a private lesson, the student saves money and the teacher earns more. Over the years, Andrew developed his eikaiwa kone and, when he decided to go it alone, his students moved with him.

Andrew now has a lot of private students. His youngest is seven, his oldest in her mid-nineties. Young people like lessons on their smartphones (which Andrew says is a nightmare to teach due to slow internet connections and the difficulties of reading text on a small screen) but older students prefer face-to-face meetings. Andrew teaches several groups of retirees in rooms he rents at municipal centres. But his favourite lessons are group classes in private homes where the housewives vie to outdo each other with expensive blends of tea and fancy pastries. Declares Andrew, 'It's a ninety-minute lesson, one hour of which is eating cakes.'

Other perks of being a private teacher are the free

gifts. He owns seven watches (he used to like wearing one on each wrist) and he's been gifted a smartphone and a computer. They're not new. His wealthier clients constantly upgrade and simply pass on their unwanted electronics to him.

Since the Covid pandemic, eighty per cent of Andrew's work has moved online, for which he offers discounts. Teaching remotely gives him several free hours every day, time that he – and his students – would otherwise spend travelling. Andrew hates commuting and lives thirty minutes outside Ōsaka in a small city called Takarazuka, between a shrine and a temple, 'so I've got green on both sides'.

He also works for a couple of despatch (temping) agencies which send him out on company jobs, teaching speech training and public speaking. He teaches classes for Kōbe University and for the immigration office, and he often judges speech contests. His most stimulating job is with the Japanese police, holding discussion-based English classes about other countries' legal systems. Sometimes they practise interviews, and Andrew roleplays an English-speaking criminal. The police seem to enjoy the classes, says Andrew, probably because it's a distraction from long hours sitting in a kōban (a neighbourhood police station). 'And hopefully it means I'll never be arrested,' he laughs. Awareness of his law enforcement connection also encouraged a 'black' talent agency to cough up his back pay.

When I first spoke with Andrew, via Zoom during the Covid pandemic, he had recently divorced from a second marriage (which lasted five months) and knew that his visa would expire in 2023. It was crunch time and he was debating whether to stay or to leave Japan. By the time we meet for lunch in Ōsaka, he has gained permanent residency and is pondering the complexities of registering a corporate address when you don't own your home. His business plan is to attract subscribers to his YouTube channel who, with the aid of a monthly workbook compiled by Andrew, can follow his lessons. He's thinking of setting the subscription at no more than 1,000 yen a month (around £5). One thousand subscribers would mean he could stop his despatch agency work, although he doesn't see that happening any time soon.

Having committed to spending his life in Japan, I ask him if the next step is to become a naturalised Japanese citizen, but this he is vehemently against. 'Because I would lose my British citizenship,' he points out. 'I'm not super patriotic but I am proud to be British.' And he does miss Wales. If he could go anywhere in the world, he tells me, he'd choose a caravan in west Wales and recreate the childhood holidays he spent with his grandmother. 'As a child, I hated it,' he remembers. 'There was no TV, no computer games. But now ah, just to sit there in the quiet, reading a book.'

He even credits his hometown with sparking his interest in astrophysics. Pentyrch is a very dark place. 'And I don't mean that in a metaphorical sense,' he says. 'It's a literal dark place.' It is so dark that, from up on Mynydd y Garth he could see all the stars in heaven.

He often wonders what his life would have been like if he hadn't dropped out of his astrophysics degree. 'I think I would be far more successful now,' he muses. 'I love physics. I love science. I love numbers. I love mathematics. And I do miss it. Because you don't use your brain much, teaching kids.' Of the 'science' friends he has kept in touch with, three now work in the medical profession as general practitioners or specialist doctors, one develops new tools for the CIA in America, and one works in engineering for MI5.

Since he left Wales in 2010, he has only been back once, for his grandfather's funeral. Now approaching forty, he has no experience of working in his home country and, outside of London, there is little call for either English language teaching or Japanese translation. Other than family – his parents, two sisters and a brother – he has nothing to go back to. And he's not sure they'd be that pleased to see him. 'I think I'm more stress than anything,' he confesses. He admits it is his pride that has kept him in Japan, working long hours, doing unusual jobs. When he left Wales, he told his parents, 'If I ever come back, it means I've failed.'

But at the same time, he loves his life in Japan. 'It's easy,' he admits. 'There are aspects I hate: houses are small, neighbours are noisy. But I love being a foreigner in Japan. I love the attention.' He shows me his schedule for the next few months. He works an average of twenty hours a week and gets paid the same as a Japanese man working sixty. He enjoys plenty of free time and he runs ten kilometres a day, measuring his heart rate with a Fitbit he received as a present.

As we finish our meal, Andrew worries that he is coming across too negatively. He has no regrets about moving to Japan. He's 'happyish'. And if his YouTube subscription business takes off, he'll be ecstatic. 'The first few years in Japan are the most difficult,' he declares. 'Once you get used to it, it's fun.'

Andrew's subscription YouTube channel is: BEK English @bekeikaiwa

Eikaiwa Teaching Chaos at Peppy Kids Club

***Gerald Gallivan** from Cardiff has an undergraduate degree in archaeology and a diploma in English with TEFL (Teaching English as a Foreign Language), both from the University of Wales Lampeter (now Trinity St David). A keen traveller, in 2014 he moved to Japan to work for an eikaiwa:*

I remember looking for English teaching jobs in Japan. I did a bit of research on the internet and ended up finding a job with a company called Peppy Kids Club. It's an eikaiwa that's based throughout Japan. They must have translated 'genki' (happy, in good health) as 'peppy'. I applied for the job online and I went to the office in London for an interview. I had to do a little teaching demonstration but I think they were taking anybody. Probably I was terrible at that time. They were like, 'Yeah, great.' And I got the job.

The first two weeks I was sent to Nagoya to train in their head office. I had to pay for the training, which I thought was cheeky. It was paid for over ten months from my pay packet: 10,000 yen every month for ten months. Paid training. Paid for by me. It was pretty much a blur of tons of material and tons of lessons and all this information just suddenly rammed in. I met loads of other foreigners from around the world. We were told beforehand where we would be staying. I was told I would be in north Japan somewhere. It ended up being in Iwate prefecture in this random little city.

Pretty much you were left to your own devices. You'd be in a classroom by yourself with loads of little kids. No co-worker. The only help you had was a telephone to call head office. But they couldn't do much besides give you some advice. Or maybe, if it was really bad, they could call the parent and have them come in.

The first few months were a blur. I remember just being 'lost in translation'. Kids would ask me things. I didn't know what they were saying. I couldn't understand anything. I used to teach kindergarten kids up to junior high school level. The earliest class at Peppy used to be at 3.45pm on weekdays and 11am on

Saturdays. So I started work late: it's an after-school club. There were group classes, up to twelve kids. So it could be me and twelve kindergarten kids by myself. Which was pretty wild. The lessons were one hour, irrespective of age, which I thought was too long for kindergarten kids. Their attention span was not good for an hour. It was pretty hard to keep them going.

I taught the fundamental basics which were colours, numbers and shapes. And 'I like...'. That's about it. Really basic, with lots of songs and dancing. It was just glorified babysitting. I don't think there were many expectations. The older ages, you taught them proper things and more grammatical stuff. And some of them could actually speak a bit more English.

They're called schools but they're not schools. They're just rooms rented out. In Tomiya city, I worked in an Aeon which is a big shopping mall. There was a brand new classroom on the second floor. It didn't have a toilet inside the classroom. The toilet was on the other side of the shopping mall. And I was dealing with ten little kids every Saturday. And every Saturday in that classroom, someone needed to go to the toilet. You're not allowed to leave the kids alone in the classroom. So I had to have them all hold hands and walk them all to the toilet together. I used to go to the disabled toilets – the multifunctional toilets – and have them all go in together. It happened one time where suddenly a Japanese voice came out of the speakers and I looked around and one of the kids was pressing the emergency button over and over. It was pretty rough, because the entire lesson would be going back and forth to the toilet. You'd get back to the classroom and then another kid would be like, 'I need to go too.' OK, back we go. It would be thirty minutes of going back and forth to the toilet.

Now I'm working in a school called Cambridge English. It's run by a British guy and his Japanese wife. It's a much better setting. You're never alone. It's only one location. So there are three classrooms and enough teachers for those classrooms. I teach all ages up to high school and adults, and it's a much more controlled setting. And we have tables and chairs. In Peppy Kids Club there were no chairs. Everybody sat on the floor. There was no technology at Peppy Kids Club: no computers, no internet. In this company now, I use TVs and Google Slides to do lessons.

I don't think I'll be going back to archaeology, ever. I think teaching is definitely the thing I like. I just love teaching kids. It's really good fun. I think I want to try and continue teaching, whether it's here or back in the UK.

Mike Kettle *from Cilycwm did an undergraduate degree in philosophy and psychology at Swansea University and followed it up with a one-month TEFL course in Prague. He moved to Tōkyō to work for NOVA in 2007*:

I was working in Shibuya, right in Hachikō Crossing because there used to be a NOVA building there. And then after about six months, I went to work one day and there was yellow police tape over the building's door. And my very limited Japanese helped me understand. I said, 'Nani o shimasu ka?' (what's happening) And this guy went, 'Ah, Nova. No money. Finish.'

I went home. An email came later that said, 'NOVA's filed for bankruptcy. You guys no longer have a job.' Something like 7,000 teachers were made redundant. The Japanese government stepped in and froze all of our bills: rent, electricity, telephone bills, everything for three months. And they gave us a pretty nice jobseeker's allowance as well. We were on about 80,000 yen – about £391 a month – as long as we went to the local ward office and attempted – *attempted* – to look for a job twice each month. Attempted meant: you go in, you say, 'Are there any jobs for English teachers?' And they go, 'I don't know.' And then that's it. That happened for three months. Then NOVA was bought out by another company and we ended up going back – fifty per cent retention. I was a newer guy so I was in the fifty per cent that wasn't retained. I ended up going back to the UK.

The reason NOVA went bankrupt was because the guy who ran it informed his secretaries to get students to sign five-year contracts for lessons and to pay up front. And most of their students were over sixty years old. So a lot of these vulnerable older people were giving them millions of yen to schedule lessons for five years. And then NOVA weren't giving them the privileges they were owed. I think that's illegal. I don't think they could actually demand five years' worth of payments up front. The government told him to give the money back but he'd already invested it in new schools. NOVA had this programme to open a school every day for a year, which they did in 2005. Basically they had no money and had to declare bankruptcy. I heard the boss skipped off to the Virgin Islands outside of Japanese jurisdiction and still hasn't been prosecuted.

I had no complaints. I came back to Wales and within about three months my salary had been put into my UK account. And I then used that to do a master's degree in marketing and management at Swansea University.

Chapter Five

'Leave the Space and Let It Be': Paul Baxter looks back on his architectural career in Japan

Paul Baxter today at Andō's 'Silence' water feature

I have known architect Paul Baxter and his wife, Kumi, for over thirty years. Paul, originally from Cricieth, was involved in the design of some of Japan's modern iconic buildings, as well as being an eyewitness to the hedonism of eighties Tōkyō. I met up with him in London after my return from Japan.

'Silence' is a circular water feature in Mount Street, Mayfair. It is the work of Tadao Andō, Japan's most famous living architect, known for the simplicity and perfection of his designs. His use of space, light and water brings a Zen-like calm to his creations, while his choice of concrete and glass gives them a clean, minimalist line. Andō is a revered figure in Japan, though less so in Britain. His only building in the UK, a pavilion in Manchester's Piccadilly Gardens, was branded one of Tripadvisor's worst tourist attractions and was saved from destruction only when the council agreed to cover its grey façade with a living wall of plants. Concrete minimalism is not everyone's idea of natural beauty. London's 'Silence', however, appears to be much more popular: with walkers, their dogs and with diners at the Connaught Hotel's restaurant which overlooks the installation. Every fifteen minutes, 'Silence' emits a cooling mist, enveloping two trees which grow out of the feature. And, as clouds of water vapour drift away on a light spring breeze, I spot a figure, tall, blond and slightly stooping, waiting on the other side.

This is architect Paul Baxter's first visit to 'Silence', although he met its architect in the eighties. As he inspects the smooth curve of its single ellipse and the reflecting pond nature of the water's surface, he gives me a running commentary of his thoughts. Paul understands Andō's choice of black granite over concrete, given how the water must flow smoothly down its sides. The trees, which presumably could have been removed, Paul believes Andō chose to incorporate. 'It's a technical feat to build around them,' he points out. The water gives the feature movement as well as sound: a white noise combination of babbling brook and the hiss of the atomisers which produce the mist. For a brief moment, traffic disappears and its roar is dulled. 'It's typically Andō,' concludes Paul. 'It's relaxing and it brings a nice calm to the centre of the square.' He likes it very much.

In a nearby coffee shop Paul opens his bag and produces books, photographs and pencil drawings on tracing paper, mementoes of a long architectural career. He spent thirteen years in Tōkyō, working on some of Japan's most iconic buildings. Paul was influenced in his choice of career by his artistic mother who ran a gift/home goods shop, and left interior design magazines lying around the family home. As his father rose in the ranks at nearby Pwllheli's Butlin's camp, the family moved from a flat on the seafront to a large detached house overlooking the bay which Paul's parents later ran as a hotel.

Paul began his education at Cricieth Primary (where he picked up schoolboy Welsh) before moving to Rydal boarding school in Colwyn Bay. At eighteen, he went up to Cambridge to study architecture, disappointing his high school teachers who thought he was wasting his brain on a frivolous subject. Qualifying as an architect in 1984, he decided to do something 'extra academic' and applied for a MEXT scholarship which funds around twenty British high-flyers to study at universities in Japan.[14] Having previously only viewed Japan through architectural magazines, he describes his desire to visit the country as a mixture of 'curiosity and opportunity'.

Paul, with latest Japanese gadget, a Walkman, at Andō's Times Building, Kyōto

At Tōkyō's University of Technology, Professor Masahiro Chatani, the head of the design laboratory, advised Paul that the best way to learn about Japanese architecture was to go out and see it.[15] Paul travelled from Hokkaidō to Kyūshū visiting Japan's most important buildings and putting a cross against them in his bible, *A Guide to Japanese Architecture.* In Kyōto, he made a pilgrimage to Katsura Imperial Villa.

Katsura Villa was built by Prince Toshihito Hachijō (1579–1629), a descendent of the Japanese imperial line and adopted son of daimyō (feudal lord) Hideyoshi Toyotomi (1537–1598), one of three great unifying leaders of Japan. When Toyotomi gifted his son land on the banks of the Katsura River, Hachijō chose to build a palace inspired by an eleventh-century tale. *Genji Monogatari* or *The Tale of Genji*, by Murasaki Shikibu narrates the romantic and political life of an illegitimate imperial son of an emperor living on the banks of that same river.

The construction of Katsura Villa was influenced by the style of Shintō shrines and the philosophy of Zen Buddhism. Modular in design, it features three connected halls. Without permanent walls, shōji (translucent sliding panels) and fusuma (opaque, often highly decorated, sliding panels) allow for a constant reconfiguring of the space. Rooms can be partitioned off or opened up to offer views of a landscape which changes with the seasons. Katsura also embodies the concept of 'ma', negative or empty space, where rooms may feature nothing more than a decorative screen. A Japanese interior designer once told me that when a western person walks into a room, they see the objects in it, whereas a Japanese person observes the space between them. Says Paul, 'A western person looks at a bare wall and says, "What can I put on it? What can I put in front of it? How can I inhabit that space?" The Japanese tradition is not to do that, necessarily. There isn't a sense that the vacuum needs to be filled.' Negative space inspires a sense of quiet contemplation because there is nothing to detract from it, and the work of architects such as Andō is recognisable not because of what they put in it but what they choose to leave out. Their natural inclination, says Paul, 'is to leave the space and let it be'.

When Japan reopened in the nineteenth century, its government raced to modernise the nation's infrastructure. Train tracks were hurriedly laid, the military was modernised and offices necessary to support a trading economy sprung up. Official buildings, particularly banks, were constructed in a neoclassical style in heavy brick and stone, which looked solid and dependable but proved disastrous during earthquakes, particularly the Great Kantō Earthquake of 1923. Then, as Japan rebuilt after the Second World War, there was much copying of modernist architecture, as popularised by Swiss–French architect Charles-Édouard Jeanneret aka Le Corbusier, hailed as the founder of modern architecture, and German–American Walter Gropius, founder of the Bauhaus school. For several decades, many Japanese prefectural offices, gymnasia and auditoria were built in this brutalist style, financed with pork barrel money, government funds targeted at rural areas hit by economic and population decline and also to curry favour with ageing regional voters.

But it is interesting to note just how much the western modernist architects were influenced by Katsura Villa. Visiting in 1933, German architect Bruno Taut, a forerunner of Le Corbusier, wrote that Katsura is 'absolutely modern and of complete validity for any contemporary architecture'.[16] Gropius, who spent three months in Japan in 1954, was stunned at how Katsura's traditional architecture embodied – and obviously predated by centuries – many of the elements of modernism that he had been developing throughout his career. When Le Corbusier visited in 1955, he was photographed taking copious notes. What's more, many of Japan's eminent architects began their careers working in the studios of these modernists. Kunio Maekawa (1905–1986, creator of the Tōkyō Metropolitan Festival Hall) trained with Le

Corbusier in Paris in the 1920s and worked with him on the National Museum of Western Art in Tōkyō. Kenzō Tange (1913–2005, designer of the Hiroshima Peace Memorial Park) then worked for Maekawa. By embracing a modernist simplicity, these architects were, in effect, rediscovering traditional Japanese design elements that are epitomised by Katsura Villa. It could even be argued that modernist architecture was warmly embraced in Japan precisely because it was nothing new. Now owned by the Imperial Household Agency, Katsura Villa, its gardens and teahouses, continue to be a place of pilgrimage for architects from all over the world. Despite its age, it remains an icon of modern architecture.

The melding of western modernism with a traditional sensibility has produced some outstanding buildings with a uniquely Japanese flavour. The Kyōto International Conference Center is a prime example, says Paul, leafing through his architecture book. Designed by Sachio Ōtani (who began his career in Tange's studio) it is a metabolist structure of connected buildings onto which others can (and have) been added. Whilst the bases of the buildings are triangular in shape, mimicking Japan's volcanic mountains, they are topped by reinterpretations of Japanese pagoda. Exposed beams constructed not of timber but in concrete give a visual fluidity typical of traditional shrines and temples. And the centre is situated by a lake, offering views of and access to nature and to a Japanese garden.

Paul's favourite building remains the Yoyogi National Gymnasium which Tange designed for the 1964 Tōkyō Olympics and which, Paul says, remains as fresh and beautiful as when it was built sixty years ago. Although constructed with reinforced concrete, it has a tensile, tent-like appearance, with cables supporting a roof which sweeps around from towers at either end. It has a fluidity, says Paul, which gives the building that 'unmistakable Japanese feel'.

The eighties, Paul recalls, was a good time to be young in Japan. In only four decades, Japan had transformed from a defeated nation into the world's second largest economy. It had achieved this through manufacturing, particularly high-quality consumer electronics which sold cheaply overseas. Having initially copied western products, Japanese companies began to innovate. The eighties was the era of the Sony Walkman, the Canon camera, JVC video recorder, and of Nintendo and Sega video games. In the eighties, Japan also became the world's largest auto producer. Smaller, fuel-efficient Nissans, Toyotas and Hondas zoomed off assembly lines and swiftly replaced big American cars. In retaliation, disgruntled American auto workers were filmed smashing Japanese electronic goods with hammers.

Japanese exports were driven by a weak yen. Seeking to ease this trade deficit and to make their exports competitive again, the United States was the motivating force behind the 1985 Plaza Accord in which the world's five richest countries (the United States, Japan, Germany, France and the UK) agreed to devalue the US dollar in relation to the yen and the deutschmark. Consequently, Japanese products became more expensive in foreign countries. To compensate, the Japanese government sought to increase demand in their domestic market by implementing monetary easing policies: cutting interest rates and encouraging banks to lend money cheaply. This sparked a national spending spree as individuals took out cheap loans to purchase real estate and to play the stock market while Japanese companies bought up foreign companies and assets. Sony purchased Columbia Pictures, Mitsubishi snapped up the Rockefeller Center, and the Yasuda Fire and Marine Insurance Company bought one of Van Gogh's 'Sunflowers' for just under US $40 million, a world record for a work of art at that time. (Another had been destroyed in an American bombing raid on Japan during the Second World War.) The Japanese stock and real estate markets tripled in value and the economy expanded like a bubble. On Black Monday 1987, the US stock market crashed but in Japan the spending spree continued. It was widely believed that it was only a matter of time before the Japanese economy overtook that of the United States, the global number one. But in December 1989, the Nikkei peaked.

With lavish spending on travel, leisure, art, clothing and cuisine, Japan also grew culturally rich. The avant-garde designs of Issey Miyake, Yōji Yamamoto, Rei Kawakubo and Kenzō Takada could be found in every fashionista's closet from Tōkyō to Paris, where many Japanese designers relocated. In the eighties, the Japanese movie industry boomed, and it was the most productive decade for two of Japan's most famous directors: Jūzō Itami, whose work included *A Taxing Woman* (1987) and *Tampopo* (1985), and Akira Kurosawa, who released *Kagemusha* (1980) and *Ran* (1985). In 1985, following the success of anime *Nausicaa of the Valley of the Wind*, Hayao Miyazaki founded Studio Ghibli and released in quick succession: *Laputa: Castle in the Sky* (1986), *Grave of the Fireflies* (1988) and *My Neighbour Totoro* (1988). Japanese novels by Ryū Murakami, Banana

Yoshimoto and Haruki Murakami were translated for an English-speaking readership who delighted in their quirky and offbeat stories. And then there were the first video games from Japan, many of which morphed into or were derived from the active manga and anime scene.

Throughout the eighties, the Japanese nation partied. Paul and his university friends joined them, dining out at bustling izakaya (Japanese pubs) before going on to nightclubs such as Club D and Maharaja, where they danced with women with bubble perms and tight bodycon dresses.[17] 'It was hedonistic in the eighties,' recalls Paul. 'Because everyone seemed to have money.'

Paul worked hard, too. He and colleagues entered several architectural competitions, submitting plans for speculative building projects, including one for a new national theatre in Tōkyō which was to include Japan's first dedicated opera house. They didn't win, but out of 230 entrants they got into the last thirty, and the experience had repercussions later in his career.

However, the highlight of Paul's time on the Monbushō programme was meeting Tadao Andō, the creator of 'Silence'. With the confidence of youth, Paul and his friends telephoned Andō's Ōsaka office and wangled themselves an invitation. Born in 1941, Andō had been a boxer before studying architecture at night classes and through correspondence courses, and Paul remembers him as an 'intimidating bloke, very tough'. Paul had heard two stories about the architect, which he admits may be apocryphal but bolstered the man's working-class reputation. Andō had installed only one telephone at his business, placing it immediately outside his office so that he could listen in on all conversations. It was rumoured that he liked to be

With Tadao Andō and others

in complete control over what his employees were doing. The other story was that, in order to instil a respect for their materials, he made them pay for their own pencils and paper. Of meeting their hero, Paul recalls, 'We were all in awe.' But Andō was friendly and accommodating, showing them around his office and talking with them about architecture. Paul holds up a photograph he took of Andō drawing, a moment Paul was so anxious to capture that his thumb is visible across the top of the frame.

When his scholarship ended, Paul decided to stay longer in Japan. He made some telephone calls and was hired by Nihon Sekkei, one of the largest design firms in Japan, with offices in the black and glass monolith of Shinjuku district's Mitsui building (which Nihon Sekkei designed), and which remains standing today despite being destroyed in *The Return of Godzilla* (1984) when the monster rampages through Tōkyō. From his desk on the fifty-fourth floor, he assisted with translations and architectural competitions, designing a golf course in Nagasaki which the owners wanted 'English style'. Golf was the hobby of the bubble years and an important element of Japanese business culture. Club memberships could cost millions of yen and were tradeable assets monitored by the Nikkei Golf Club Membership Index. By the time the bubble burst, two thousand new golf courses had been built in Japan. Paul unfolds a large piece of tracing paper and moves his finger over a design for a pseudo-Tudor clubhouse with a half-timbered wedding hall attached. 'It was ridiculous, actually,' Paul admits. 'Bonkers.' But in the eighties an addiction for all things new and foreign could be fed by ample money. 'It was a symptom of the decadence of the times.'

At Nihon Sekkei

In the bubble economy, land values rocketed while building costs remained comparatively low. This enabled wealthy landowners to be adventurous, encouraging architects to experiment with opulent designs that corresponded with the indulgent mood of the decade. The eighties produced many visionary, avant-garde buildings; some iconic such as Andō's Church of the Light, and others 'ghastly', which is how Paul describes Kengo Kuma's M2 building with its bizarre ionic column. 'It was a postmodern free-for-all,' he grimaces.

In urban areas, the tiny size of building plots also spurred innovation, as architects were compelled to reimagine liveable layouts within tightly constrained building envelopes. Now, small houses in Tōkyō are so iconic they are the subjects of books and YouTube channels.

When his work at Nihon Sekkei ended, Paul returned to the UK where he expected to settle. However, his résumé was picked up by a Japanese architect who had been tasked with finding a foreigner for a big assignment back in Japan. By autumn 1988, Paul found himself back in Tōkyō working at a company called TAK. TAK's big assignment turned out to be the New National Theatre, the project for which Paul had competed several years earlier. Getting into the last thirty got him hired.

Paul pulls out a coffee table book on the New National Theatre and points to several of his own design contributions, particularly in the main foyer where bush-hammered concrete flows seamlessly into warm wood panels, which in turn feed into timber inserts in the travertine marble floors.[18] It was also Paul's idea to mimic the pattern of the timber formwork used to create a wood grain on the building's concrete walls in the actual timber panels that line the theatre's main foyer. And TAK also went with his suggestion to feature apertures in walls that offered different views and lighting effects. As the building took shape, Paul and new wife, Kumi, moved into a small apartment close to the theatre site in Yoyogi, so he could walk over regularly and inspect progress.

Life as a Japanese salaryman could be gruelling. Working until the last train was – and still is – common practice in Japanese companies. When the company was bidding for new design projects, TAK employees would work through the night. Paul recalls regularly dragging himself home in the morning, having a shower, eating a quick breakfast and then heading straight back to the office. He'd do this for several days, including Saturdays, which back then was a regular working day (and until 2002, a school half-day) in Japan.

The boss of TAK was Takahiko Yanagisawa, a

god-like figure whose lightning visits to the office to inspect new drawings provoked 'a frantic, slightly fearful atmosphere' as, with a wave of his hand, he could render weeks of work void. 'We're going in a different direction,' he'd announce to employees who had been pulling all-nighters for a week. 'Go off and start again.' But if he liked an idea, it was immediately incorporated into a design, and this made TAK an exciting place to work. The company was awarded several culturally important projects, and Paul – as a western-trained architect and the only foreigner in the office – played a key role, hired to offer fresh ideas with a western perspective. 'It was incredibly bright of them because it's about cognitive diversity,' he points out. 'They were looking for people to bring along ideas that they wouldn't have thought of.'

By 1992, the Japanese economic bubble had burst. In December that year, the Japanese stock market, the Nikkei 225 Index, dropped by more than half. People defaulted on their loans. The real estate market crashed. Companies went bankrupt. Banks found holes in their accounts. The following ten years were labelled the Lost Decade. But TAK specialised in cultural buildings such as theatres and museums which, Paul points out, was a lucrative specialism to have, just as the economy crashed. 'There was still money around, pork barrel money which allowed them to build these rather glitzy museums, with not so much to put in them.' For a time, TAK employees were kept busy with a new project, Tōkyō Opera City, which included a spectacular world-class concert hall, a fifty-four-storey office tower and a shopping mall. After that, they worked on the Tōkyō Museum of Contemporary Art and the Kōriyama City Museum of Art. But, as fewer large building projects were commissioned, staff numbers at TAK fell. 'It did feel like the end of an era,' Paul admits. In 1998, when Paul turned forty, 'there was definitely a sense that the peak had gone'. With Kumi and their three children – Sian, Owen and Ceri – he returned to London, to work for Nicholas Hare Architects where he later became a partner.

Looking back, Paul realises he was witness to a significant era in Japanese history. Having recovered from total devastation after the Second World War, the Japanese economy was threatening to surpass that of the United States and the nation seemed hellbent on celebrating prematurely. 'There was a certain hubris about it which was understandable because they'd come from nothing and they were challenging to be Number One,' he says. 'But it was remarkable how quickly it could go downhill.' Although he did not know it then, Japan was experiencing its 'last days of Rome'. 'Japan was at the very peak of its economic power, but with cracks beginning to appear,' he recalls. 'I was blissfully ignorant of that.'

He was also an observer of – and contributor to – an exciting period in Japanese architectural history, when ideas and money converged to produce culturally significant designs. Ninety-five per cent of buildings – office blocks and mass housing – look the same anywhere in the world. But as Japan rebuilt, Japanese architects, funded by the Japanese postwar economic miracle, created iconic structures, what Paul calls Architecture with a capital A.

After Covid restrictions were lifted in 2022, Paul flew back to Tōkyō and wandered around the New National Theatre. Twenty-five years after it opened, Paul is pleased at how well the building, and the elements he designed for it, are holding up. Japan is a nation constantly under construction. Each generation wants a new house, and buildings are expected to last no more than thirty to forty years before they are pulled down and replaced, sometimes aided by typhoons and earthquakes. But for as long as the New National Theatre stands, Paul can know that something he designed remains part of Tōkyō's architectural history.

British Hills The British theme park on top of a Japanese mountain

In 2014, former eikaiwa teacher ***Mike Kettle*** *took a job at British Hills, a sixty-acre English language immersion village on top of a mountain in Ōkawa Hatori Park in Fukushima prefecture. It is seventy miles from the Dai-ichi Nuclear Power Plant:*

My friend saw a job advertisement for this ridiculous-sounding place, a British theme park in the north of Fukushima. This eccentric, rich Japanese guy wanted to recreate Britain on a mountain top. Apparently, the climate of the mountain top was similar to the Scottish Highlands. The rumour was that he and his wife were anglophiles and that, when she got too old to travel, he decided to bring Britain to her. And he recreated her favourite areas. It cost millions of pounds in the eighties and it took ten years to build.

They wanted to use original British oak. And they used so much oak that maintenance of the Globe Theatre in Stratford had to be put on hold because British Hills had acquired almost all the oak that was available at the time.

There's a village with eight guest houses and they all look like they've come out of Stratford-upon-Avon. The huge manor house has been modelled partly on the front doors of Westminster Abbey. The interior has all been done with official Wedgwood designs. And they've got these Chesterfield sofas, really low wide-backed ones with the big button indentations, real hallmarks of British sofas. And then upstairs they've got a full library with one of the original pressings of the *Strand Magazine* with all the original Arthur Conan Doyle instalments of Sherlock Holmes in them.

They also have two bedrooms in the manor house that were modelled on guest houses in Buckingham Palace. I don't know if this is true but I heard that they asked the palace if they could model them on their guest houses. Buckingham Palace refused and they did it anyway. They just said, 'What are they going to do? Come to this random mountain top in Japan to check?' No. So there are these amazing, really beautiful, luxurious rooms with pictures of Queen Elizabeth.

There's also a snooker room with three full-size

tables which were built in Liverpool and transported to Japan. They are three of only nine full-size snooker tables in Japan. They hold the national snooker tournament at British Hills because they've got three of the big ones. No expense spared at this place.

Also there's a pub that is quintessentially British. And a dining hall that was modelled after Christ Church College, Oxford University. It also looks a bit like Hogwarts. All the kids love that. They go in there and say, 'Oh, Harry Potter mitai (lookalike)!' And they take pictures of it.

I think originally British Hills was supposed to be a bit of an escape for CEOs and people of that ilk to get out of the city and have a relaxing time. The snooker room has a whisky bar and there's also a room for 'gentlemen' downstairs with these beautiful sofas and tables. And there were smoking areas where the gentlemen could smoke cigars and have a whisky. As time went on, these all became unprofitable, so they changed tack and turned it into an immersive English school. When I was working there, every week they'd have three or four high schools come up, and they'd bring about two hundred students each. We'd teach them in four ninety-minute classes a day. And we used the environment to help them feel immersed in the culture. It was fun.

One of the most popular lessons was scone cooking. There are these old kitchens that they fitted with beautiful oak beams running through them, and these old ovens. We'd teach the students how to make scones and put jam and cream on them, and then they'd take them off to the teahouse and enjoy them. There was an 'Ascot' teahouse where they'd have high tea on these little trays. Often they'd be taking pictures outside the teahouse with their scones. 'Ah, kawaii! Hontō ni igirisu-jin!' (Cute! Like real English people!) That was really fun.

A big part of my shtick when I'd meet the kids used to be me telling them about crazy Welsh names like Llanfairpwllgwyngyllgogerychwyrndrobwll-llantysiliogogogoch. And that we have dragons. Oh, yeah, we all have pet dragons in Wales. If you go there, you need to feed them. There was a big copper statue of a love spoon. That was part of our tour as well. We'd show them the love spoon and give them a bit of its history. Apart from the love spoon, there were not a lot of Welsh things there. Just me.

I loved it. It was amazing. But you definitely knew your role was to be a performer. These kids would come up and you were wheeled out to do your little performance and they'd go, 'Ooh!' [furious clapping]. You felt like a celebrity. The kids would chase you around and want to get pictures with you. But if you looked at them directly, they'd go, 'Waah!' They'd freak out.

It was a popular place for film studios to come and shoot movies. Do you know a guy called Odagiri Joe? He's been in a couple of movies here and there. People found out that he was going to be in this television show that they were filming, and we were asked whether we wanted to volunteer. I really enjoyed his performances in a couple of movies so I said, 'Yeah, I want to be in that.' He was playing a Japanese prime minister. At the turn of the century, during the Russo–Japanese War, Japan needed to build warships to fight against the Russian Navy. So the prime minister went to the UK to get finance and ask them to help build what they needed. We were playing British bankers, and we were like [posh banker's voice] 'Oh, welcome, welcome. Yes, you've had a very good idea, investing in our British companies. Good luck with those Ruskies.' That kind of stuff. It was great. I got to meet Odagiri Joe. He's really short.

People back home said, 'You're going to Fukushima? Ooooh, be careful up there. Make sure you wear a hazmat suit.' Every morning, staff would have to go out with these machines and check for radiation because they had guests coming up constantly, so they always had to make sure it was completely safe. They had these little machines that made that kind of 'rrrrrrr' noise. And they'd stick them into trees, roots and soil. Because that's generally where the radiation is. If it's there, it's being pulled up into the roots. But they always, *always* had a lower background radiation than the average reading in America, which is kind of interesting. So it was not a problem. But where we were was very far away from where the nuclear fallout had been. Having said that, when I moved there, you could see the fallout, the social fallout. So many people had abandoned Fukushima. There were many areas where houses had just been abandoned. People had just moved out of that area. And there were these big blue bales of soil. They looked like massive hay bales in this blue packaging. They had been identified as radioactive. They had traces of radiation. And they'd been putting these at the edges of fields.

There are certain areas in Fukushima where the government have done things like offer free houses to people who will live in the area. If you move to certain areas of Fukushima and you stay for ten years, they'll pay back your mortgage and give you the house. They're trying to get people back. They need people back because businesses are drying up. And it's a massive crop area as well. I think it supplies something like a third of Japanese tobacco. The biggest tobacco manufacturer in Japan is in Fukushima. There's a lot of tobacco grown up there. The Japanese government is one of the only governments in the world where the tobacco industry is run by the finance department, not the health department. The finance department gave billions of yen to Fukushima for rehousing, trying to rejuvenate it. And when you find out that a lot of their tobacco crops are grown there, you go, 'Ah okay, I see why they did that.' There was a dark joke that if you do smoke, you're automatically getting free radiotherapy.

It was totally fine. Absolutely fine. They'd done as much research as they could, to know that it was safe. The whole area where we were, there were never any issues. We'll find out, I guess, in thirty years. But at the time, it was fine. Absolutely fine.

Chapter Six

Big Man Jitsu: In the dōjō with seventh kyū black belt, Jaime Morrish

Jaime Morrish, jiu jitsu seventh kyū black belt

It's a crisp spring evening and a fading light filters through the windows of the dōjō (training hall) at the Nagoya City East Sports Center. To our left, a group of men spar with single sticks. To our right, a lone teen rehearses his J-Pop dance moves in front of a mirror. We warm up on the soft mats in the centre then gather to watch our sensei, a third dan black belt, demonstrate a roundhouse kick. Pairing up, we practise, me in a pair of Marks & Spencer leggings, the other students in white gi (pyjama-style martial arts training wear). The walls echo to the cries of 'Hyah!' as we repeatedly land blows on our opponents who are cushioned in padded gloves and punch pads. Our sensei, in a long black hakama (pleated trousers), glides between us correcting stances and refining technique. It's a typical martial arts training session that might happen on any evening in Japan. Except that our sensei is Welsh.

Jaime Morrish doesn't strike you as a man who could kill you with his bare hands. Sure, he's six feet tall and built like a prop forward (the position he plays in rugby). But he's a cheerful, smiling character. He tells stories against himself with good humour. He laughs more than he talks. And he talks with a laugh. He seems permanently relaxed. But if you're an eighteen stone jiu jitsu master, little intimidates you.

It was his mother who introduced Jaime and his older brother, Hywel, to martial arts. When she discovered that their local policeman in Aberaman was a jūdō teacher, she joined his class and took the boys with her. Jaime was two. 'I could do jūdō before I could walk,' he laughs.

Jaime and his brother are close. As kids they sparred with each other, 'running around the house trying to be Bruce Lee'. It was Hywel who first joined a jiu jitsu class at university. Home for the holidays he'd teach Jaime wrist and arm locks. So, in 1996, when Jaime went up to Manchester University to study applied biological sciences, he headed straight to the freshers' fair and signed up to learn the same style, shōrinji kan.

Originating in India, jiu jitsu or the 'gentle art'

developed in Japan in the fifteenth century as a fighting discipline practised by samurai, the warrior class. Samurai protected their regional feudal lords, the daimyō, and were the only class permitted to wear two swords and to execute commoners at will. Over time, jiu jitsu split into distinct fighting styles known as ryū, including jiujitsu and aikijitsu, kenjitsu and karate.

With the arrival of the western powers in the late nineteenth century, the Japanese government realised it needed to modernise its army. The samurai class was abolished and its martial arts were forced underground or else adapted from 'jitsu' (an art) to 'dō' (a way). Martial arts had developed to maim and to kill but as 'dō', practitioners could develop them as more spiritual pursuits concentrating on the mental and physical health benefits. And as sports they could be included in the school curriculum. Aikijitsu developed into aikidō, kenjitsu became kendō, and jiujitsu evolved into jūdō.

Traditional jiu jitsu fell out of favour until it resurfaced in Brazil, carried there by poor Japanese immigrants before being taken up nationally and adapted. Today when most Japanese hear the term jiu jitsu they think of the Brazilian style popularised in MMA – mixed martial arts – fighting, in UFC (Ultimate Fighting Championships) and in cage fighting. There are several Brazilian jiu jitsu dōjō in Nagoya but the original Japanese style remains a somewhat clandestine practice. Unlike other martial arts clubs, Japanese jiu jitsu classes are difficult to join. 'It's a closed environment,' says Jaime.

As the older of the martial arts, jiu jitsu developed techniques which are now fundamental to other disciplines, such aikidō locks, jūdō throws, karate strikes and kickboxing kicks. Jaime describes shōrinji kan jiu jitsu as a 'jack of all trades' martial art, ideal for practical self-defence. He would know. One evening, while returning from a training session in Manchester, he was seated on the top deck of a bus when he found himself confronted by a gang of fifteen teenagers. After stealing his Walkman and headphones, one boy, his jacket zipped to his chin and hat pulled low, blocked Jaime's escape route, saying, 'Yo man, if you don't give me your wallet, I'm going to knife you.' Jaime knows he should have just handed over his wallet. Even in martial arts, the smartest move is to run. Confrontation is the last line of defence. But that night, Jaime had had enough. 'I just kind of went, naaaah,' he recalls. Before he knew it, he'd pushed the boy out of the way with a basic ōsotogari takedown (tipping him back and throwing him to the floor), and leaped from the bus. Jaime was only an orange belt at the time. 'That made me think, this is a good form of self-defence,' he explains. 'Even though I was only six months into learning it, I'd already managed to defend myself.'

Jiu jitsu also came in handy when he worked as a bouncer outside nightclubs and bars in Manchester, Cardiff and Swansea. Life behind the red rope was never dull, and he used martial art moves to subdue the violent and control the drunk. Manning the doors on international day with rugby and football fans jostling to get in, 'could be... hectic,' he admits, chuckling.

Jaime enjoyed his time in Manchester 'on the mat'. There were three university clubs in the city so he was able to train six days a week. He competed in national competitions and won medals. After six years, he gained his brown belt, which allowed him to don the hakama over his white gi. But his enthusiasm for jiu jitsu affected his university studies and was, he admits, the reason he eventually dropped out. By this time, his brother was a first dan with his own club in Swansea. Jaime moved back and became second in charge.

Jaime and his brother travelled to Japan for the first time in the summer of 1999. 'Back then, no one went to Japan,' he points out. But their interest in martial arts, and the fortunate coincidence of having a friend on the JET Programme, prompted them to make the trip. Jaime's instant love of the country and his desperation to return impelled him to return to university, this time to Swansea where he studied for a degree in applied linguistics and TEFL. Two weeks after graduation, he was on a plane to Gifu prefecture where the JET Programme placed him as a roving teacher in several high schools, some academically high level, others considerably less so. Jaime wasn't intimidated. Warned by a teacher that the class of students he was about to face were crazy, he replied, 'They might be, but they won't be as wild as twenty people stood outside a nightclub in Cardiff at two o'clock in the morning.' Unsurprisingly, he had no problems with discipline. Indeed, in one of the schools where he taught English, he was also roped in to teach jūdō.

Jaime remained on the JET programme for four years, although this was not without a wobble. At the end of his first year, an embezzlement scandal hit Gifu city and, low on funds, the prefectural government was forced to drastically reduce its JET participant numbers. Jaime was one of the few retained. At the end of his contract, he decided to further his education and returned briefly to Swansea to study for a master's degree in TEFL and then a CELTA

In action

qualification (Certificate of English Language Teaching to Adults). He now lives in Nagoya with his Japanese wife and daughter, and teaches at Sugiyama Jogakuen University.

As soon as Jaime moved to Japan, he sought out a dōjō. Wandering into his local budōkan (martial arts hall) he came upon a class training in jūdō so he joined it. He is now a second dan black belt in jūdō, and credits the lessons with helping him to make friends and to learn Japanese. A few years later, in a Nagoya training hall, he discovered a group practising yōshinkan aikidō. This is the style utilised in crime fighting by the Japanese police, as explained in Robert Twigger's award-winning book, *Angry White Pyjamas*.[19] Jaime picked that up too (attaining a first kyū ranking). Recently, he has started training in kyokushin karate (he's a fifth kyū). (Dan are rankings for black belts, kyū are rankings for other colour – lower ranking – belts.)

It was in Nagoya that Jaime decided to set up a dōjō for both Japanese and foreigners. In Japan, a lot of non-Japanese want to learn martial arts but lack the confidence. 'To go to a Japanese dōjō is intimidating, especially if you don't have any Japanese skills,' Jaime explains. He offers classes in shōrinji kan jiu jitsu with some modern variations. Although jitsuka (jiu jitsu students) sometimes train with weaponry, they're not articles you might have to hand if you find yourself in a combative situation. In Jaime's classes, the katana (wooden or metal sword) has been replaced with a baseball bat and the short-bladed side sword with knuckle dusters.

As it is spring vacation time in Japan, there are only eight people in Jaime's class this evening: four men and two small Japanese women, one of whom is a first-timer like me. The other, Anna, says she's usually the only woman in the class and, when I witness her hitting the floor hard in an ukemi (a break fall), I wonder if this is the reason why. Is jiu jitsu more suited to those with more bulk and muscle? Jaime shakes his head. As a beginner, he was regularly told off for doing 'big man jitsu', picking people up and throwing them around. He soon realised it was the smaller, nimble people – particularly women – who progressed more rapidly by developing and refining techniques such as joint locks and wrist releases which did not rely on their size or strength. 'It doesn't matter how much muscle you've got, you can't build muscle on a wrist or knee joint,' Jaime points out. And while karate involves hard blocks, practitioners of jiu jitsu (and aikidō) learn to manoeuvre away from an attack and to turn their opponent's momentum against them. Jaime feels that jiu jitsu and aikidō are ideally suited to smaller frames and is eager to start a women's self-defence class, similar to one he used to run for students at Swansea University.

Perfecting one's technique is vital because it doesn't take much knowledge to do serious damage. There are twenty-four dangerous parts on the human body: eight on the head, eight on the front of the body, and eight on the back. A well-aimed strike to the nose, solar plexus, groin or kneecaps will cause an opponent to think twice about continuing an assault.

Even a glancing blow to the carotid artery can knock an opponent unconscious while a hard punch can kill (by sending a massive spurt of blood to the brain). In the UK, you can only legally defend yourself 'within reasonable force'. If you are attacked, 'use the heel of your hand or a fist to the nose,' Jaime advises. 'That will break it. There will be blood everywhere, their eyes will be streaming and they won't be able to see. That's OK. But if you hit someone on the neck and break their trachea, you may be in trouble with the police.' He always teaches with caution.

After two hours, I feel exhausted but exhilarated. We have practised kicks, wrist locks and throws. I have learned about 'weakeners': jabs and twists (particularly to pressure points) that will steadily exhaust your opponent. And now I know why drunks who get into fights outside pubs often fracture the bones in their hands. They take curving swings and 'buckle' their wrists which, I can tell you, hurts like hell. The trick is to keep a straight arm and to strike with your two main knuckles not your ring or little fingers.

As Jaime packs up the punch pads, our conversation turns to his day job. Jaime is now an associate professor and is completing his doctorate (on the efficacy of the JET Programme) on the side. I ask him why he doesn't quit his university and teach jiu jitsu full time, and am surprised to learn that Jaime does not charge for lessons. 'I do it for kicks,' he says, as always, with a laugh.

If you would like to join Jaime's class, you can contact him via the Jiu Jitsu Foundation website: jitsufoundation.org or on Facebook at: KKSRKJP (Nagoya Karate & Jiu-jitsu Dojo).

Jaime's jiu jitsu class

The 2019 Rugby World Cup 'Fifteen thousand turned up to watch a training game'

Japan hosted the Rugby World Cup for the first time in 2019. It is estimated that 53,000 Welsh fans travelled to Japan for the tournament.

Takeshi Koike: I came to love rugby. Especially after Japan won against South Africa (in 2015), I became more interested. Many people in Japan became fans of rugby after that. It became very big. We watched every Welsh game in the World Cup. [Who did you support?] Yeah, that was hard. Both. I'm glad Japan and Wales didn't play each other.

Paul Baxter: We bought the tickets about a year prior to the event and decided to make a big thing of it. We had a great time. It was absolutely fantastic. We booked all the Welsh matches. They were in Tōkyō, Yokohama, and then two in Kyūshū.

It was absolutely wonderful and bizarre at the same time. The Welsh following was terrific and it was bizarre to pitch up at a railway station and see the forecourt full of Welsh people in red rugby shirts. Absolutely bizarre in rural or semi-rural Japan. But it was all very friendly and everyone was enjoying themselves.

Richard O'Shea: I had an absolutely brilliant time, especially going down to Ōita (in Kyūshū). Wales played Fiji down there. The Kyūshū area was the Welsh base for the World Cup. So when you were walking round, there were Welsh flags everywhere and it was like everyone was supporting Wales. It was great. I met a lot of Welsh players. And I bumped into my old rugby coach at one of the games as well.

Gareth Jenkins: Best time of my life, basically. Just insane. I was lucky in that I have a friend who works part time at the British Consulate in Kitakyūshū. [That] was where the Wales rugby team was based before the World Cup. A few months before, the WRU decided to send over some delegations, to make connections and do exchanges. They included famous players like Rhys Williams and Brian Jones. I was lucky enough to be allowed to interpret for a few of them. I would help interpret when they did rugby classes. Having been given the chance to do that, when the official delegation arrived in Kitakyūshū, I got in touch with Rhys Williams, who I'd got to know, and he invited me to the official welcome party for the team, which was in the nicest hotel you can imagine, The RIHGA. The players sang a few songs. It was just unbelievable. It was really special.

I think, as the hosts, the Japanese wanted to show they had an interest. So you'd have people who had never seen any rugby, buying tickets just for the experience of seeing a major rugby game. With the pre-camp in Kitakyūshū, they had 15,000 people turn up just to watch a training game. Just to watch them practise. You never have anything like that back in the UK. The Japanese are so quiet and benign, usually, but when a big festival like the Rugby World Cup or the Olympics comes along, they tend to go crazy. It's the same with Japanese festivals. They're a quiet and peaceful people but, when it gets to festival time, everyone just goes crazy. It's insane. Any excuse to go crazy and they do.

Simon Whalley: Kumamoto, where I was living at the time, had the Wales vs Uruguay game. It seems I was the only Welsh person living in the town because, every time they wanted to have a Welsh guy talking, I was invited onto all the television shows. I was on TV a few times. Then a friend of mine said, 'Hey Simon, they're looking for a Welsh guy who can be on TV talking about rugby,' and then they came and interviewed me at my house. And then I was at the city hall. They came to the university as well, and interviewed me. They wanted to know what they can say to Welsh people to make them feel at home.

We went out the night after the Uruguay game. There was one tiny bar, like a karaoke bar, and there must have been 150 Welsh people in there. There were Welsh people behind the bar, helping out because there were only two girls working by themselves, so all the Welsh were behind, helping pour pints. And the singing. Oh, it was amazing. It really was. It made me proud. It was rugby so there's not going to be any trouble, anyway. But they loved Japan. Every Welsh person I spoke to said this is an amazing country. They'd had such an incredible experience.

John Llywelyn: It was amazing. The Japanese don't have a culture of going to the pub, so you'd go to the fan zones in the city and there'd be Welsh fans in their rugby shirts. You'd go to the pubs and you could immediately meet, talk and make friends with Welsh people. 'Where are you from? Where have you been? I'll see you at the next game.' And you'd see people at the next games, you'd see them in the next cities or you'd see them at some other location.

Joe Cairnes: One or two places in the local area would get taken over for the rugby. You'd be walking around and there would be these little pockets of really loud noise at these small corner pubs. The locals were really getting into it when Japan was on, and some were getting into it when the other games were on.

The thing about rugby is, it's such a melting pot for all the fans. It's wonderful. You get to meet fans from all over the world and everyone's in a really good mood. The tension, the rivalry; it's there, but – unlike football which can be somewhat confrontational in its fanbase – rugby is very much a friendly back and forth, if ever there is one. I think that's just the nature of rugby and rugby fans.

Ursula Bartlett-Imadegawa: It was the very air you breathed. You couldn't go down the street without seeing a rugby banner fluttering. And you got on any train and the doors would close and there would be posters. It was everywhere. The city was alive. I'd get into taxis wearing my Welsh rugby T-shirt and taxi drivers would say, 'Oh Wales, Wales, ganbatte, ganbatte! (do your best)' It was remarkable.

Geraint M: The company had seats for corporate entertaining and staff. So I went to several games. Thinking about it now, it's funny because I went and bought a Welsh flag. I was thinking, 'Why am I doing this? Because I'm not English, that's why I'm doing it.' I went to the Wales vs Australia match. There are lots of Australians that work for the company here, and there's me, the lone Welsh guy. And I'm there with my flag. They play the Welsh national anthem and I'm clearly the only person in my particular group who can sing it. 'Advance Australia Fair' drowns everybody else. Of course, we beat the Australians. And I was thinking, 'Well, that's really interesting, because people now understand – at least in this sporting environment – that we are a country, a nation. And we have an identity that can be clearly distinguished within the four nations and from other parts of the English-speaking world.'

Lily Crossley-Baxter: Rugby made my life so much easier. Because the Japanese already know Ireland, which is frustrating. They sort of know Scotland.

It was always Wales. They never knew Wales. It was annoying. It was like a transformation, because the Rugby World Cup was such a big thing here. They really went for it. It was everywhere. Now everyone knows what Wales is. They know what the flag is like. I wish we'd won. That would have been even better.

Chapter Seven

Powder to the People! The philosophy of capitalist ski bum, Jac Phillips

Jac Phillips, 'capitalist ski bum'

When I exit the train station, I panic. It has taken me two days to reach this place from Tōkyō: four hours and 823 kilometres on the northbound Hayabusa Shinkansen (twenty-three kilometres of which was through an undersea tunnel), three and a half hours on the Super Hokuto limited express to Sapporo city, another hour on a 'Lilac' train, and finally one more hour on a local – one carriage, one driver, five passengers – train to the town of Furano. It is cold, it is sleeting, and there is no one here to meet me.

Ten minutes later, a white van pulls up and a man in khaki fleece and a beanie hat leaps out. 'Sorry about the mess,' says Jac Phillips as I survey a jagged pile of skis in the back. Ignoring red traffic lights, we speed along Furano's main street, an uphill slope of low-lying buildings that end at the foot of a mountain. A ski lift disappears into the mists but I can just make out one or two hardy skiers snowploughing downhill through the slush. Furano is experiencing a heat event which could signal the end of the season. But before setting out from Sapporo this morning, I had checked the forecast. It said that a temperature drop around lunchtime would result in snow later in the day. 'Awesome!' says Jac.

Jac's introduction to snow came early. His mother, a French and Spanish teacher, took the family to Europe during the school holidays. While she enjoyed the culture and the cuisine, her son immediately took to the slopes. After one year at Cardiff University, Jac – to his parents' dismay – dropped out and moved to Austria, where he trained and worked as a ski instructor and backcountry (off-piste) skiing guide. For the next five years he chased winter in Europe and New Zealand. In 2016, he arrived in Hokkaidō.

Comprising twenty-two per cent of its land area, Hokkaidō is Japan's second largest island. Originally the province of Japan's indigenous population, the Ainu, who knew their lands (Hokkaidō and surrounding islands) as Yezo (or Ezo), it was swiftly annexed by Japan in the nineteenth century in the face of Russian expansionism. In an effort to persuade the mainlanders of Honshū to settle here, the Japanese government gave away parcels of (previously Ainu) land. But Hokkaidō's inhospitable climate deterred many. Today only five per cent (5.7 million) of the Japanese population call Hokkaidō home and, after being physically stuffed into trains in Tōkyō, I find the empty roads disconcerting.

Hokkaidō in the summer is pleasantly cool. North of North Korea and only forty-three kilometres from Russia, the island – unlike the rest of Japan – lacks humidity and a rainy season. Also unlike the rest of Japan, Hokkaidō has green grass on which cows graze to supply the country with wagyū beef and creamy, vanilla-flavoured milk. With a summer temperature in the mid twenties, Hokkaidō is a retreat for frazzled urbanites escaping the heat and humidity of Japan's sub-tropical climate. Visitors can hike in the mountain ranges, go white water rafting on the rivers, and visit wineries, farms and colourful flower meadows reminiscent of the tulip fields in Holland. If they bring a wetsuit, they can even surf.

But in winter, the temperature plummets and the island is transformed by snow. Between November and April, upwards of fifteen metres of it covers the mountain ranges, many of which are volcanically active. The capital city of Sapporo, the second snowiest city in the world, holds an annual festival where international teams compete to create the most spectacular ice sculptures. Hokkaidō snow is considered to be the best in the world, and Jac moved to Hokkaidō because he wanted to experience it for himself. His immediate reaction was, 'This is Mecca.'

'What's so good about it?' I ask suspiciously, looking out of the van window at heaps of the stuff piled high on pavements and in car parks. Surely snow is ice water everywhere in the world. Apparently not. Japanese snow is formed by a meteorological phenomenon caused by bitter Siberian winds blowing down across the warm Sea of Japan, sucking up the moisture and creating giant clouds. When these clouds reach land, they cluster over the Japanese mountains and, as they rise up over the peaks (a movement known as orographic lift), they cool and release huge amounts of a powder snow known as 'Japow'.

Japow falls over the mountains all across Japan. Honshū has a volcanic spine which stretches from the north to the centre of the mainland, encompassing three distinct mountain areas known collectively as the Japanese Alps. Skiing and snowboarding are popular winter pastimes, and the major Honshū resorts – Hakuba, Shiga Kōgen and Nozawa Onsen – are only three hours from Tōkyō by train, close enough for weekend getaways. But it is worth venturing further north, says Jac, because the Japow in Hokkaidō is deeper and more consistent. When Jac realised he wanted to make ski instructing and guiding his career, he briefly considered New Zealand but ruled it out because recent winters have been blighted by warm, wet weather caused by climate change. Hokkaidō has so far remained unaffected by the fluctuations in temperature that have ruined ski seasons elsewhere in the world. Consequently, the snowpack – fallen snow that is compressed and hardened by its own weight – is thicker and safer in Hokkaidō. Avalanches are less likely here than on Honshū, where the temperature is a few degrees warmer. Winter temperatures in Hokkaidō hover around minus five degrees Celsius (but can drop into the minus twenties) and the slopes are continuously blanketed in soft, fresh snowfalls.

Jac began ski instructing in the town of Niseko, on the western side of the island in the Annupuri mountain range. Gathered around the slopes of Mount Niseko Annupuri (1,308 metres), Niseko United is a collective of four interconnected resorts offering sixty-one ski runs and twelve terrain parks. Back in the nineties, as Japan fell into recession, ski resorts lost money. The Niseko Hanazono resort was purchased by a group of Australian investors, and Qantas-owned Australian Airlines began twice-weekly ski season flights into Sapporo. With basic facilities and an undeveloped terrain, the resort was a big hit with Aussie snowboarders.

But in recent years, new faces have appeared on the piste, the wealthy citizens of the burgeoning Asian economies: mainland Chinese (often British educated and carrying American passports), Hong Kong Chinese, Singaporeans and Malaysians. As the French Alps are to the British middle classes, so Niseko has developed as the premier winter vacation destination for the Asian nouveau riche. Jac estimates that around three-quarters of the ski tourists in Niseko are foreign, wealthy and highly educated.

In Niseko, well-heeled vacationers like to spend their money. They demand five-star accommodation: at the Ritz Carlton, the Park Hyatt or their own luxury chalets. They eat only the freshest Hokkaidō sushi at the resort's fifteen Michelin-starred or recommended restaurants. And they require ski instructors on call, offering lessons in the global elite's common language, English. Some of the über rich have skied all their lives, others are beginners, Asia having no traditional ski culture. And not everyone wants ski lessons. Jac admits he sometimes acts solely as a sherpa, carrying equipment. Or else he will drive them to the slopes so they can pose in designer gear to show off on Instagram. Jac has sometimes sat for hours in hotel receptions, not knowing if his clients will appear or if he will simply be paid off and told to come back tomorrow. But there are perks. Tipping is not the custom in Japan but in Niseko a foreign culture prevails, with a wad of cash in the hand at the end of the day. Instructors who introduce clients to local restaurants can also find themselves seated at their table, enjoying a free meal. As long as they don't join the conversation. 'You're there to sit and be quiet,' warns Jac.

After nine winters (Jac counts in units of seasons), he and British wife Makenzie (who he met in Austria) moved over to Furano. The resort sits in the dead centre, or belly button, of Hokkaidō and the locals celebrate this fact with an annual belly button festival, painting happy faces on their torsos and donning low straw hats. Compared to Niseko, Furano remains relatively unknown and undeveloped, and I wonder why the couple would relocate away from a major client base to a rural outpost which even Jac describes as 'a farming town with a ski hill'. 'There is more opportunity over here in Furano,' he says, parking the van. 'I thought I'd get a foothold in.'

In late 2019, Jac and Makenzie founded their own ski business, Summit. They have recently opened a shop and office, conveniently located at the base of the resort's main ski slope. Inside, the walls are lined with skis and snowboards for sale and for rent. With hot coffees in hand, Jac and his office manager, Gabil, list Furano's attractions.

At Summit Ski School

Furano, begins Jac, has the deepest snow he has ever encountered. At high season, two months of whiteout is not unusual. In the mornings, Jac shovels half a metre of it from his driveway to get the van out and the same amount again to park it at night.

Consequently, with fewer people on Furano's runs, there is still powder aplenty after lunch when Niseko is skied out.

The snow is also drier. Dry snow is formed in colder temperatures. Also known as champagne snow, it creates optimum conditions for skiing or snowboarding, giving a feeling of floating over the terrain rather than slicing through it. 'The product is powder, and you want to deliver the product,' Jac points out.

But the biggest draw for Jac is not Furano's curated ski fields but its hinterland. Furano borders the largest national park in Japan, Daisetsuzan, home to Hokkaidō's highest mountains, a range of eight dormant stratovolcanoes situated in an actively volcanic landscape. It is a vast, unexplored wilderness of steep fir- and birch-covered slopes, frozen creeks and even the odd steaming fumarole. It offers 'rocky, craggy' skiing and the excitement of plunging down narrow chutes and near-vertical couloirs (seams or fissures in the mountainside). 'It's some of the craziest terrain I've ever seen,' says Jac with a grin. There are even opportunities for 'first ascents', to ski where no one has skied before.

Backcountry skiing is a relatively new phenomenon in Japan, where ski resorts are highly regulated. On groomed slopes, resort operators feel they can control everything. Off-piste is labelled 'abunai' (dangerous). Accidents suggest a resort is badly managed and Japanese skiers will go elsewhere. 'They don't like risk,' says Gabil. 'They like being safe.'

Japan's collectivist culture promotes social harmony and rewards conformity. Its citizens will not inconvenience those around them by breaking the rules. Japanese skiers stay within the ropes and keep to the approved trails and runs. 'For some reason, Japanese love being cordoned off,' Jac explains with a frown. In other countries, he points out, it is down to the individual to look after themselves, to decide whether they have the knowledge and experience to venture off supervised trails. And when foreigners come to the Japanese ski fields and see virgin snow on the other side of the ropes, they duck them, heading off-piste and disappearing into the trees. Recently, Japanese operators have begun bowing to the inevitable, establishing a gate system which allows access to areas that are not completely groomed.

Backcountry is extreme skiing and not without risk. The previous month, three foreigners had died in avalanches on Japan's off-piste slopes, two in Hakuba and one near Niseko. 'It *is* dangerous out there,' agrees Jac. Which is why Hokkaidō needs experienced guides. Japanese guides do not always have the expertise required to take clients off-piste. Qualified as a backcountry guide, a wilderness first responder (equipped to handle medical emergencies in remote locations) and trained in avalanche risk management, Jac has that expertise. He understands the local terrain and the weather conditions. Avalanches are 'the dragon you play with', he warns. 'But if it goes well, it's a lot of fun.'

In hindsight, winter 2019–20 was the worst time to start a business. Although under constitutional law the Japanese government was unable to enforce a Covid pandemic lockdown, gatherings were discouraged, and locals took to checking car number plates (which display the prefecture in which they were registered) for signs of out-of-towners. When Japan closed its national borders, resort hotels emptied and Hokkaidō's foreign-directed tourism industry all but collapsed. Now the tourists have returned and Summit is enjoying a busy season, welcoming not only the super-rich Asians but also French, Italians, Swiss, Scandinavians, Kiwis, Australians and Americans who want to spend their holidays ripping up the powder. Summit has taken on two office staff and several ski instructors, and is looking to recruit a Chinese speaker.

Summit provides a concierge service tailored

to each client's desire, be it skiing (day or night), backcountry exploration, photographic or film-making tours (popular with Americans who like to make Hollywood-style ski movies), onsen trips, sightseeing and even visits to local festivals. 'We're not just a numbers game,' states Jac. 'We take pride in what we do.' The company maintains a foothold in Niseko but in Furano it caters to the powder hounds, adventurous skiers who travel the globe seeking that next white powder high.

After ski-bumming for a decade and living on seasonal salaries plus tips, Jac wants to monetise his (and Makenzie's) experience and expertise. He is fortunate, he says, that Makenzie is organised. 'She's the operations manager,' chips in Gabil. Jac has the big ideas, Makenzie figures out how to make them happen. 'It's weird because now I've turned into a capitalist ski bum,' says Jac, laughing hysterically as we climb back into the van.

As we head out of town, we pass vacant lots with signboards announcing the imminent construction of modern condo-hotels, opulent chalets and managed villas, top-end real estate that will soon replace the old minshuku, traditional Japanese guesthouses. Foreign developers are moving in, keen to buy into the lucrative luxury Hokkaidō tourist business.

'Furano is just kicking off,' says Jac. I wonder out loud what Furano locals think about newcomers, and Jac admits they are wary. Having seen the Aussies in Niseko (which he likens to the British in Spain) they have become 'leery' and complain that there's more talk of money than there is of skiing. 'They're scared we won't uphold their values or morals,' he adds. He acknowledges the paradox of encouraging foreign skiers to ditch the Niseko tourist trap and follow him to Furano. It is only a matter of time before Furano's slopes fill up. 'But for the time being there's powder in abundance for everyone,' he says.

Over lunch (in a renovated wooden farm shed – one of those places that only locals know) Jac lays out his strategy for Summit in Furano. He plans to offer a unique adventure to clients: to take them out into the wilderness of the backcountry – initially on snowmobiles but later in snowcats and even heliskiing – to hike in nature, to encounter herds of wild deer and to ski in waist-deep snow. The terrain around Furano is 'raw' and undeveloped, and he wants more people to enjoy it. 'I want to bring powder to the people,' he announces with a wide grin.

Before we head into Daisetsuzan National Park, we make a stop at Jac and Makenzie's home in the village of Nunobe. When we arrive, my first thought

Jac outside the akiya with Nalu and Griff

is that the couple has been robbed. The front door is wide open. Then two giant Akita dogs, large as bears and just as hairy, appear in the doorway, blinking curiously through the sleet. The house, a former akiya, was once the village shop and the front, which used to be the shopfloor, is left open for Nalu and Griff. The living area is in the back. Constructed in the eighties, like most Japanese homes, it is made of wood. Wooden houses are expected to last no more than thirty to forty years and, when adult children inherit their parents' property, they generally knock down the old and build new. 'Japanese like new stuff,' says Jac. 'They even teach in schools that your electrical kitchen appliances should be renewed every three years.' But like most akiya buyers I have met, Jac and Makenzie are in the process of renovating. As the walls are too thin to insulate, Jac has fixed cladding to the outside. Much in the same way as many Japanese place new rugs over old, he is adding layers to keep in the warmth. And to stop the water pipes freezing.

Inside, they heat the traditional Japanese way, with kerosene. Kerosene heaters are smelly and greasy and liable to singe your eyebrows off if you get too close, but the oil doesn't freeze in low temperatures. The heat, however, does not reach everywhere. The house has a unit bathroom, a metal capsule containing a shower, bath and basin. In winter, Jac admits, it's like washing inside an ice cube.

Jac feeds his dogs. Nalu and Griff are oblivious to the driving sleet. In fact, they seem to enjoy it. Akita are hardy animals with a strong prey drive. They recently disappeared for four days, chasing wild deer in the mountains, and returned none the worse. This morning, from the window of the local train, I had seen numerous deer tracks tracing around white birch trees, the bark stripped. Deer numbers are increasing because Japan's ageing human population means there are fewer hunters left with the energy to trek into the mountains to find them. But the deer have other predators. Hokkaidō is home to the Ussuri or Ezo brown bear, a near relative of the grizzly and almost as big. There are estimated to be between three and fifteen thousand bears living in Hokkaidō's remote and environmentally protected wilderness and, as hunting them is prohibited, they are becoming braver, wandering into towns and attacking the locals. Northern Hokkaidō is the scene of Japan's most notorious bear attack. In 1915, in the village of Sankebetsu, a nearly nine-foot-tall Ezo bear killed seven residents in less than a week.

Recently, while out driving on one of the nearby forest trails, Jac encountered a giant Ezo bear, its rump higher than the bonnet of the car he was rapidly reversing. He had earlier come across scattered deer legs while walking his dogs, and his close encounter was followed by a note through his letterbox warning Nunobe residents that a mother and cub were using the village as a short cut to reach a nearby river.

Deer and bears aside, Jac and Makenzie assumed their rural life would be quiet. At Nunobe's tiny station, the train stops only four times a day. But when tour buses began arriving, they discovered that the village was a place of pilgrimage for viewers of a long-running Fuji television series, *Kita no Kuni Kara* (*From a Northern Country*) about the idyllic rural life of a divorced man who returns with his two children to his hometown. 'We need to open a tea shop,' announces Jac.

Nunobe is a village with a dwindling number of elderly residents. The previous occupant of Jac and Makenzie's home was a ninety-year-old woman who moved to a retirement complex. But Jac and Makenzie are not the only foreigners in the area. Their neighbour, and sometime employee, is also Welsh. Later, I chat with him on Zoom.

John Llywelyn arrived in Hokkaidō in 2019. He learned to ski on the dry slopes of Llandudno, and instructed there while he was in the sixth form. After five years in the merchant navy, he worked winter seasons in Canada and New Zealand before arriving in Japan. 'That's the next step,' he explains. 'If you've done North America and you don't want to do Europe, then you go east to Japan.' He had no problem finding a job. He estimates there are over a thousand foreign instructors in Hokkaidō during the winter season.

During the Covid pandemic, other instructors left the country but John had just married his Japanese wife. He found work in a food processing factory, sorting and bagging onions from local farms. The couple bought a house near Jac and Makenzie's because it was cheap (2.7 million yen: £13,196, which they paid for in cash) and convenient, although it doesn't have mains sewage.

Another outdoors type, John loves Hokkaidō: skiing, white water rafting (which he teaches in the summer), driving up into the mountains to soak in the onsen. 'It's beautiful,' he says. 'I can't recommend it enough.' It even reminds him of Wales. 'I tell people I live in the Anglesey of Japan. Because it's not densely populated, just little villages and farms everywhere. Nobody knows about it.' As Jac's van pulls away, we pass John's house. It is shut up and Jac doesn't think John has visited in a long time. 'He's bought a bar in Niseko,' he says, sadly. 'For the après-ski.'

By the time we arrive at the summit of Mount Tokachi (2,077 metres), one of the eight active volcanoes in the Daisetsuzan national park, the sleet has whipped itself into a blizzard. A tractor and a giant snowblower are attempting to clear the car park but are dwarfed by the height of the snow around them. I slither across a road glazed with ice, trying to take photographs, my hair freezing to my forehead. But Jac stands happily on the edge of a sheer drop and, as the storm rages around him, smokes a cigarette. He's not even wearing a coat. In his element, he is eager to share his thoughts, shouting over the howl of the wind. When he was younger, he says, he always 'hiked to ride', meaning he sought the shortest walking distance in order to find the longest ski line. Impatient to ski, he considered it boring to walk in nature. Now that he is older, he confesses that hiking has become a pilgrimage. Spending time in nature has become a meditation for him. It is in these mountains where he encounters his 'Zen monk' moments, and in the backcountry that he finds peace. He frowns, struggling to explain. 'I don't know if I'm doing it justice.' Lost for the right words, he pulls out his smartphone and shows me a video of a giant stag he encountered on a recent hike in the Daisetsuzan wilderness. Its tree-like antlers shudder as it leaps along a frozen creek bed and dives through the snow, fearful of Jac's camera. But when the stag realises he is in no danger he stops, and the watcher becomes the watched. 'Awesome,' says Jac.

Prompted, he admits that he misses Wales and Llanharan, his hometown. But on his last visit home, he felt estranged from Welsh-speaking friends and detected an animosity over his decision to leave, as if his departure was a rejection of the country. His experience echoes that of other interviewees who went home and found they no longer belonged. Jac doesn't see himself going back. 'What would I do there?' he muses. Jac is one of those people who must always be in motion. As skateboarders seek the smoothest concrete, and surfers live for the perfect wave, skiers like Jac pursue that perfect line: the steepest, most exhilarating downhill run. He knows it sounds 'dudeish' but he doesn't care. 'There's a beautiful line that does exist,' he says, making it sound mythical. 'And that's what I'm chasing.'

Descending the mountain, we speed across the flat expanse of Furano Valley. I gaze out of the window at the undulating white fields and the occasional farmhouse with a snowblower parked in the driveway. In early summer, when the snow turns to rain, it will refresh the soil, and these fields will bloom with rows of lavender, tulips, zinnia, marigolds, dahlias, pansies, irises and sunflowers. Giant striped beach towels of colour. 'Have you ever driven this fast before?' Jac asks. I look at the speedometer. He's doing 125 kilometres an hour. Through a blizzard. With all the skis sliding around in the back. But the road is flat and there are no other cars. 'The speed limits round here are a joke,' he says and puts his foot down. Jac Phillips is an adrenaline junkie. And a white powder addict. But he is also a backcountry pilgrim, seeking meditative moments of peace in a harsh mountain wilderness. Very dudeish.

Two hours and two trains later I am back in Sapporo city, inhaling a steaming bowl of miso ramen noodles and enjoying the restaurant's free wifi. Consulting a weather website, I see that the temperature has dropped rapidly and snow is falling again in Furano. The ski season is not yet over. Awesome!

Jac and Makenzie can be contacted at: summitski.jp

The Day the Tōkyō 2020 Olympic Games Were Cancelled 'His attitude was so Japanese – shōganai'

***Abby Hall** moved to Japan in 2017 to work for an eikaiwa. Via an internship at the British Embassy, she discovered a love for public relations*:

As my internship was coming to an end, my manager said to me, 'I think you would be great working for the communications team at the 2019 Rugby World Cup.' I said, 'I'm so sorry, I'm Welsh but I know nothing about rugby.' To me, Welshness is here. (She points to her heart.) It isn't the fanfare; it isn't putting on the red jersey or the daffodil hats whenever there is the Six Nations. This kind of rugby culture wasn't speaking to me at all. So when she said, 'I'll get in touch with [the organising committee],' I was very apprehensive.

It must have been about three weeks later that I had an interview. He asked me, 'What's a ruck?' I said,

'I don't bloody know!' He said, 'Do you know what a maul is?' And I didn't know what a maul is. How was I supposed to work there? I was underqualified.

A couple of weeks later, he offered me a full-time position as fan engagement and communications manager for the Rugby World Cup. And I actually turned him down. I said I couldn't get over the fact that I didn't know enough about rugby. He said, 'This is the biggest mistake you'll ever make in your life.' I thought, 'Who the hell are you, sir?!' He said, 'Come in tomorrow. We'll have a good offer for you.' So in May 2019 I started working there. And it was one of the most amazing and memorable experiences of my life.

One day, I walked into the office and my manager said, 'Abby, we're taking you to your first rugby match.' It was Wales vs Australia and it was in Tōkyō stadium. They got me a Welsh rugby jersey and gave me my ticket. It was a VIP ticket and at the stadium we got all this VIP treatment. I thought, 'Is this normal for a rugby match?' I had no idea. I'd worked at the organising committee for five months but still hadn't been to a match. I sat down in my Welsh jersey and, of course, sang the national anthem. All of a sudden, these Welsh people in Welsh jerseys, about fifteen of them, came walking along and they sat a couple of seats behind me. My manager tapped me on the shoulder and said,

'That's the Welsh team. They're the players who are not playing right now. Do you want to go say hi?' Me, I didn't know any of their names or any of their faces. And I've had three beers at this point. I walked up to them and said, 'Apparently, you're Welsh rugby players. Can I get your picture?' They were like, 'Yeah, go on.' So my Twitter background picture is me and them. I look so clueless. I'm sitting there with Leigh Halfpenny and Dan Biggar. Looking back I think, 'Oh my God, how could you, Abby?' I realise now how naïve I was.

Abby Hall with Welsh rugby players at the 2019 World Cup in Japan

It was a really great match, my first ever rugby match. I just remember trying to follow the game as much as

I could but, at the end of the day, I was still a novice. I didn't know any of the rules. I couldn't even tell you what the score was. All I knew was I was having fun and everyone around me was having fun. And I knew I liked it. It's that simple.

My time at the organising committee was spent as a spectator communications manager, handling all aspects of communication to each and every rugby fan: from social media, web content, app content, email marketing – you name it. I was soon an expert in rugby and it felt as though I'd found my rather unexpected calling.

After the Rugby World Cup, Abby moved to the Tōkyō 2020 Olympics organisation. But as the Covid pandemic spread across the globe, rumours began to circulate that the games might be cancelled:

I was an international federations communications manager, so I was the go-between between the Tōkyō 2020 organising committee and all of the international sporting federations in terms of press releases and announcements and social media.

We used to have almost daily press conferences and the press were asking, 'Are you cancelling? What's the situation?' We just said, 'The games are not going to be cancelled. We have information that Covid will die down by June.' We were told to keep our heads down and keep working. We'd constantly see people running out of the room and people having quiet meetings looking very grim. But we had no idea what was going to happen.

We knew there was going to be a big press conference. People higher than us were scattering and stressing the whole day, and you could see the looks on their faces. Myself and one other translator – because I used to do some of the translations – were sent an email and it said, 'Classified: Do not send to anyone. Do not forward' in massive red letters. I remember glancing at it but it wasn't actually hitting me. We were sitting in the office at about 8 or 9pm when the press conference started right next door to us. There were hundreds of media there. We'd got these massive television screens in our office and we were watching it. And I'm looking at the email as they're saying it. And I'm reading it as they're saying it. And I just thought, 'Wait. What?' Then they said it in Japanese, 'We are here to officially announce that Tōkyō 2020 will be postponed.'

I'll never forget that moment. I was sitting next to my manager and he leaned back in his chair, looked at me and just smiled. He wasn't upset. He was very calm. His attitude was so Japanese: shōganai (it can't be helped). There was utter silence in the office. No one said anything.

We all stayed in the office until 1am, just in silence. We didn't have anything to say to each other. We didn't know what to say. You couldn't make light of it. You couldn't continue working. I mean, there was nothing to do anymore. We all went out to whatever bar might have been open at that time and we just drank in silence. I think at about four o'clock we went home, saying, 'Okay, see you... tomorrow?'

One of my roles at the time was working with international sporting federations, for example, FIFA and World Rugby and FINA, but also smaller federations and ones that were new to the Olympic roster such as surfing and skateboarding. I'd be emailing them saying, 'Obviously the games have been postponed so maybe we can pick up on this another time.' And I'd get an email back straightaway saying, 'I'm sorry but our federation doesn't have the money to sustain itself so my position no longer exists. I've been let go.' It was constant. Automatic emails coming in from smaller federations. It was just a very strange and very sad time.

There were no clear visuals on anything. We had team meetings and every day we'd ask our managers,

'Are the games going to be held?' They would just say, 'Plan as if they are.' That's all they could say. And I could understand that. But, at the same time, so many people were deciding to leave for better things.

It was about three weeks later that they decided everyone would work from home. I have a heart condition so I asked to work from home sooner than everyone else. Funnily enough, when I said, 'Look, I'm working from home. I have health problems and I need to be way more concerned about this,' a lot of other people started speaking up about the same thing. Japanese people don't like to speak up but as soon as someone else does, they feel more comfortable. So I feel that I was able to pave the way for people who didn't want to keep coming into the office during the pandemic.

We didn't know whether the games were going to be postponed until spring or summer 2021. When Japan did the bid for Tōkyō 2020 they said Japan has a nice cool summer in July and August. It's actually very hot. Temperatures of forty degrees are common and so are deaths related to heatstroke, often elderly people running errands without proper protection. I'm sure every marathon runner was glad when the race was moved to the northern and far cooler city of Sapporo. There was the potential that, if the games were going to be postponed, maybe they'd postpone them to the following springtime to mitigate any potential heat-related concerns for athletes. Because if spectators were sitting in the heat and if a lot of athletes were taken ill or fainted, they could pull out of the competitions. Fortunately, a lot of teams and their staff were prepared for Japan's heat and came as early as travel restrictions could allow, to ensure they acclimatised before their event.

The Tōkyō 2020 Olympic Games were eventually held in July and August 2021 in an enclosed 'bubble' without spectators and with competitors confined to the Olympic Village. It was the hottest Olympics ever.

Chapter Eight

'A Quiet Murmur of Buddhist Thought': Japanese influences in the career of Welsh independent writer/director/producer, John Williams

Writer, director, producer, John Williams

John Harford Williams is an award-winning film writer, director and producer. His first feature, *ichiban utsukushii natsu (Firefly Dreams,* 2001), was a coming-of-age story set in rural Japan. It reflected traditional Japanese cultural themes: the evil of the city versus the simple, honest ways of the countryside, a love of nature, and nostalgia for a way of life that is disappearing. *Variety* declared it was 'astutely crafted... [with] strong human appeal and emotional resonance'.[20] Screen International called it 'beautifully shot'.[21] The film won six international film festival awards, was voted best film at the twenty-first Hawaiian International Film Festival, and was the audience's choice for Best Dramatic Feature at the twelfth Cinequest San Jose Film Festival in 2002.[22] John was even nominated for best new director by the Director's Guild of

Japan. But the movie would never have been made if the small-town Welshman had not moved to Japan. And John might still be teaching in a north London comprehensive.

When not making movies, John teaches film production and translation at Sophia University in central Tōkyō. To learn more about his work, I visit him in his office. John's office is a mess. There are movie posters covering the walls, and DVDs, video tapes and film books stacked on tables, chairs and in piles on the floor. With nowhere to sit, we move to a bright, empty meeting room and John chooses a seat which frames him perfectly in the window which overlooks a campus frothing pink with cherry blossoms.

Born in 1962, John was raised in Llantrisant and went to school in the nearby mining town of Beddau. He was a movie fan from a young age. When he was fourteen, BBC2 ran a late-night Sunday slot showing foreign films such as Jean-Luc Godard's *Alphaville* (1965) and Akira Kurosawa's *Dersu Uzala* (1975) which he watched on his tiny black-and-white television. *Aguirre, the Wrath of God* (1972) made such an impact that at school he told his German teacher about it. 'That was directed by Werner Herzog,' his teacher replied. 'Okay,' said John. 'What's a director and how can I get that job?'

John knew he wanted to be a film director. But he had no idea how to become one and knew no one who could help. 'Every time I asked people they said, "Oh no, you can't get that job, a country boy like you."' So he read French and German literature at Trinity College, Cambridge instead. But he took with him a 16mm Bolex camera that his father had bought for him and, when he could afford the film, he made surrealist, experimental shorts.

Graduating in 1984, John thought that he could just knock on a few doors in Soho and get his first job as a runner. He was wrong. It was the year of the miners' strike and the Brighton bombing. It was also the year that Margaret Thatcher's Conservative government ended its subsidisation of the film industry. In 1984, film production and box office takings fell to their lowest level ever. John also didn't realise that the industry he was trying to break into was a closed shop. Entry level jobs were given to those with connections, and nearly all skills were unionised. Recalls John, 'I had that feeling that I was not going to get anywhere in this country because I am a country boy, and – although I went to an elite university – I was still not of those people.' For a time he washed dishes in a Cardiff hotel and hung around Chapter Arts Centre trying to find work on independent films.

He even knocked on Karl Francis' door but the Welsh film and television director sadly informed him that things were so bad, he doubted he himself would ever be able to make another film.

John found a job teaching French and German at a secondary school in London. In his free time, he went to the Everyman theatre in Hampstead where he saw Japanese films by Kenji Mizoguchi, Yasujirō Ozu and Kurosawa. He particularly enjoyed the wackiness of Ishii Sōgo's black comedy, *The Crazy Family* (1984) and the strange humour of Jūzō Itami's tribute to ramen noodles, *Tampopo* (1985). So in 1988, when he saw a newspaper advertisement which suggested that he 'Come and teach English in Japan', he packed his bags. 'I'd pretty much psychologically committed to not going back to Britain for some time,' he admits.

John began teaching English with the Interac company in the central city of Nagoya. He had only been there for two weeks when one morning, looking out the window of a restaurant, he saw a group of young men making a film in the street. They were students at the Nagoya University of the Arts. He spoke no Japanese and they spoke no English, yet he conveyed his desire to join them. He began by holding lights and carrying bags, all the while learning Japanese and receiving a film school education from his new friends. After a year he told them that he'd like to write and direct his own film and they in turn crewed for him.

Nagoya's vibrant independent film culture was centred around Cinema Skhole, one of a chain of art house cinemas founded by controversial director Kōji Wakamatsu, primarily known for his sixties pinku (soft porn) films and also for films with increasingly political messages. (Wakamatsu was killed in 2012 when he was hit by a taxi on his way home from a meeting about his next feature. It was to be a film about the Japanese nuclear lobby and Tepco, the owners of the Fukushima Dai-ichi Nuclear Power Plant.) Having rejected the studio system, Wakamatsu was known to support young independent filmmakers, and Cinema Skhole was the place where they could get a late night or Saturday morning slot and fill the theatre with their friends and colleagues. Skhole was managed by director/producer, Junji Kimata, who watched their films and gave comments. 'He was very honest,' admits John. 'If he didn't like it, he said, "Okay, you can show it but it's not a good film." Or "That was interesting. But you should change the ending."' John made three short 8mm films, two of which – to avoid translation issues and because he was going through a David Lynch phase – were dreamlike and without language.

The third, *Promises*, was a human drama about an American man who comes to Japan and tracks down his Vietnam veteran father's Japanese mistress.

John included these films in his portfolio when applying to the film school at New York University and was delighted when he was accepted. Unfortunately, he was travelling in India when he received his offer and by the time he'd returned to Japan, they had given his place away. Initially devastated, he now says it was the best thing that ever happened to him. Back in Nagoya, at a meeting of Amnesty International, he met a group of Sri Lankan asylum seekers who persuaded him to fly there and make a documentary about the political killings and disappearances. John arrived shortly after the assassination of President Premadasa in 1993. He carried only a video camera and did his editing on a small two-deck machine but his documentary, *Voices from Sri Lanka*, was well-received at Amnesty events in Japan. With his new-found interest in documentary filmmaking he took himself to the Yamagata International Documentary Film Festival in Tōhoku. One night he was sitting in a sake brewery listening to a discussion between a Palestinian and an Israeli filmmaker when he realised he did not want to go to America after all. Japan was a much more interesting place to make films. 'Perhaps this is the only place I can make [films],' he thought, 'because there's so much I like about this place and so much I want to say.' He decided to take the four million yen (£19,550) he had saved for film school and make a feature in Japan.

With traditional gentō (magic lantern) shows already popular in nineteenth-century Japan, the Japanese were ready for the era of moving pictures. The first Japanese film (a ghost story called *Bake Jizō* or *Jizo the Spook*) was made in 1898, only two years after the arrival of Thomas Edison's Kinetoscope and the Lumière brothers' Cinematograph. Japan has one of the oldest film industries in the world, and currently the fourth largest by number of films produced (after India, the United States and China). John believes that the Japanese film industry succeeds because it is run like the American studio systems of the past. It is commercially minded and quick to invest in other avenues for profit such as multimedia, song tie-ins and merchandising. Many Japanese movies are adaptations of manga comic stories and bestselling books or have been adapted from the small screen. Consequently, Japanese studios don't need to look to Hollywood for financing. Says John, 'In terms of keeping Hollywood at bay, Japan's domestic industry is bigger and more successful than most other film industries in the world.'

Japanese audiences also want to see their own culture reflected on film, and native filmmakers know their nation's tastes and preferences. More than half of Japanese films are anime, such as those created by Hayao Miyazaki's Studio Ghibli. Japan also has a rich literary tradition of ghost stories and horror tales, a genre which Japan's earliest filmmakers were quick to put onto celluloid, and which remains popular today with movies such as *Ring* (1998). With *Brother* (2000), Takeshi Kitano (aka television's Beat Takeshi) has tapped into another traditional genre, the Yakuza or gangster movie. He has also explored jidaigeki or period dramas, with *Zatoichi* (2003), a remake of a long-running film and television series. Then there are pinku movies, idol movies (springboards for popular talents of the day), and kaiju (monster) movies of which the most famous is *Godzilla* (1954).

But the British do not seem to have this preference for home-grown productions. 'Look at the reports in *Screen International*,' says John. 'British people go and see American films.' Consequently, it is to Hollywood that British filmmakers look for financing and for box office success, remaining largely unaware of the creativity and productivity of the film industry in Japan. When John first started going to film festivals, he found some people in the British film industry to be very narrow-minded. 'They seemed to have no idea that there was this other film industry on the other side of the world that's much more successful at winning a local audience,' says John. 'And it just happened to be in another language.' In recent years however, the promotion of the idea of Japan as 'cool' and/or 'cute' has increased interest in Japanese films: in horror, arthouse, anime and, more recently, in movies and streaming series made by women directors.

John's first feature, shot in 16mm, was a seventy-minute comedy thriller called *Midnight Spin* (1996). It was the story of an American bar hostess having a bad night which gets steadily worse as she fails to understand Japanese culture and some of the characters she meets. The film was picked up by the Raindance Film Festival in London but John couldn't afford to attend as he'd already spent the entire budget, plus two million yen he'd borrowed from a friend. John realised it wasn't enough to just make a film. He'd put all his time and energy into writing and directing his feature but had given little thought to its promotion or distribution. 'A lot of filmmakers don't think about that,' says John. 'They think the film is going to have a life of its own. You can make a really fantastic film and then it can just not go anywhere.' As well as being a writer and director, John realised he needed to become a producer as well.

His next film was a full hundred-minute feature. He raised forty-five million yen (£220,000) from investors: fifty per cent Japanese financing, fifty per cent foreign. He set up a company, 100 Meter Films. And he drew up a festival and distribution strategy. The film was shot over six weeks at the height of summer (when John was on vacation from his teaching job) in the village of Hōraichō, in the central Japanese prefecture of Aichi.

Firefly Dreams is the story of seventeen-year-old Naomi, a teen tearaway who prefers hanging out with her friends to attending school. When her parents divorce, she is sent away for the summer to help at a countryside ryokan run by her maternal aunt's family. There she is tasked with looking after frail Mrs Koide, an old neighbour with creeping dementia whose deteriorating mind pulls her back to her wartime past and to a secret she'd rather forget. The two form a close friendship.

Situated in a rural valley, Hōraichō is a place few Japanese know. Migration to the cities has left the area depopulated and unmodernised. The roads are narrow, the hills steep and dense with foliage, but there is a nearby hot spring resort, Yuya, and there are sweetfish in the river. John and his crew were welcomed by the local government and village community who offered them an old house in which to stay, while the Association of Ryokan Owners allowed filming in a nearby inn. Mrs Koide's home was an abandoned wooden house in Hōraichō village, possibly the former site of a traditional cottage industry in Japan, silk production. On a location visit, John found spinning wheels and looms on the upper floor which in the nineteenth century would also have housed vats of silkworms. A scene in which Naomi pokes around the dilapidated interior, sliding open fusuma and lifting the lids of dusty chests and boxes, features an old globe and a mirror. John also found these items in the house and wrote them into the script. The globe symbolises Mrs Koide's world in her younger days while the mirror expresses how Naomi and Mrs Koide are mirrors for each other, transporting Mrs Koide back to her youth while Naomi, realising her own mortality, grows up. For John, the mirror also represents cinema itself and the way in which, on gazing into it, the flow of time is stopped, as it is on celluloid. While making *Firefly*, John had in his mind the Horoshige ukiyo-e woodblock print of people running across a bridge in the rain, a moment in time captured forever.[23]

But time does not stop, and John also acknowledges this. A scene, in which Mrs Koide helps Naomi to put on a yukata, made women in cinema audiences cry, evoking personal memories of being helped to dress for shichi-go-san, a coming-of-age festival for young people when they are dressed up and taken to the local shrine. In Japanese aesthetics there is a term for this nostalgia, mono no aware, literally the 'transience of things'. Mono no aware represents that feeling of deep sadness at the passing of time and the impermanence of all life. From the way the cherry blossom is blown away on the first strong breeze to the death of an aged parent, all are representations of mono no aware.[24] Mono no aware is an old term for a bittersweet feeling that remains potent within modern Japanese culture. Yet, despite it being a key scene in the film, John claims to have hit upon the significance of the dressing ritual by chance.

As John was both director and producer of *Firefly*, he had final say on the actors hired. For his lead he chose Maho Ukai, a young woman with no acting experience. When she first auditioned, he was hesitant because he didn't think she was acting at all – she didn't appear to be giving a performance – but John wanted authenticity, and her natural style won her the part. His Japanese assistant director thought he had 'shot the film in the foot' by not hiring a more famous or conventionally pretty woman but, two days into the shoot, he admitted that John had been right.

The role of Mrs Koide was played by a national treasure, film, television and stage actress, Yoshie Minami, who had begun her career in 1934 playing the male roles in the all-female Takarazuka acting troupe. She had appeared in numerous Japanese movies including Akira Kurosawa's, *Ikiru* (1952). Minami was an enthusiastic wine drinker and at dinner regaled John and the crew with stories of her life and career. Minami's memories of witnessing the wartime bombing of Tōkyō were written into the script as Mrs Koide's reminiscences. Born in 1915, Minami was eighty-five when she filmed *Firefly Dreams*. It was her last film role; she died in 2010.

The ways in which John drew on historical ukiyo-e range from creating framing devices to playing with light and shade. A scene in which Naomi talks with a delivery boy in the inn kitchen is framed in such a way that two-thirds of the shot, a darkened corridor in which a shadowy Naomi stands and smokes, is completely black while in the other third a boy carries a crate of empty beer bottles through a bright white kitchen. John believes that the problem with a lot of contemporary cinema, and television in particular, is that everything is shown. 'The beauty of traditional woodblock prints is not what is shown but what is left in darkness,' he explains.

In modern film, when a character walks out of frame, the scene generally cuts to that character in another place. In *Firefly*, when Naomi goes to the local hospital to pay her respects at Mrs Koide's bedside, the camera and thus the audience are left waiting in the corridor. We are left to imagine what is occurring off-screen. 'It leaves space for imagination,' says John.

The partially obstructed view, the voyeuristic peek through the shōji, the shadow on the wall, are all elements that are commonly utilised in Japanese films. *Firefly* too is told in an oblique story-telling style. Not only must the audience imagine what could be happening off-screen but also what conversations may be taking place. At the inn, Naomi's aunt answers the telephone. The scene then cuts to a funeral, and the audience gradually becomes aware that Naomi's father has committed suicide. Indirectness is a strong tradition in many Japanese arts.

In another scene, Naomi and her relatives eat a meal without speaking. This so-called 'silent' cinema of long pauses and slow, meandering dialogue is a key feature of cinema Japanesque. Subtlety and silence – not saying what can be surmised – are key facets of the nation's language, where it is silence not words which facilitate understanding. Elements of non-verbal communication may include haragei, the concept of 'belly talk', of people communicating through their stomachs without the need for dialogue. Ishin-denshin is a shared understanding between two people without the need for words. This concept is also represented spatially, as 'ma' or negative space. The aesthetic of emptiness is a key concept in the Japanese art world.

Although proficient in written and spoken Japanese, John wrote the script for *Firefly* in English, had it translated and then worked on it with the actors and even the locals in Hōraichō. Observations, such as that of a ryokan owner who noted that guests didn't go out in the evenings anymore but stayed in their rooms watching television, were written straight into a scene in which two of the characters discuss this whilst hanging out washing. The dialogue in *Firefly* is sparing. Yet each scene is rich in sound: the electric hum of cicadas, the creak of tatami rush matting, and the soft crackle of a fire as Mrs Koide burns her old photographs.

Even though *Firefly Dreams* appears very Japanese in style and content, John warns against 'orientalising' cinematic techniques, of reading too much into a commonly perceived dichotomy between east and west. He is quick to point out that many apparently Japanese techniques are also utilised by non-Japanese filmmakers. A famous scene in Roman Polanski's *Rosemary's Baby* is used in film schools throughout the world to demonstrate the power of off-screen action. Polanski shoots through a door but places the camera so that the audience cannot see the figure talking on the other side. The effect causes the audience to lean en masse to the right in their attempt to see around the door. John also feels that much of the use of long pauses and of silence is a relatively recent invention in Japanese film, prompted by directors such Takeshi Kitano who edit with a distinct off-beat rhythm, 'almost like jazz'. Old Japanese studio films of the fifties were much faster. Nevertheless, a group of Sony executives who saw rough cuts of *Firefly Dreams* refused to believe it had been written and directed by a foreigner. And John doesn't believe he would have made the movie if he had remained in Britain. 'I don't think I would have *attempted* to make *Firefly Dreams* in Britain,' he admits.

As a schoolboy growing up in Wales, John loved poetry, particularly French poetry, but felt that it was considered 'funny' for a boy to admit to this. 'Where I came from it was like *Billy Elliot*,' he recalls. 'I went to school in a mining community and that goes deep.' John associates British films with a political realism (such as the works of Ken Loach which he loves) but he didn't want to make political cinema just because he grew up in a working-class community (even if he did share Loach's values and politics). He feels temperamentally closer to more poetic directors such as Lindsay Anderson and Lynne Ramsay, or even Mike Leigh. 'He's a very similar director to Ozu in many ways.' Yet John feels that the very idea that you're trying to do something artistic in Britain throws you into being associated with the 'snobby middle class'. 'I wouldn't want to feel that what I was doing was just pretentious,' he says. Relocating to Japan gave John the freedom to make the films he wanted to make, films about society that are both imaginative and engaged. Japan, he believes, gives him 'a bigger latitude to do things that are poetic'. Writing haiku is a national pastime in Japan and, if John admits to liking poetry, no one here calls him a 'ponce'. In Japan, the idea of a metaphorical and philosophical cinema, a cinema of ideas, is more accepted than in Britain and, having lived and worked in Japan for twenty-five years, John is now more 'at home' in Japan than he is at home. 'Because I've been here so long, somehow I've become a Japanese filmmaker,' he admits.

After *Firefly Dreams*, John has directed five more films including the surrealist noir ghost story *Starfish Hotel* (2006) which won best film at the Luxembourg International Film Festival and which the Sydney Film Festival called 'handsomely stylish, hypnotically atmospheric and, no question, very weird indeed.'[25] He wrote it after his traumatic move to the 'inferno' of Tōkyō after his summer filming in the idyll of Hōraichō. Recent productions are Japanese interpretations of western works. *Arashi*

(*Sado Tempest* in English, 2012) is a science-fiction reworking of Shakespeare's *The Tempest*, while *Shinpan* (2018) is an adaptation of Kafka's *The Trial*. His latest cross-cultural project may be the closest to his heart. It began as a Japanese version of *Under Milk Wood* which he planned to stage as a play in a remote fishing village on Sado Island. When Covid dashed any hope of a live performance, he rewrote it as a film, incorporating local island legends. 'By the time we shot the film in the summer of 2022 it was no longer recognisable as *Under Milk Wood*,' John says. 'But the spirit of the original play remains.' The film *Tabi* (English title, *Another Time*) and a documentary about the fishing village where it was shot, *North Cormorant Island*, were both released in 2024.

A still from *Tabi* (*Another Time*)

Now John is writing a television series. While making single feature films is becoming harder, John sees opportunities to tell compelling narratives in long-form. Recent productions such as *Giri/Haji* and *Tokyo Vice* have created fresh interest in stories about Japan, 'though they are still recycling a lot of clichés,' he points out. John would like to make a home-grown Japanese streaming series that would work internationally. 'The rise of the streaming services has changed everything,' he believes.

Surprisingly, John puts the fulfilment of his childhood dream of becoming a director – and a writer and producer – down to lucky breaks. After some gentle probing, he admits that he grabbed opportunities in Japan that might never have come his way in Britain. In the UK, he would never have walked up to a film crew and asked to join in. Whereas, as a foreigner in Japan, he was able to distance himself from the limitations that held him back at home. As an outsider, he was not constrained by 'insider' rules and was quick to grasp all the opportunities that came his way. There is a Japanese saying, 'tabi no haji wa kakisute' ('Shame is cast off on a journey'). In John Williams' case, he seems to have cast off not just shame but also nationality.

Does John Williams have any regrets about leaving

Britain? He says he would not have been unhappy if he could have found a way to become a filmmaker in the UK, and he believes that opportunities have expanded since he left, particularly with the advent of YouTube and Netflix. While he has no plans to move back, he is currently working with a British producer on a horror film which will be filmed in the UK. At the same time, he realises that it was not simply a question of departing but of actively following his interests. 'Something pulled me towards Japan,' he believes. Japanese history, cinema and culture, all the things about Japan that he loves, are underpinned by 'an undercurrent of Buddhist thought.' It's not obvious, it's not in your face. 'It's just there,' he says. 'A quiet murmur.'

The Foreign Extra 'More big! More black!'

After meeting his future Japanese wife at a music concert in London, Llangadog-native **Clive Davies** *moved to Japan in 1999 where he works as a gaitare, a foreign talent aka an extra or background artiste*:

A saigen is a reconstruction drama. In the UK we used to have a programme called *999* which was a reconstruction of events where the emergency services were involved and it was dramatised. Saigen are like that but it's mostly stuff out of the States. And it's bizarre crimes and strange murders. The big one is called *Kiseki Taiken! Unbelievable* (miracle experiences! unbelievable). And there's *Za! Sekai Gyōten News* (the world's astonishing news). There's quite a few of them. They love saigen here.

I was on a train coming back from a Japanese-language class. I bumped into a guy who told me about the Inagawa Motoko Talent Agency (IMO). Inagawa Motoko – that's the name of the lady who runs it. It's notorious for not paying the talent. I went to the office and registered. Then the agent phoned me and he said, 'You have a job next Sunday.'

'Okay, good. What's the job?'

'It's unbelievable.'

Unbelievable! I was like, 'That sounds great. What is it?'

And he kept saying it's unbelievable. I didn't get it for a while. And then finally I got it. The first job I had was for *Unbelievable!*

That ended up being a real trial by fire or, actually, ice. It was a World War Two story about a Japanese ship that had sunk a British ship. And they actually took prisoners of war on board which I don't think they often did at the time. They just let people drown. So it was a notable story. We shot it down in Yokosuka on the deck of a real battleship. It was March and we had to be in the water for two days straight. It was horribly cold. I even did a stunt. Everyone else had been doing this kind of work for a while and they were jaded. But I, being a film fan, was Mr Eager Beaver.

They said, 'Does anyone want to do this stunt?'

Everyone else, 'Er...'

And I'm like, 'Yeah, I'll do it.' And I jumped off the deck of the battleship into the sea.

Normally, they overdub everything in Japanese. So you can say pretty much whatever you like as long as it fits the length of the Japanese line they want to dub it in. They tell you what the line is and then you get an idea. Some people take it too seriously and they hold up production because they're trying to get the right translation. Why? They're not gonna hear it. You could literally just recite fruit and no one would know.

It's overacting as well. They don't hear your voice, for one thing. And then it's all big. For instance, if you find a dead body you have to go, 'Oh my God!' They like big, big reactions.

I remember the first time I learned the lesson. I had lines. I had something to say. 'More! More!' the director kept saying. 'More big! More big!' I got a bit fed up and decided to take the piss, basically. All right, you want more? Okay, here: 'Oh my God! Aaaaah!'

And they were like, 'Great.'

From then on, I just brought it big from the get-go. I suppose silent film is the closest thing to it. It's not rocket science. But, oddly enough, it is a skill because you do occasionally meet people who can't do it. It seems easy to overact but even that is beyond certain people. They're shy or they have something I've heard of called 'dignity'.

The crazy thing is you often don't know your role until you turn up, so you can't prepare. When I was John Wayne Gacy, for example, I didn't know I was John Wayne Gacy because they just said, 'You have a job tomorrow.' That's it. Okay. Turned up. And then the guy's trying to explain to me, 'You're a clown and you kill people.'

I said, 'Are you talking about John Wayne Gacy?'

'Ah yes, Gacy-san, it says here.'

Okay, now I know. But you get that information at the very last minute.

I once played Captain Mahmud of the Bangladeshi Air Force in brownface. Until I turned up, I didn't know what the story was. And it was the same guy who directed the John Wayne Gacy thing. I think he liked me after John Wayne Gacy.

He said, 'Okay, you're playing a Bangladeshi guy.'

I said, 'Ah okay, how's that gonna work?'

They took me into make-up and put brownface on me. I came out and there was a Bangladeshi guy there as an extra. I said to the director, 'This guy's Bangladeshi and he looks a bit like the guy. Why don't you get him to play the main part?' But the director said, 'No, the acting's important.' The acting is important? Riiight.

This is just nonsense. But I asked this Bangladeshi guy and he seemed comfortable. So I went ahead and I did it. It did feel very weird and wrong. But the thing is, if I had walked, I would not have worked again. I would have been labelled a troublemaker.

I think the saigen world view is slightly racist. We do all these stories set in the United States which is a cultural melting pot, but rarely is it people who aren't white. Only if it's specifically a story where everyone's black in it. We did this story once. Somewhere in the States there was a gang of bank robbers and they were a bunch of black guys. And they disguised themselves as white guys. They had the *Mission Impossible*-style masks. And the way the film crew did the story was they just had white people play them in masks, and then they had black actors play them as themselves. So I suddenly turned into a black man, much thinner and more muscular than me and about a foot taller. There was a scene where we were supposed to be outside the house of a woman who worked in the bank. We were casing where she lived. And of course, in saigen world we're black Americans so we listened to extremely loud hip-hop in the car while casing this joint and, no word of a lie, they had the guy in the back seat spin a basketball on his finger. And they kept saying to us, 'More black! More black!' They wanted us to act more black. They were trying to teach us to do handshakes and things. I don't know what they did on the day when they were shooting with the real black guys. I don't know if the director asked them to act more black.

What have I done commercialwise? Docomo – but that was just the back of my head. Nike – an extra for that one. Shiseido – just an extra for that one but Orlando Bloom was in it. And I managed to annoy him, which was worth it. We were shooting in the winter and it was in a warehouse down in Kawasaki. It was a really big warehouse and there were loads of extras including myself. And Orlando Bloom. One half of the warehouse was all us extras crammed in with a few heaters trying to keep warm, and on the other side was Orlando Bloom's motorhome. And he had a big screen TV with Wii on it. And the whole day he didn't come out. They had an Orlando Bloom stand-in. And then eventually, when we got to doing the actual honban (the real take), he comes out and tries to get this fake camaraderie going with us. He was saying to the sound men, 'Yeah, hurry up guys because we're freezing our bollocks out here, aren't we guys?' I said, 'Isn't it nice and warm in your trailer?' I didn't realise I was saying it out loud. I thought I was just thinking it. A bunch of people laughed around me and Orlando Bloom was like, 'Who said that?! Who said that?!' He was furious.

Saigen work, I'm proud to say, is the lowest rung of the ladder if you're a foreign talent. You really want the big-paying television commercials. But when they get bored of you, you end up doing saigen. Or stop. I haven't landed many big commercial jobs because I just don't have the look that they want, to be honest. And I'm pudgy as well. So I get the character roles. 'We're looking for someone with character,' which means, 'You. Ugly. Get in.' Nothing is going to change that much for me.

The going rate is 12,000 yen (£58) for the first eight hours unless you're the main part, then it's double that. And then over eight hours, it's ten per cent. You're not going to get rich doing it. Certain jobs will be spread across a few days but then you won't work for a couple more. It probably averages about a day a week. I've never understood how to make money. That's one of my bad points.

Voice work. That's something I'd like to do but the voice acting world here is more cliquey. When I did the first *Unbelievable* job, I met all these other people and they were very generous with telling me the names of all the other agencies. Because there's a lot of agencies you can join as a foreign talent or gaitare as they call us, and you don't have to be exclusive to any of them. I blitzed the other agencies and joined them all. But I've noticed voice people are a bit more cagey and it's tricky to get in. I've done a few bits but they have their own specific voice talent agencies and I've never been able to join one. I've just been thrown a bone here and there by a regular.

When I first joined Inagawa Motoko, the main reason was because I wanted to do voice work and the guy I'd met on the train said to me, 'Oh, you've got a strong regional accent. That's great. They're always looking for stuff like that.' Not interested, apparently. Because when I have done voice work, they've never asked me about it. Or they don't seem aware of my accent. I mean, Wales is a pretty small place, right? And unless you have some connection to it, most people probably wouldn't know. People never guess my accent right. It's always, 'Are you Dutch? Or Scottish?'

When you join the offices of Inagawa Motoko in Roppongi you have to open an account at the Roppongi branch of Sumitomo Bank for them to pay you. I'd heard the rumours from everyone, 'You have to chase them', or 'You have to go down to the office and sit there until they can't ignore you'. I thought, okay, fair enough. I'm not desperate for this money.

And I don't have the time to go running around after people. So I'll check the account every now and again, assuming it'll come in dribs and drabs. I totally forgot about it. I'm a terrible procrastinator. About four years later I thought, 'I'll have a look. How much is in there?' Zero. Nothing at all. They hadn't paid me in four years. So I wrote them a very official legal-sounding, threatening email and got paid everything in a lump sum the next day. And I never worked for them again.

Clive Davies (centre) as an *Unbelievable!* American cop

Chapter Nine

Discovering Dō: How the Japanese experiences of Dan Bradley and Eluned Gramich shaped their creative careers

Eluned Gramich at Nijūbashi Bridge in Tōkyō

Dan Bradley at Ōhira nursery school

You can't spend time in Japan without bumping into an aspiring writer. Practising poets pore over technical translations by day and write in the windows of cheap kissaten (traditional coffee shops) until the last train home at midnight. Budding scriptwriters teach English conversation to office workers before heading out to table reads. And you can always find would-be novelists scanning the shelves for inspiration in the crevasse-like aisles of Infinity Books in the Sumida district of Tōkyō. There is even an annual English language writers' conference (Japan Writers Conference) where Japan-based authors can exchange knowledge and offer support.[26]

I'm not immune. When, during my travels, I find myself with an hour to spare, I head to the nearest Book Off, a nationwide chain of second-hand bookstores.

Signposted by a giant red and white 本 (hon, meaning book), they are easy to find in most towns. The Japanese second-hand book trade survives because, unlike in the UK where the Net Book Agreement was abolished in the nineties, new books cannot be sold at a discount. In Tōkyō, the place to go for used books of all kinds and prices is the Jinbōchō district. Maps are available which indicate whether shops are antiquarian or just cheap, and which carry foreign language works and art prints. I've just spent an afternoon there.

Back in my hotel room, I wonder what is it about Japan that attracts foreign writers? And what can Japan and Japanese literature offer those seeking the creative life? To answer my questions, I call up Eluned Gramich and Dan Bradley. Eluned won the New Welsh Writing Awards 2015 WWF Cymru Prize for Writing on Nature and the Environment for her memoir of a homestay on the northernmost island of Hokkaidō (published in book form by *New Welsh Review* as *Woman Who Brings the Rain* and now available in a new edition from Parthian). A versatile writer whose work also includes literary translation, short stories, the literary novel and gothic fiction, she has since published the haunting novels, *Sleep Training* and *Windstill.* Dan began his career as a Japanese–English translator before discovering a love of short fiction. His work has appeared in *Ambit* and *Granta,* and during the Covid pandemic he appeared in *The Guardian* describing the joys and trials of being a postman during lockdown. Now back in Wales, Eluned and Dan are pursuing different creative journeys. But they both credit Japan with inspiring their writing careers. We chat on Zoom.

Dark-haired with delicate features, Eluned from Haverfordwest says she always wanted to be a fiction writer. She began composing short stories as a teenager then followed an undergraduate degree in English literature from the University of Oxford with a master's degree in fiction from the University of East Anglia. Eluned first became aware of Japan as a child when she discovered her German grandfather's albums, full of colour photographs of Japanese gardens and castles, and group shots of men in flared trousers. In the seventies, he had worked for a Munich pharmaceutical company, travelling around Asia on sales trips. In 2012, within two weeks of handing in her master's dissertation, Eluned was on a plane to Tōkyō.

Eluned travelled to Japan as a Daiwa scholar on a two-year programme designed to foster interest and develop expertise in the country. For twelve months she studied Japanese intensively before being assigned two six-month internships. The first was at the Welsh Government Office where she was tasked with researching English-language teaching opportunities in Wales. The second was at the Japanese Literary Translation Agency.

But it was a homestay which sparked the idea for her first book. Eluned stayed with a retired couple in the town of Niseko at the foot of Mount Yōtei. After two years in the neon megalopolis of Tōkyō, her move to the rural north could have proved a culture shock. Instead it seemed very familiar: the mountainous terrain, the forest landscapes in muted colours, the small communities, the sense of not being part of the mainland, the indigenous culture and language. And the constant rain. Six thousand miles away from home, Hokkaidō reminded Eluned of Wales.

In Niseko, Eluned encountered the locals: hardy retirees whose children had deserted them, rich Tōkyōites with second homes, Aussie snowboarders awaiting the start of the ski season, and anyone seeking an escape from the modern urban lifestyle. They reminded her of communities in west Wales: the Welsh farmers, the English hippies seeking the good life, and those who came for a rave and never left. Both places, Eluned recalls, have that 'end of the line feeling'. But it is just such places that attract an interesting mix of people.

In Hokkaidō, places have two names: one Japanese,

the other their original Ainu moniker. When the Ainu, the indigenous people of the northern islands of Hokkaidō, Sakhalin and the Kuril Islands, were displaced by mainlanders (both the Yamato 'mainland' Japanese, and Russians) their language was banned and their culture suppressed. Through forced intermarriage and the redistribution of their lands to mainlanders, they were assimilated into the Japanese nation. A visit to an Ainu museum reminded Eluned of San Ffagan (St Fagans), the Welsh Museum of History, (a genuine 'folk museum' with rebuilt and transplanted buildings). 'All these parallels,' she remembers. 'I thought something here will ring true to a Welsh readership.'

Looking back, Eluned believes she had been too young for the extremely critical, competitive environment of UEA writing workshops. She graduated with her confidence in tatters, admitting, 'I couldn't even put down a sentence without thinking it was terrible.' Moving to Japan allowed her to reflect and regroup. It also presented her with something new to write about, enabling her to challenge cultural assumptions. 'That really helps writing because you're not fixed on one way of seeing the world,' she says. 'There is always a sense that we can turn it on its head and look at it another way.' This, she believes, is very important to the development of any artist, especially a writer.

Japan also gave her a new perspective on her craft. In Tōkyō, she attended museums, exhibitions, galleries and theatres. She particularly enjoyed the weirdness of butō dance and the high drama of kabuki plays that were so long, audiences had to pack a lunch. 'You go through boredom and reach a Zen state,' she says of the experience. Through attending so many artistic events, she came to realise how seriously Japanese follow their creative interests. Actors, dancers, potters, calligraphers, flower arrangers, musicians and martial artists, whether they pursue an art form as a job or as a hobby, they follow 'dō' (the way), growing and developing their craft with lifelong dedication. 'It is,' says Eluned, 'almost a quasi-religious experience.' 'Dō' gave Eluned a fresh perspective on life and on her craft. It restored her confidence and enabled her to write again.

In contrast, Dan Bradley did not go to Japan in order to write. The first in his family to go to university, he studied English at the University of Cambridge but found its elitism and snobbery destroyed his love of reading and discouraged him from writing for many years. He even admits he had no real interest in Japan or its culture before moving there in his mid-twenties. In 2006, he joined the JET Programme on a friend's recommendation, simply as a way to experience another culture.

He was posted to Ōhira, a village of less than six thousand people in an agricultural, predominantly rice-growing, area of Miyagi prefecture. As an ALT, he taught English at the local elementary and junior high schools where, in such a small community, he often found himself teaching brothers, sisters and cousins. Discovering that their English capacity was low, he set himself the task of mastering Japanese – which he did through total immersion – eschewing a home internet connection in favour of watching Japanese television and movies, listening to Japanese music, reading manga and attending conversation classes in the nearby city of Sendai. He achieved Level 1 (the highest) in the Japanese Language Proficiency Test (JLPT) in under three years.

Towards the end of his third and final year on the programme, he was sitting in a career seminar on translation when 'a lightbulb went on'. After all his work mastering the language, translating seemed the obvious career choice, a field in which he would get paid to read and learn new things. 'I could see myself excited about being a translator for twenty, thirty, forty years,' he says. Returning to the UK, he survived for a couple of years doing freelance commercial translation work, deciphering 'very dry' business documents and the occasional bit of marketing copy.

What he hadn't yet realised was that the market for Japanese to English translation was small and unstable. At one financial translation job, his entire team was fired the first week back after Christmas.

In the first two years after returning to the UK, Dan also experienced reverse culture shock. Because he had been working in the Japanese language and socialising mainly with Japanese friends, not only did he begin to suffer from first language decay – to forget English – but he had few local friends through whom he could rediscover his Welsh identity. Like many expatriates who return after a long time overseas, he felt alienated. 'I was meant to be back home but I still felt like I was in a foreign country,' he admits.

It was in Japan that Dan suffered his first serious bout of depression. In the winter of 2008, when his closest friends were leaving to embark on careers back home, he started to wonder what he was doing in a country where he had invested so much time and effort integrating himself into the language and culture, but where he still felt deeply alienated. Beefy and bearded, everyone stared at him wherever he went. In Japan, Dan recalls, 'It's easy to feel like a constant novelty, which isn't good for your long-term mental health.' Several years of precarious freelance translation later and facing extreme burnout, these feelings of depression resurfaced, and he became 'lobotomised by deep depression' and too ill to work.

In 2013, he moved back to his parents' house in Port Talbot where the depression began to lift. He started writing in earnest, filling notebooks with ideas and images, sketches and poetry, and conversations overheard on the bus. 'It was amazing to have my voice back,' he declares. From these notes, he began creating short stories which captured the issues he was experiencing: the disconnection and defamiliarisation, and that liminal experience of existing between cultures. Having struggled with learning an unfamiliar language from scratch, he is particularly interested in inarticulacy and is drawn to elliptical and impressionistic short-form fiction.

In 2014, Dan interned at *Granta* magazine to assist with the publication of their first dual English/Japanese edition. Out of eighty applicants, he was selected because he was the only one who could read Japanese. The internship gave him a solid grounding in how publishing and literary magazines work, and he still reads submissions for them.

Dan believes that his experiences in Japan – both good and bad – set him on course to become a writer, helping him to reconnect with his love of language, of writing and the telling of stories. Through translation, even that dry marketing copy, he has been able to master the technicalities of good writing and to shape his own short fiction forms. 'Translating and writing go together,' he says. This is especially true of literary translation. Having translated Japanese short stories for *Granta* and *The Book of Tokyo* anthology (Comma Press) he has learned to recreate voice and tone and atmosphere. 'Literary translation is effectively creative rewriting,' he notes.

More than this, he rediscovered his creative voice. At Cambridge, for fear of being mocked or excluded, he had hidden his Welsh accent and his working-class roots. Japan released him from the financial and class barriers that had held him back, the same barriers that make the arts, literary publishing, academia and many other fields 'so off-putting and inaccessible for working-class people in the UK'. Distanced from them, he was able to explore elements of his personality that had long been stifled, to express himself freely, and to rediscover his creative inspiration.

Both Eluned and Dan agree that reading Japanese novels, either in Japanese or in translation, has also influenced their writing. Dan likes the deadpan weirdness of Japanese literature: the supernatural, the uncanny, anything that deals with the ellipsis, where much – like the Japanese language itself – is unspoken. Stories that are 'like looking at the surface of a dark pond knowing there's all this stuff going on under the surface that you can't quite capture – that is too elusive.' He offers up *Yukiguni* (*Snow Country* by Yasunari Kawabata) as one of his favourites, 'very depressing but beautifully written – a story about not expressing how you feel.' Ironically, not expressing how you feel is one reason why Dan found it difficult to live there. In Japan, 'it can be a real test to work out people's motives or true feelings.' And yet, as he points out, quoting the writer Lorrie Moore, 'Most things good for writing are bad for life'.

As a teenager, Eluned was drawn to classic Japanese authors such as Yukio Mishima and Jun'ichirō Tanizaki. But in many of these, women are depicted as geisha, or ghosts, or – in the case of Kawabata's *House of the Sleeping Beauties* – as unconscious. For a long time, she found it difficult to find contemporary works in translation by Japanese women. Having interned at the Literary Translation Agency (now defunct due to lack of funding), she came to appreciate how patriarchal the translation industry can be and how female novelists are continually overlooked. Recently, however, translated works by Japanese female writers have been enjoying a boom in popularity outside

Japan. Novels by authors such as Sayaka Murata (*Convenience Store Woman, Earthlings*), Hiromi Kawakami (*The Nakano Thrift Shop, Strange Weather in Tokyo*) and Mieko Kawakami (*Breast and Eggs, Heaven*) have all been translated into English. As Eluned observes, these Japanese female novelists express different concerns, and often with a quirky outlook or a veiled message. 'These feminist symbols are registering dissatisfaction with patriarchal society through these allegories and symbols. It's something that is missing in Japanese male literature.'

Moving to Japan was a formative experience in Dan and Eluned's writing journeys. Japan played a role in developing them as writers. Eluned wonders if she would have become a writer – if she could ever have been published – if she had stayed in Wales. 'Going to Japan gave me time to think, to study, to reflect, to read, and it also gave me a subject matter that allowed me to explore writing more seriously.' Dan's route to creative writing came through language. 'Learning Japanese was huge for me,' he admits. 'It changed the way my brain works.' His mastery of Japanese to English translation also brought him opportunities such as the *Granta* internship, which introduced him into the literary world and gave him confidence that a working-class boy from Wales has something to contribute. For both, having that Japan experience gave them that all important USP, the unique selling point that moves a writer's work to the top of an editor's reading list.

This begs the question why they are both now living outside Japan. For *Woman who Brings the Rain*, Eluned said that, once again, she needed distance to gain perspective and to write. Dan didn't even consider writing until brought low by reverse culture shock. He's currently working on a master's thesis in English literature at Cardiff University on Welsh folk horror, landscape and national identity, and is putting together a collection of weird and uncanny short stories. Having experienced life abroad, he is keen to move on again soon. Wherever these writers settle, it is clear that Dan and Eluned continue to be influenced by their Japan sojourns.

Eluned can be contacted via her website at: elunedgramich.com

Dan can be contacted via his website at: dan-bradley.co.uk

On Learning Japanese 'A gigantic magic eye picture slowly coming into focus'

The Japanese language consists of three writing systems: hiragana, katakana and kanji. Hiragana is the Japanese alphabet, katakana is the alphabet for foreign words. Kanji are pictographs derived from the Chinese language. There are 2,136 'jōyō' kanji, kanji prescribed for 'everyday' use in Japan.

There are several Japanese examinations for foreigners. The most well-known is the JLPT in grades from N5 (beginner level) to N1 (advanced). Japanese companies and universities generally require applicants to hold N2 or above.

Many of the interviewees in this book are proficient in Japanese. As they made it clear that near fluency in Japanese is a prerequisite for successful employment outside of language teaching, I asked them for their views on the language as well as tips for studying.

Gareth Jenkins: Despite being a developed country, there's a very low rate of fluent English speakers, even in Tōkyō. They have the expatriate community and other foreigners but, if you want to get friendly with Japanese people, you need Japanese. It'd be a waste not to learn the basics at least. Having said that, I was very lucky in that I did the first two years of my Japanese university education back in Wales before coming to Japan.

Dan Bradley: When I got [to Japan], I decided not to get internet installed in my apartment. I decided if I'm going to be here, I want to completely be here. I don't want to be on Facebook with my friends back home. So I went complete immersion. I made sure there was no escape. I set my phone and computer to Japanese operating systems. I always carried a Japanese book. I made sure that my MP3 player was full of Japanese music. So I was getting exposure all the time. I had my Nintendo DS as well, and I was playing kanji video games. It was exhilarating. Because the more you understand, the more I was connecting and the more I was able to have genuine conversations.

I did the kanji kentei, the exam they have for kids. I got Japanese kids' textbooks on how to write kanji and I was able to write and memorise the readings of about 1100 kanji. I remember doing one of the kanji exams in

Sendai. I had to catch a bus into the city on a Saturday afternoon. I was in this big exam hall with all these desks. It was me and forty eight-year-olds. I remember all these kids looking at me like I'd arrived from another planet. It was surreal. They had invigilators and they kept stopping when they got behind me and looking over my shoulder thinking, 'a foreigner knows kanji?'

I met a lot of people who enjoyed talking about learning Japanese but then, when it came down to it, they were like, 'Ah I'm a bit tired. I'm gonna watch the film in English.' I think there's a certain amount of masochism: you have to be willing to watch a film and be happy to only understand forty per cent of it. For me, it was amazing. It was like a gigantic magic eye picture very slowly coming into focus.

Eluned Gramich *was a Daiwa Foundation scholar who studied Japanese using the controversial Naganuma Method. For one year, Daiwa scholars were taught the method at a school in Shibuya, Tōkyō, after which time they were expected to pass the JLPT at N2 level. (Writer and artist, Edmund de Waal, recipient of one of the first Daiwa Foundation scholarships in 1991 also studied the Naganuma Method. In* The Hare with the Amber Eyes, *he recalls kicking the school's green metal gates on his way to the school.)*:

It was very controversial even when I was going there. The idea is that you're not allowed to speak your native language in the classroom. Everything is in Japanese. The method is very rigid and you're never supposed to know more than what they've taught you, so you're not supposed to bring in words you already know. That's not allowed. You had to really adhere to the method and to the rules in order to advance. But it was a very effective method for learning Japanese. Very intensive. You had to speak Japanese every day. There were lots of advantages. You really started to tune in to the way Japanese works. There was phrase-making and structure and syntax rather than always translating. But one problem was a lot of people from the Daiwa scholarship, people who were used to being seen as clever or successful, didn't like being treated like children in this way. So there was always a lot of annoyance about the rigidity and patronising nature of the method. But I liked it.

In the JLPT examination, there's no speaking element. It's all writing and reading. But it was a rather unfair test because other scholars were much better than me at speaking. They were the sort of people who naturally picked up the language by speaking. I was always much too nervous or reserved to do that but, in terms of reading, I could do that better and that's why N2 was simpler for me.

Gerald Gallivan*'s first teaching job was located in Iwate prefecture, a rural area*: I studied a lot up in Iwate because there's nothing else to do. I had a lot of free time. My main motivation was being able to speak to the children and to know what they were saying. It helps to have a goal. After six months, I managed to get a private one-on-one teacher. But for me, it was having notebooks. I used to write in notebooks everything I was learning: grammar and vocabulary. Because I lived in the country, it was so much easier to practise because I could use it straightaway. In Iwate, there weren't many English-speaking people or services so I had to learn Japanese. So I'm happy I moved to the countryside first. Living in the country helps a lot. Being thrown in the deep end.

John Llywelyn: Last spring, I went to work at a restaurant on the coast. Me and a friend of mine from Scotland worked there as the only foreigners. The place was called Kaki Goya which means 'oyster shack'. It's a really interesting restaurant. All the tables have got a big hot plate in the middle. And it's all shellfish. So you've got your scallops, oysters, whelks, even the big snow crabs that you get here in Hokkaidō. Really delicious stuff. And one of the things they served there was tabehōdai – 'all you can eat' – oysters. So the customers would shout, 'Tabehōdai! Tabehōdai!' And me or my friend would answer, 'Hai!' and we'd come with a wheelbarrow full of oysters and a shovel. And we'd shovel two or three scoops onto the hot plate. It was amazing. Working there, my Japanese had to improve. But then you kind of plateau because you learn everything you need to do that job. Then I worked in a hotel and did building and maintenance work. So, again, my Japanese went up and then it plateaued. And now with the [white water] rafting, I've got to do a safety speech to the Japanese clients in Japanese. Some of my friends, their Japanese is basically rafting based. They can only say: forward paddle, backward paddle, turn left, turn right, duck your head, stand up, move this way.

Pred Evans: I used to go round to a local okonomiyaki place where the owner was fluent in English. And he used to teach me lots of – I was going to say useful Japanese – probably not very useful Japanese, but Japanese that people would be surprised that I'd know. So my Japanese came on fast.

Bethany Cummings *studied Japanese at the University of Edinburgh*: One of the things that helped me learn Japanese was karaoke. Because even in Edinburgh we used to go a lot. And obviously if you're singing in Japanese you have to read really fast, and so I trained myself to be able to read that fast. I love singing. I always sing 'Kiseki' by GReeeeN. And Mr. Children songs such as 'Shirushi'.

***Geraint M** is a professional linguist. In Japan he works for a multinational company, revising and editing Japanese to English translations into understandable English*:

I don't think there is anything intrinsically difficult about the Japanese language other than as an expression of culture. And by that, I mean the direct or indirect statement. What's said or not said. It's the use of the passive voice which I find very interesting. 'It has been decided that...'. When I'm writing in English, part of the job I do is to ask, 'Who said that? Who is thinking it? And why?'

Sometimes I've gone back to [my Japanese colleagues] and said, 'It's unclear. Can you tell me what the tone was in Japanese?' And sometimes the answer is, 'We don't know.' And I say, 'We're publishing this comment and there is no clarity of expression in Japanese for a reason to be determined. And you want me to come up with something equally vague in

English? It just won't work.' There's an ambiguity that Japanese people enjoy, experience, exploit – I'm not sure what the correct word would be.

I think that the sense of collective decision-making here in Japan is a real thing. When it has been decided, it's understood that it is the group that has decided. Whereas when you need to express that in English, there needs to be an agent. There needs to be an identifiable, 'I think this' or 'I said that' or 'We as a firm think this'.

Obviously, three writing systems, two reading systems – it's not the simplest language in that sense. But I think it's less about the mechanics of the language, I think it's more an expression of culture. The expression of culture is the true heart of the difficulty.

Clive Davies: I find Japanese immensely difficult, I have to admit. I always have done. But then again, I always found Welsh a bit difficult even though it's my mother tongue. I like to say I'm bilingual across three languages. My English is solid. And if you put the Welsh and the Japanese together, that might pass muster.

Chapter Ten

Welsh at Heart: Chikako Hirono and the Kansai St David's Society

Chikako Hirono in the classroom with students of St Nicholas Church in Wales primary school, Cardiff

Chikako Hirono is annoyed about the Welsh cakes. They were advertised on a major Japanese department store's website at two packets for 2,000 yen. That's £9.77. There are six in a packet meaning they cost 166 yen (81 pence) per cake. Chikako looked online and found them for £1.20 for a whole packet at Waitrose in the UK. And the store's photograph showed them served with butter and jam. 'With jam?' she wails. 'I worked for that store's advertising company. They could have asked me, right?'

So, although we meet at the store's Ōsaka branch, we go elsewhere: to a retro coffee shop located in a mall under the train tracks. At Hoshino, the lighting is dimmed and the tables vibrate whenever a Kyōto line train rumbles into the station. Hoshino offers hand-dripped coffee in three signature blends. I order the sweeter Hoshino blend with a side of apple pie and a scoop of vanilla ice-cream. Chikako orders the heavier Hikoboshi blend and a piece of strawberry cheesecake.

Chikako is a freelance advertising copywriter. She is also an expert on Wales and contributor to the Japanese language book, *Sixty Chapters to Get to Know Wales*.[27] And she is a founder member of the Kansai branch of the St David's Society Japan (Cymdeithas Dewi Sant Siapan Kansai or Kansai CDS). In 1990, she joined an international internship programme and was sent to St Nicholas Church in Wales primary school in Cardiff. 'Because Japan was a rising sun economically, the headmistress thought it would be interesting for her pupils to know about Japan,' recalls Chikako. 'And also there were so many Japanese companies already in Wales.'

Chikako taught her pupils origami, calligraphy, how to wear kimono, how to use an abacus (she carried a giant 'soroban' from Japan), about festivals such as setsubun (a cleansing spring ritual when people throw beans to repel demons) and hinamatsuri (a doll festival in celebration of Girls' Day in March). Students decorated the school with drawings of Japanese castles and koinobori (giant carp windsocks flown in celebration of Children's Day – originally

Boys' Day – in May). She also used the school's small kitchen to prepare sticky Japanese mochi (sweetened rice) cakes to eat with green tea. Mochi filled with anko (red bean paste) is a popular sweet in Japan but it was a strange taste for Welsh pupils who took one bite and ran away.

One day, when Chikako happened to mention that her birthday was on the first of March, 'there was a silence first and then yelling all over the staff room'. Chikako was stunned to discover that her birthday coincided with St David's Day. 'You were destined to come to Wales!' declared the headmistress.

On that first trip Chikako saw little of the nation. Back then, Japanese-language guidebooks of Britain contained few pages about Wales, so she followed the standard trail for Japanese tourists: the Lake District, Edinburgh and London. 'It was so foolish of me,' she now admits. Instead of the country, she fell in love with Welsh people. Welcomed by several homestay families whose children attended the school, she found everyone to be warm and friendly. She was never homesick for Japan.

After nine months in Wales, Chikako went back to Japan and returned to her original career as an advertising copywriter. Now she works freelance, producing copy for flyers, travel guides and department store catalogues. One January, her mother received a New Year's card from an old friend who mentioned that her daughter-in-law was Welsh. Marilyn Amoko was living nearby in Nara. In 2000, Chikako and Marilyn met and established a Kansai branch of the St David's Society Japan for those who could not travel to the Tōkyō meetings.

Now an independent organisation, Kansai CDS differs from the society in Tōkyō. As the majority of Welsh residents of Japan live in or around the Kantō (eastern) area, the Tōkyō branch is a meeting place for them to socialise, network and maintain their Welsh language. Whereas Kansai (central) area branch members are based in or around the city of Ōsaka and are mostly Japanese expatriates who have returned from postings to their company's factory in Wales. These include families from Panasonic which has had a factory in Cardiff (originally producing analogue televisions and microwaves) since 1976. Panasonic's main television division is based in Ōsaka. The construction company Takenaka is also well-represented. And there is a sprinkling of old girls and boys from the Saturday school in Whitchurch Upper High School in Cardiff, where the children of Japanese executives went to study their native language and to keep up with the Japanese educational syllabus.

Chikako believes that Welsh and Kansai people have more in common than economic ties. While teaching at the primary school, she recognised in local people 'a strong awareness of being Welsh', which made her feel very comfortable. Ōsakans too have their own defiant identity, she says. And they are just as patriotic. Ōsaka may only be the second biggest city in Japan but it has a longer history and a richer culture than Tōkyō. 'Tōkyō is our rival,' she explains. 'People in Tōkyō look down on us. But Ōsaka people think "we won't lose". That feeling towards Tōkyō is something like Welsh people's feeling towards England.'

The Kansai CDS provides a forum for returnees to reminisce about their expatriate experiences. But its other objective is to introduce Welsh culture to Japanese people. Chikako finds it kuyashii (frustrating, regrettable – our conversation takes place in a mixture of English and Japanese) that the other three countries of the United Kingdom are well known in Japan but not Wales. Japanese know that Ireland is recognised for its Guinness and for St Patrick's Day which is celebrated with a parade in Tōkyō. Scotland is famous for bagpipes, whisky and golf. 'So many things they show off, but Wales is not so fashionable,' she laments. 'The biggest attractive point of Wales is Welsh people,' she says, but that is not easy to convey.

The Kansai CDS has sixty official members but only twelve people attended the Christmas party last year. Since the Covid pandemic, numbers for in-person society events have declined. However, by moving online, the society is discovering a new audience. During Japan's (unofficial) lockdown, Kansai CDS along with the Academic Society of Welsh Studies chairman, Dr Takeshi Koike, and Yūko Nakauchi, the founder of Bore da Kikaku ('good morning' in Welsh followed by a reference to Yūko's event-planning remit) began running regular language and culture classes, quizzes, movie nights and talk shows on Zoom and YouTube. With these events open to all, non-members with an interest in Welsh culture are also able to tune in from anywhere in the world. They include fans of Welsh rugby, movies, language, and admirers of Katherine Jenkins and particularly, Luke Evans. (In hushed tones, Chikako reveals that one married housewife is such a Luke Evans fan that she even flies to Britain to see his concerts. And, having bought an online meeting with him, she is eager to become fluent in his native tongue.) For anyone who wants to discuss and share information about Wales, Chikako also runs a closed Facebook group: Talks on Wales (in English) or Wales Nandemo Kandemo ('anything and everything on Wales' in Japanese). It has around seventy members.

The Kansai St David's Society also invites returnees to talk online about their memories of Welsh life and culture. The most recent event took place the week before I flew to Japan so I tuned in. *Me & Wales* was a slideshow talk given by professional photographer Hidetoshi Ochiai who in 1983 lived in an attic in Romilly Crescent, Cardiff, and studied photography at the local arts centre.

Ochiai had arrived in Cardiff with a book of beautiful colour photographs of Japan but, when a friend told him that there was no philosophy in them, he began instead to record everyday images of local life: strings of onions hanging from the handlebars of a bicycle in Cardiff market, his downstairs neighbour who (he thought) looked like Princess Diana, and his landlord's Morris Minor with an armchair where the passenger seat should have been. There is even a photograph of Prince Philip, the late Duke of Edinburgh, gesticulating at Ochiai's camera as he asks him what a Japanese man is doing with a German Leica.

Many of these images are in black and white, and Ochiai gave an explanation of the difference between western and Japanese eyes which I later ask Chikako to clarify. Japanese people have black (they say black, we say brown) eyes which are more sensitive to colours and able to recognise a wider variation of tones. Western Europeans are more likely to have blue or grey eyes which tend to recognise variations in light, and so are more attuned to black-and-white images. I have no idea whether this is true or not. But I do know that Japanese people rarely wear sunglasses in Japan (unless they are gangsters) whereas I have to wear them all year round, even in winter.

After Ochiai's talk, the online audience chipped in with memories of their own. Some remembered the Laura Ashley shop on Queen Street. Others recalled the locomotive scrapyard in Barry, in the Vale of Glamorgan, where the GWR 5972 Olton Hall steam locomotive sat rusting until it was restored and became Harry Potter's Hogwarts Express.

Marilyn Amoko returned to Wales and passed away many years ago. Now Chikako has to keep the society going by herself. Next year, she is hoping to bring back the society's annual cultural festival and party as an in-person event. Previous gatherings have featured performances by the Ōsaka male voice choir, harp recitals, talks and sales of homemade Welsh foods, including Welsh cakes. It is tiring work but, having just celebrated her birthday (we meet on the second of March), she says it warmed her heart to receive so many birthday greetings from society members and from friends in Wales. These include the teachers from St Nicholas Primary with whom she stays whenever she travels back. 'I think it is my destiny to be bound to Wales,' she concedes, as we head out into a damp, rainy (rather Welsh) Ōsaka morning.

Later Chikako emails me with more thoughts about her experiences in Wales. Back when she was a teacher and lodging with a local family, she watched a boxing match on television with her host father. Pointing to one of the boxers who was black, her host father said, 'He is Welsh!' 'I was puzzled so much!' writes Chikako. 'How could a person of African origin be Welsh??' And when she moved to live with another host family, she discovered that – while their parents were English – both daughters declared they were Welsh. At that moment, Chikako realised, 'to be Welsh, you don't need to have Welsh racial blood.' Where you were born and raised is the most important element in deciding who you are. 'This is an eye-opener to me because most of the inhabitants in Japan are Japanese racially,' she admits. 'Anyway, since then I sometimes introduce myself as "Welsh at heart"!'

The 2011 Tōhoku Earthquake and Tsunami The day that got shortened by 1.8 microseconds

On Friday 11 March at 2.46pm, a magnitude nine earthquake struck the eastern seaboard of Japan. So powerful was the sudden jolt of tectonic plates that it shifted the earth on its axis by seventeen centimetres and shortened the length of a day by 1.8 microseconds. After water from tidal waves engulfed the Dai-ichi Nuclear Power Plant in Fukushima, three of its reactors exploded and went into meltdown, releasing radiation across eastern Japan and the Pacific Ocean. Approximately 20,000 people were killed in the disaster. Many others were left homeless or evacuated from their homes in exclusion zones and have still not returned.

As the disaster occurred during the winter academic vacation period, some foreigners were out of the country. Others were working as usual.

Tim Pelham Williams: It was kind of weird, man. I was teaching in Temple University, in a class, and suddenly everything started shaking. Obviously, in Japan, an earthquake is an earthquake. But this was different. Usually when there's an earthquake, I take my reaction from those Japanese people around me. And honestly, on that day, the colour drained from their faces. And I was like, fuck, that's bad. We went downstairs and outside and – actually I went to a pub, an English pub – and drank Guinness. Eventually I got to Nakano station and that's where the train stopped. So I went outside and I just asked a fella on a motorbike to take me to Ogikubo and he did. I said, 'Oh, go on fella,' and he drove me home. I got home at 9pm.

Nery Rees Asai: I was teaching at the time at the Pure English international kindergarten in Toda Kōen which admits children from eighteen months to six years old. School was finishing for the day and we'd just sent most of the younger kids home. There were around ten older kids left and most of them were in my class on the ground floor, having a snack or doing some crafts. I just remember some of the other teachers coming downstairs and the Hawaiian teacher was like, 'Everybody out!' We went outside to the car park and the cars were jumping up and down.

Once I went outside and saw the school building going 'whoosh', I really thought it was coming down. It was very intense. We were just looking round and up and [wondering], 'What's going to happen?' The students were confused because they were not old enough to grasp how terrible this was. Some of them were laughing.

Then it stopped. Of course we knew there were going to be aftershocks but in the meantime we [said], 'Okay, we have to go back in. We have to get water, snacks, blankets.' So two of the male teachers went back in and collected everything we needed. Me and some other teachers stayed with the kids. In the car park there were electrical poles above us so we said, 'Okay, we can't stay here.' There was a park nearby and so [we said], 'Let's go somewhere a bit more open.' Eventually the parents came and by 4pm all the kids had gone.

I went to the train station and the trains were stopped but luckily, because it was so early, I could line up and get a taxi. I went to the bank and I took out 300,000 yen *(£1,466)*. I just thought, I don't know what's going to happen because if the cashpoints and the electric goes off, I need money. At the beginning, people were just getting in taxis by themselves. In the end this one man [said], 'I'm going towards here, who wants to go in the same direction? Let's go together.' So that set a precedent for other people to do the same.

I remember being in a taxi with one of the other teachers and this Japanese salaryman, and he was on the phone. [The district of] Odaiba was on fire and his kids were in Odaiba at school. It was just insane. I didn't know who the guy was and I've never seen him since. [We were] listening to him trying to phone the school and the TV was on in the taxi and seeing all the destruction and then the helicopters flying over and we were like, 'Oh my God.' He couldn't get through to the school because all the phones had gone down but I had Skype on my iPhone. So I [said to him], 'Do you want to use my Skype?' In the end he managed to get through on Skype. He was able to communicate with the school and they [told him], 'It's okay.'

The taxi ride was about thirty minutes. I got out at Itabashi near the twenty-four-hour post office because that's where the guy got out. It was probably a fifteen-minute walk to my house in Higashi Ikebukuro but, because I didn't know where I was, I ended up walking for thirty minutes. I just remember I was really glad to get home because when you're walking by yourself, what if it happens again? I was by myself in a random street and I didn't know where I was.

I got home and then we stayed in Tōkyō to

begin with. My bookshelves and stuff were down, and there was a slight crack in my wall. Then there was the explosion at the nuclear plant and, after that happened, I tried to go and get supplies. I remember going to the store and trying to buy stuff and every [shelf] was empty. In the end, we decided to go up to Toyama, which is where my husband is from, and we stayed there for a week or so.

A lot of people left Japan during that time. Many foreigners got the nickname 'flyjin'. I guess it was scary, especially with the nuclear incident. Many people were worried – especially people with kids – whether the government was being transparent about the nuclear fallout. If I had had [my son] Keita at the time I might have done the same. But just being one person, it was different.

Joe Cairnes: I was at the office. Our office was down on the waterfront in Toyosu, near the fish market. The earthquake was clearly bigger than anything anyone in the office had experienced. It's an open plan office of thirty-forty people, and people quickly made it known, 'Oh my God, this is the big one.' It was big. It lasted a long time and then it went bigger. Clearly something was up. We were told to evacuate the building immediately. We were all stood outside

and another shake came a few minutes later, and in all those glass-fronted buildings you could see the glass waving under the vibrations.

Everyone was told to go home and I went on a long walk with a colleague, from the waterfront all the way home to Ichigaya. We stopped at a few pubs on the way. It was probably a two- to three-hour walk [that] we extended to about six or seven hours. We were young guys. We were confident we would be fine. Maybe it was a bit irresponsible and not something I'd do now but there were pubs that were open so we just made our merry way. A lot of the convenience stores were open although some of the key items like water quickly emptied off the shelves.

For a couple of weeks, I was up in Ishinomaki city, helping with the clean-up. I heard there was a charity that was organising volunteers to go up. They organised a coach, you took your own camping equipment, your own batteries for charging your mobile phone, your own everything, essentially, for the whole trip. And then they brought you back at the end of it. We got placed in a university or some kind of college. The grounds were up on a hill, and we were working in the gym that had been converted into a warehouse. We were organising the donations. Early in the morning we would borrow some bikes

and ride down into town just to see for ourselves what was happening. The first day we rode down we were shocked. There were just piles of rubble. People had emptied out the first floor of their houses and there were just piles of stuff on the side of the road, clocks that had stopped at different times and trash all across the road. It was shocking.

The next day we went a bit further into town and it was up another notch again. We realised that we were just getting shocked by the outer edge of what the disaster was. We rode deep into town and there were boats in the middle of the road. There were buildings that didn't exist anymore. There was a whole plain of rubble closest to the waterfront which had been a residential development that was not there anymore. It had just been converted into its constituent parts. It was harrowing.

We were helping people get clothes and doling out some food here and there. So there were different tasks to be done. The warehouse stuff was up at the university, [and] some folks would come up and get the clothes there. There would be other times when we would take the bikes to people we'd met in the town and, if they had specific needs like toothpaste, the following day we'd go down and give them a kind of bespoke delivery. Then there would be other times when we'd just be going down in the truck with loads of stuff in the back and setting up a food or donation stall. There was just an infinite amount of work to be done. Any expectations that things could be resolved in the one or two weeks I was volunteering for [had gone]; you do what you can, right, and then hand over to other folks who can be there for longer.

Andy Moore: The British Embassy did actually provide iodine tablets. To get them, we had to go to an office building in central Tōkyō. You had to bring your passport to prove you were British. And just queue up. There were lots of people. It was probably a couple of hours' wait. The British are very good at queuing so it wasn't dreadful, but I think it was one of the biggest groups of British people that has ever been in Tōkyō. There was a form we had to fill in, probably just to make sure people didn't go twice. And they gave us a silver packet with the tablets in and instructions on how and when to take them, which simply said, 'don't take them yet'. It said, 'wait for further instructions'. The idea is they would saturate your thyroid with iodine so that if there was a radiation leak it wouldn't cause thyroid cancer. Doing this kind of thing, it's a nice gesture but then it makes you think, 'Oh my God, if I need these then what is the situation?' There was definitely this sense of tension. This was not a normal situation to be in. We were all trying our best to be calm but I think there was definitely a feeling of, there's something going on here that is out of our control.

On the TV, I saw these long queues of foreigners at the immigration centre getting re-entry permits because they all wanted to leave. I just felt no, I don't want to leave because life's not that easy. You can't just run away when something happens. I've made this place my home and I'm going to have to deal with it. I thought, my [Japanese] girlfriend can't leave. She can't just walk away. So why should I? I thought, I'm just gonna stay and deal with it as best I can.

Joe Cairnes: To be honest we'd borne the brunt of some pretty poor communication from various embassies. I still recall the French embassy describing some kind of nuclear death wind on the way to Tōkyō. When those kinds of articles are coming out in the press you're like, 'Really? Okay, let's think this through.' And, granted, it was one of those situations which we faced again with Corona. The suspicion was that the Japanese government really didn't have its act together in terms of reporting. In the early days it had a motive for not reporting the true numbers. In the case of Covid, it was the Olympics. At this time, it was in relation to a massive nuclear disaster and of keeping that under wraps. But there were good sources around for actual hard data on the ground. There were Geiger counters set up and you could see what kind of readings people were getting across the country. You sift through the noise from various embassies and try to hear people who you think are compelling in times of disaster.

Richard O'Shea: The Sunday after, we had rugby training and it was the first time getting back together with everyone. We played rugby and then someone brought a cricket bat and ball, and we were playing cricket and having a few beers. And it was just really good to see everyone again because everyone got stuck at home and didn't want to go out. Of course, at that time, there were the flyjin and a few of my teammates had run away, escaped the country. So there was a lot of talk about them. Not positive at all. It was more the international businesspeople – where the company's paying for them to leave – who were leaving. And the teachers and mid-level salarymen were stuck.

Chapter Eleven

'Wales Is My Eternal Theme': The teaching life of Dr Takeshi Koike

Dr Takeshi Koike with his Welsh textbook

There's a sign on the bus that says we're not allowed to speak. It's a pity because I'm sitting next to Takeshi Koike and I've been waiting to talk to him for three years. At the entrance to his university, Daitō Bunka, we stand in front of a machine to have our temperatures taken. Only then can we take the elevator to Takeshi's office on the eighth floor and remove our masks. There's no actual law that says we have to wear them but Japanese people wore masks before the Covid pandemic (against colds and hay fever) and they're not going to stop now.

I suppose we are taking a risk. Takeshi's office is small, and made narrower by the bookshelves which line both walls. There are also books piled on his desk, stacked on the table and spilling out of boxes on the floor. I peruse the shelves. On one side are works on linguistics and the Anglo–Saxon language. On the other are books about Wales: history books, academic tomes, myths and legends. Some are in English but most are in Welsh. There are more books at home, Takeshi tells me. He has no idea how many books he owns. Probably thousands. Takeshi removes a box of books from a chair so I can sit down. I clear a space on the table for my digital recorder and ask him to tell his story.

In 1992, when Takeshi was a twenty-one-year-old undergraduate studying at Ōbirin University in Tōkyō, he was sent abroad for one year to improve his English. Having grown up with a love of music (his cousin is the opera director, Aguni Jun) Takeshi requested he be sent anywhere he could sing. Having heard that Wales was the 'land of song', his supervisor sent him to St David's University College (now the University of Wales Trinity St David) in Lampeter. 'At that time I didn't know anything about Wales,' admits Takeshi. 'I just wanted to improve my English.'

His first impressions of Wales were not positive. Sat jetlagged on a two-carriage train from Swansea to Carmarthen, all he could make out was an iron-grey sea and castle ruins glowering under a murky sky. In Lampeter, he found the campus deserted (it was the summer holidays) and, with students making up half the local population of 4,000, the town felt just as empty. 'I felt I came to a very gloomy, dark, remote place,' Takeshi recalls. He says he felt like Pwyll who goes deer-hunting, finds himself alone, meets a man from the other world and is invited there. 'Do you know the Mabinogion?' he asks me in what is to become a recurring motif in my interview with Takeshi. He knows a great deal about Welsh culture.

That first night, wandering through the silent streets in search of somewhere to eat, he found a fish and chip shop where, because of his Asian looks – a rarity in Wales at that time – a gang of local youths took an immediate interest in him. When he told them he was going to study Welsh, they taught him his first Welsh phrase, 'Catchyaladamate'.

Takeshi was looking forward to learning some real Welsh, and in Lampeter he found his ideal teacher. Gwendreth Morgan was a strict linguist who was precise about pronunciation. This suited Takeshi because he wanted to speak Welsh 'as precisely as possible'. Every time he learned a new phrase he would venture into Lampeter to try it out. When he learned, 'Alla'i gael bara?' (can I have bread) he wandered around asking the local people, 'and they were so happy to hear me speaking Welsh, they said, "Oh, diolch, diolch."' Takeshi found he could go anywhere with his new language and make friends. 'I loved that atmosphere, being part of the community. So I learned more and more,' he remembers. Takeshi searches his bookshelves and locates his original beginner's textbook, *Catchphrase*, now filled with pencilled annotations. Thanks to Gwendreth Morgan's efforts, 'I felt I could really accept it,' he says, flicking through the pages.

One of the places he made new friends was at church. Despite having been brought up in a non-religious family, Takeshi became interested in religion. (He is now a practising Catholic.) Since Gwendreth Morgan's husband was the vicar of the local Anglican church, it was only natural that Takeshi joined the choir. He didn't always understand what he was singing but it improved his Welsh pronunciation. Every Sunday after service he was invited to lunch at the Morgan's home where he became immersed in family life and the local community.

For Takeshi's birthday, the vicar's son gave him a cassette tape of Welsh harp music, through which he discovered the bardic craft of Cerdd Dant (in which a poem is sung to a harp melody). One poem, Waldo Williams' *Y Tangnefeddwyr* (the peacemakers) refers to the German bombing of Swansea in 1941, and talks about the importance of love, forgiveness and a dream of universal peace. Takeshi admits there were times when he became a bit fed up with Welsh jingoism, 'because it was too passionate, too patriotic.' And too anti-British. But the poem's Christian message helped him to realise this was not the case, after all. 'When I read the poem, I felt that I found some kind of treasure,' he says. And he realised that mastering the Welsh language, 'could be a key to a huge wealth of rich culture.'

After his first 'gloomy' view of Wales, Takeshi began to explore it in earnest, walking and cycling through the countryside, although he regularly miscalculated distances. Discovering he had to wait seven hours for a coach to return to Lampeter from Swansea, he opted to walk instead. 'Many things I didn't know,' he admits ruefully. 'One thing is in the UK you use mileage not kilometres. So I miscalculated the distance.' Another thing he didn't know was that he was walking on the layby of the motorway. Since in Japan you must pay to take an expressway, Takeshi had expected that Welsh motorways would be clearly marked with tollgates. When a man pulled over and offered to give Takeshi a lift, he thought he was being kidnapped. The man dropped him at Carmarthen.

One day in a Lampeter street, Takeshi encountered another Japanese man. So rare an occurrence was this that they went to lunch together and Takeshi discovered that the man was not a tourist but a scholar, Professor Hiroshi Mizutani of Kinjō Gakuin University in Nagoya. Mizutani, Japan's first Welsh expert, had been studying Welsh language and culture for over twenty-five years and was travelling in Wales on sabbatical in order to complete a book. He gave Takeshi an early draft and, after his return to Japan, Takeshi regularly rode the night bus down to Nagoya to learn more from Mizutani about the grammar, culture and history of Wales.

Takeshi admits that meeting Professor Mizutani was an important moment in his life. 'People in Japan were saying, "We have learned enough about the UK. There is nothing to learn anymore from them."' But Mizutani convinced him that Welsh was not a minor postscript to British studies. Takeshi must dedicate himself wholly to Welsh language and culture, Mizutani said, and strive to understand everything.

Since there were no postgraduate courses for Welsh in Japan, Takeshi instead studied historical linguistics for his doctorate and spent time researching and teaching at Edinburgh University. Upon graduation in 2004, he was hired by Daitō Bunka University in Tōkyō. The year after the Tōhoku Earthquake, Takeshi was given the task of reorganising the curriculum in his faculty, the Department of English and American Literature. He decided that every lecturer should offer a course in their specialist area of study. One was an expert in film studies, another a specialist in old manuscripts. Takeshi was adamant. 'I'm teaching Welsh,' he announced.

In the first year, sixty students enrolled on his course, Wales: Its Culture and Its Language. They learned about the Welsh flag, songs, ancient literature and of course, rugby. By the second year, he had them writing and making PowerPoint and video presentations introducing Japanese culture in Welsh. Takeshi filmed their presentations on subjects such as Studio Ghibli and sumō wrestling, and uploaded them to Facebook. In 2023, Takeshi had the students record self-introductions. He plays me a couple and they're good, with words clearly enunciated and r's rolled, which is difficult for Japanese speakers as there is no letter r in the Japanese alphabet. (They use a soft mix of r and l.)

Of course, I have to ask him what use the Welsh language can be to Japanese university students. 'It's a constant question for me,' admits Takeshi, especially as Daitō Bunka is a private university and his students are paying a million yen a year in tuition fees. In Japan, students begin learning the English language at elementary school, although most schools teach American – not British – English. Nevertheless there is much interest, even a certain snobbery, in being knowledgeable about British culture. Japanese housewives learn about England from the *Downton Abbey* television series and enjoy the English afternoon tea service offered in international hotels. Salarymen know Scotland from the shelves of their local bar, whisky and water being the drink of choice for middle management. Irish pubs serve Guinness, and on St Patrick's Day there is a parade through the streets of Tōkyō. But until the Rugby World Cup in 2019, the Japanese knew very little about Wales, which Takeshi finds disappointing but not surprising, since it often seems to get written out of British history. 'Look at the Union Jack!' Takeshi cries. 'There's elements of St George, St Patrick, and St Andrew. But where's Wales?'

Takeshi's justification for running his course is that he is introducing Welsh in the context of teaching English. He maintains that you cannot truly understand British culture unless you also understand the impact of the Welsh, their history, their landscape and their poetic tradition. Consider the Welsh influence in the plays of England's most famous playwright, he suggests. In William Shakespeare's *Henry IV*, both Lady Mortimer (a Welsh monoglot) and Owen

Glendower (bilingual) speak lines in Welsh, although this is indicated only by stage direction. Luckily, there were several contemporaneous Welsh actors in Shakespeare's company to fill in the Welsh dialogue. (It is also likely that Shakespeare's maternal grandmother was Welsh.) Shakespeare was not the only artist to seek inspiration from Wales. Many English poets and writers have mined Celtic myths and legends for their own works, not least of them JRR Tolkien, who borrowed Welsh sounds for his Elvish languages in *The Lord of the Rings* and *The Hobbit*. 'So, to really talk in depth about Britain, you need to mention Wales because that is where the British root of Great Britain is,' states Takeshi.

In his office at Daitō Bunka University

But equally his lessons are a way to show how different Wales is from England. Professor Mizutani lamented that Japanese people felt they knew all there was to know about British culture when all they really knew was England. Takeshi has even produced video interviews of himself interviewing Welsh people in their own language. 'And that's how I can really drive home how different Wales is.'

Takeshi's efforts have borne fruit. When one of his first-year students gained a scholarship to England to study English, he took the opportunity to visit Wales and wrote back:

> Dear Professor Koike, to be honest last year I didn't really understand why you're so crazy about the Welsh language. But I know why. I can see the people here speaking Welsh and I regret now that I didn't learn as hard as I should have done. Only people who have been to Wales and been welcomed by Welsh people, come to realise how great Wales is.

The letter left Takeshi invigorated and enthusiastic to introduce the country and its culture to a new generation of students.

Now married with five children, Takeshi is unable

to travel back to Wales as much as he would like. Instead he puts his energy into organising Welsh-themed events in Japan. During the Rugby World Cup in 2019, he gave a one-hour Welsh lesson in the Welsh Dome in the Shinjuku district of Tōkyō. And with another Japanese Welsh expert, Yoshifumi Nagata, he has produced a Japanese-language primer called *Basics of the Welsh Language.*[28] Takeshi wrote twenty short language lessons for beginners, while Nagata wrote pieces about the culture. 'But many people who bought the book said they enjoyed the columns more than the lessons!' he exclaims in exasperation.

Takeshi seems bemused at the way his life has turned out. He never chose to go to Wales; the university chose for him, and their original idea had been to send him to North Carolina. 'If they had sent me there, my life would have been totally different,' he says. Having reached his fifties, Takeshi is aware that his time as an academic is running out. While the university 'doesn't mind' him teaching Welsh, a member of administration has already expressed concern about what will happen when Takeshi retires in eighteen years' time. But Takeshi has a dream. There is currently no comprehensive Welsh-language textbook for Japanese learners. His students have to use an English book, which means they must master English before they can understand all the grammar explanations. Takeshi's dream is to write a coursebook especially for Japanese learners so they can learn Welsh directly. To accompany it, he will compile a grammar with Japanese explanations. And they'll also need a Welsh–Japanese, Japanese–Welsh dictionary, so he'll need to draft one of those too. 'It's a big job,' he admits. 'I will need lots of help from Welsh people, so you can advertise!' Then perhaps by the time he retires, one of his own students can take over his classes. When they do, he can pass on his collection of Welsh books. Many of the books in his office have been sent by retiring Japanese colleagues such as Mizutani, eager for Takeshi to carry on the study of Wales in Japan. 'I don't think I can read them all while I am alive,' he says, looking around his office. 'All I can do is pass on the means for the next generation to read these things.'

Takeshi has already made a start on his great task. He is currently a member of a book group which gathers to read the Mabinogion. For this he is compiling a glossary of words which could become a base for his dictionary. And at Daitō Bunka he is continually planning new Welsh lessons, trying to find ways to bring Wales alive for his students, to help them to understand that Wales is not a footnote to British history but a distinct land with its own language, culture and people. 'I have to think what I can offer them, something useful, something interesting,' he states. 'It's my eternal theme.'

Cross-cultural Communication Nemawashi, karōshi and the male-dominated workplace

***Andy Moore** began his career as an eikaiwa teacher before becoming a freelance corporate trainer for Japanese companies, teaching the differences between Japanese and western business cultures and the misunderstandings that can arise:*

The obvious one that most people talk about is low context and high context cultures. The idea that Japanese read the air. Basically they don't say what they think, they hint at it and the listener has to fill in the blanks and try to understand the meaning. Whereas, as a general rule, English speakers take things very literally. And problems can arise from that.

I think the classic one is when Japanese say, 'Oh, that's very difficult,' meaning no. An English speaker hears, 'That's very difficult,' and thinks, 'Okay, so you need a bit more time.' Or if an English speaker says, 'That's difficult,' meaning I need more time, the Japanese person is going to think they said no.

Japanese decision making is different. Nemawashi is the Japanese way where, if you have an idea and you want consensus, rather than having a meeting and discussing it in a group and getting everyone's opinions and looking at pros and cons and beating it around, what you do is you go up to one person and you say, 'I've got this idea, what do you think about this?' And then that person says, 'Yeah, I think that sounds okay.' Okay, good. And then you go to the next person and you say, 'I've got this idea. What do you think about this?' And you do that with everyone. Once everyone has said, 'Oh, I think that's a good idea,' then in the meeting you say, 'I've got this idea. What do you all think?' And everyone's already agreed.

There's the idea that westerners don't do this and I think maybe we do. If we want to get support for an idea, we might do this but we don't have a name for it. If your language has a word for it, it means it is a tangible thing. For example, the fact that Welsh has this word hiraeth means that in Welsh culture this is a tangible thing. One of the well-known ones in Japan is karōshi, death from overwork. The fact that they have a word for this clearly shows that this is an acknowledged part of society. We don't have a word for that because, as a concept, it doesn't really exist. It may exist in practice for some people but not enough for us to have a word for it.

Japanese are not very good at disagreeing with each other, being confrontational, saying no or openly disagreeing. Because, if you disagree with someone's opinion, you are directly attacking them. It's like someone's idea is a part of them. So by saying, 'I disagree with your opinion,' it's almost like saying, 'I don't like your hair.'

In Scandinavian and Germanic cultures, they're able to disassociate ideas and opinions from them as people. So if you disagree with someone's opinion, it's just an opinion, it's just an idea. You're not, to use a modern phrase, throwing shade on the person. You're just showing a different opinion. And obviously, you've got some logical reason for that. You've got some way to support it.

The British like to use the term 'with the greatest respect' and then disagree with someone. So we do it but we'll try to use some diplomatic language to warn people, 'I'm about to disagree with you here. So please don't get too offended.' Whereas the Japanese, they just avoid doing it. In most cases. I'm sure there will be cases where people do that, if they know each other well enough. But, culturally, how your opinions are connected to you is different in Japan.

Asian cultures in general, and Japan especially, are founded on relationships. And in Japanese business culture, there's the tradition of 'nomunication'. It's a portmanteau of nomu, to drink, and communication. It's the idea of communicating through drinking. So it's after-work drinks with your team. Or, if you're working in sales, with your client. The drinks with your clients are really important, not just when you're trying to seal a deal but when you want to maintain the relationship between deals and contracts. It's basically the way to say that, when the contract comes up for renewal, they will continue with you because you're friends. It's not real friendship but it's a relationship. They put a lot of effort into building those relationships. And they tend to stick with those relationships. They prefer to do business with people they know rather than someone they don't know who may potentially offer them something better. If you're a purchaser for a company and you're buying some raw materials, in most cases that purchaser would continue buying from the supplier they know rather than changing to an unknown supplier, even if the unknown supplier offers a better price or faster delivery. Whereas western cultures tend to be task based. And in a task-based culture, we tend to prefer to do business with people that we believe can do the job. It's not so much about who you are, it's 'Can you do the job? Can you deliver on time? What kind of price can you give us?' We shop around. So when businesspeople are trying to do a deal, the task-based people will go into negotiations and try to get the deal done today if possible. Whereas the Japanese will go in thinking, our goal today is to find out who you are. Are you someone we want to make a second meeting with? They've got no intention of making a deal today.

Japan loves its clubs. In universities, everyone does an extracurricular activity. No one goes home at 3.30pm. Everyone's there till six or later in whatever club they're in. And again, they have nomunication there. They have events with the team. It's showing your loyalty to the team by attending these events. There's a lot of pressure now in Japan to try to stop this. Covid's had a big effect on it. But a lot of companies are trying to stop it because it puts pressure on people: people who don't drink, people who have families. It's difficult for them to go home and see their families. It seems to affect female staff a lot more. Even if they're working, they still have a traditional role at home as well. So it's difficult to fit everything in. And if women do attend the drinking, they're pouring the drinks for the senior male workers which is not really a good environment to be in, in this day and age. So there's a lot of companies now that are trying to stop nomunication.

This idea of the Japanese working hard is something that's open to debate. They work long hours. A lot of people work from 8am until 10pm or midnight. There are people who even have to stay in the office overnight, occasionally. This does happen. The reason for it is that the management style is so different. And also the way tasks are allocated. A Japanese worker is expected to do anything their manager tells them to do. They tend not to have job titles. Unless you are very specifically an accountant or you're IT support then you're just an office worker, and that entails doing anything that could be thrown at you. And your workload will just be increasing all the time. It's not like, 'This is what you do today' or 'This is your job and you finish at five o'clock and you go home and then you can carry on the next morning.' They're continually being given more things to do. And it piles up.

Something that's very different is the relationship between the person and their company. It is changing but Japan still has that concept of – you join a company and you stay in that company for life. So it's a really long relationship. And you have to commit to that relationship. Especially when you're a relatively new or junior worker, you shouldn't go home before your boss. That's rude to your boss. You should always be there to show your dedication to the company and be thankful for it. If you do that then you will be in line for promotions. And promotions tend to be age-related.

Traditional Japanese companies hire people straight from university. They don't often hire people mid-career and, if you didn't go to university, it's very difficult to get an office job. It's just a continuation: you go to school, you go to university, you start your job, and then you work your way through the company. It's a straight line.

Traditionally, if a woman wants to marry, she would be expected to quit her job and become a housewife and mother. If she does want to return to work, it's very difficult because she's missed out. She's not starting from university and they don't hire mid-career. It's a difficult thing but it's changing. More companies are allowing women to take maternity leave. Legally, they have to. It's the law but extended maternity leave is relatively rare.

A lot of the companies I've taught at are technology or engineering companies so they tend to be male dominated. When you enter the building, there's a reception desk and there is a female receptionist dressed in a uniform whose job is basically to greet visitors and to tell them to take a seat while they call the person that they're meeting. And there may be other female staff whose job is to serve tea during meetings. There are relatively few female managers. That's not to say there aren't any. But it's certainly not a fifty per cent balance.

I did work at a cosmetics company which was ninety-nine per cent female. I think a company like that does give a lot more opportunities to women. And there were a lot of married women and mothers who worked there, so they would have opportunities to get a good career in that environment.

I've noticed a difference in male–female communication styles. In the company that was mostly female staff, they were a lot more relaxed, more proactive in the way they talked to each other. Because there's a lot of hierarchy in Japan, and communication is very coded. The way you speak to someone, even someone that you may have known for a long time, you still speak to them with a certain amount of formality. But I found, in those all-female groups, there tended to be fewer barriers, which was more comfortable for me because that's more like what we're used to back home, that slightly less formal, more relaxed atmosphere. Obviously, still professional, still business-like but definitely a more open feeling. That could just have been that one company. I'm not sure. But definitely, I'd say it was a more comfortable, familiar kind of feeling for me, more like working in a British office environment.

Few Japanese employees work from home. Even at the height of the Covid pandemic, only thirty per cent of Japanese workers stayed home:

Again it goes back to this idea of the relationship with your company and the relationship with the people you're working with. If you're not having regular face-to-face contact with your boss you might get passed over for promotion, or you might not be considered a team player because you're working from home. Whether this is true or not, this is how people are feeling. They're getting this pressure to go back into the office, so the work-from-home figures compared to other countries are low.

There are other issues. Traditionally, Japanese homes are small, so finding a space to work from home is tough. If you have to work from your kitchen table that's an uncomfortable place to be working all day. Sometimes we just need a change of scene, but we can't always go for a nice walk down to the park or sit in the garden. Back in Wales, how many people have a garden? I guess most people. But in Japan not that many people have gardens.

Chapter Twelve

One Moonlit Night, Yūko Nakauchi Encounters Wales

Yūko Nakauchi in Caernarfon with Rhys Mwyn,
rock musician, music producer and archaeologist

It is a Sunday in high summer. Across Japan, high school students are playing tennis in 37-degree Celsius heat, young singles are shopping for designer brands in air-conditioned boutiques, and families are queuing at food stands for cups of shaved ice. And on this sweltering afternoon, twelve Japanese people are sitting in front of their computers, with their curtains or shōji closed, taking an online beginners' lesson in Welsh.

Among the students there are several rugby supporters, a couple of ladies who want to read the Mabinogion, and a 'dai' (big) fan of the actor Luke Evans. There is even a *Lord of the Rings* enthusiast with an interest in elf language.

The one-day course is being run by Dr Takeshi Koike who begins with a self-introduction in Welsh,

English and Japanese: 'Here is Takeshi. He likes bread. He likes beer. He likes dogs.' He guides the students through letters and pronunciation, gives a lecture on eisteddfodau and teaches them to sing *Land of my Fathers*.

Emceeing the day's events is a young Japanese woman with a professional manner and a smooth, encouraging voice. This is not surprising, as for many years Yūko Nakauchi was a radio presenter for Tōkyō's commercial radio station, InterFM. What is surprising is that she learned her media skills in Wales. In Welsh.

A native of the Tōkyō ward of Shibuya, home to the busiest intersection in the world, Yūko grew up with a love of British culture, particularly film and music. (Her favourite band is *Take That* but she would rather I didn't mention it.) As a junior high school student, she would ride the Tōkyō subway to any movie theatre that was showing *Four Weddings and a Funeral, Love Actually* or any other British movie, even skipping her evening cram school classes to do so. One evening in 1992, she slipped into a small cinema in the Ginza district to see a movie called *One Moonlit Night* and was puzzled when she couldn't understand a single word of the dialogue. After purchasing a pamphlet at the box office, she discovered that the film was based on the novel *Un Nos Ola' Leuad* (*One*

Moonlit Night) by Welsh poet and novelist, Caradog Prichard, and written in a language of which she had no knowledge. A fan of all things British, she had never even heard of Wales. 'I was so shocked that there was another culture apart from English culture in Britain,' she admits.

In Japan, there are many independent educational organisations providing fee-paying schooling from kindergarten through to tertiary level. Known as escalator schools, they are elite and highly selective, since admission enables students to rise smoothly through Japan's notoriously competitive education system without going through 'exam hell' at every stage. Students who gain places at an organisation's private kindergarten, for example, are assured a stress-free progression through their affiliated elementary, junior and senior high school to university. After moving through the Jissen private school system, Yūko found herself heading to Jissen University to study art history, a subject in which she had little interest. Yūko dreamed of studying in Britain but her parents were protective of their only child. They insisted there was nothing a British college could offer that a Japanese university could not teach equally well.

Yūko had an arubaito (part-time job) at McDonalds, selling Teriyaki McBurgers and the famous '0 yen Smile'. (It's written on the menu – you can even request one for home delivery.) She saved her wages and, before the start of her first semester, took a brief solo trip to England, visiting London and Manchester. She enjoyed her visit so much she was determined to return. Hearing that a university in Wales was offering an eight-week summer course in Welsh, she hurried to the British Council office to obtain the addresses of Welsh universities. After writing to them all, she discovered that the summer course was offered by Cardiff University. Here was something that a Japanese university could not offer. Her parents could not deny her this trip. In the summer of 1996, she boarded a plane for Wales.

Stepping off the bus in Lampeter, the city girl was stunned to find herself in a 'small, small village' with a square. It was, she recalls, 'totally another planet'. With only high school English, Yūko was worried she might not be able to communicate but, after eight weeks in classes from 8.45am to 8.30pm every day including weekends, she and her classmates (who came from North America, Patagonia and various European countries) were able to hold a conversation in Welsh.[29] 'That made me confident in myself,' she says.

By the time she flew back to Japan, she had decided to master the Welsh language and informed her parents that she was going to drop out of university. 'After I told them, I went upstairs to my room,' she recalls. 'I could hear my mother crying.' The following year she was back in Wales, studying for a degree in Theatre, Film and Television Studies at the University of Aberystwyth. In Welsh. By her second year, she was reading the Mabinogion. Reading Welsh literature, she admits, was very hard. 'Because I still didn't have much English vocabulary. So I was always carrying two dictionaries: Welsh–English, and English–Japanese.' (There is currently no Japanese–Welsh dictionary in existence.) She studied hard. She also enjoyed socialising. For this Shibuya girl, small-town life – going to the pub, making friends with the locals – suited her. 'When I moved to Aberystwyth, the society is so small. You just bumped into someone you knew on the street and started having a chat. That would never happen in Shibuya.' But it is how she met her Swedish husband.

Returning to Japan after graduation, Yūko found work first as a television researcher, then as a translator for the *Asahi Shimbun* newspaper. After successfully auditioning as a radio presenter and DJ, she was hired by InterFM in Tōkyō. Radio work brought her into contact with Welsh media. She began acting as a fixer for S4C and BBC Radio, driving journalists around

Tōkyō and introducing them to local culture and cuisine. Through them she met Welsh stars on tour. The Super Furry Animals were 'really relaxed and super nice' – and Welsh speakers. After her producer got her a ticket to Duffy's secret gig, she was even able to exchange a few words in Welsh with the singer before the record company people whisked her away. Katherine Jenkins doesn't speak Welsh but 'was very beautiful, actually'. Yūko says the Welsh stars she met seemed surprised when fluent Welsh came out of her mouth. 'No one would expect me to speak Welsh, right? Considering how I look?'

By 2011, Yūko's career was prospering. She had married her Swedish husband who had moved to join her in Japan. They had a son, and Yūko was expecting a second child. Then, on 11 March, the Tōhoku Earthquake struck and the Dai-ichi Nuclear Power Plant, inundated with water from the subsequent tsunami, exploded, sending radiation across Japan and towards Tōkyō. Like many international families, the Nakauchis escaped Japan for several months, moving to Sweden. As the crisis and radiation fallout continued, the decision was made to remain there.

Yūko never wanted to leave Japan: it meant quitting her job and losing all her Welsh media contacts. For a long time she floundered, trying to keep her Welsh connections alive but feeling too distanced from both Wales and Japan. Then, in 2020, the Covid pandemic struck and brought unexpected opportunities. With the world in lockdown and people confined to their homes, there was increased interest in learning about foreign countries and cultures online. As noted in Chapter Ten, Yūko founded Bore Da Kikaku (boredakikaku.com), offering translation and event planning services which connect Japan and Wales. In her emcee voice, she also produces a regular Japanese language podcast commenting on aspects of Welsh culture, from the Olympics, VJ Day (which is unknown in Japan) to Welsh connections in the James Bond movies (Q was formerly played by Desmond Llewelyn). And she emcees Kansai St David's Society's online events.

Six hours later, the Welsh lesson concludes with all the students raising their glasses (of beer or green tea) and calling out across the internet, 'Iechyd da!' Afterwards, Yūko and I chat online. I tell her that I have noticed a tendency of Japanese people to want to study something offbeat, niche. 'That's the otaku (nerd) nature in every Japanese person,' explains Yūko. 'If you know something that only a few people know, that's appreciated in society.' She tells me that the one-day course was oversubscribed, and more online classes are planned, as well as an online autumn festival, a Christmas party and of course, a St David's Day event.

There is another connection she believes should be made between Wales and Japan. While numbers of Welsh speakers are rising, it is estimated that fewer than one hundred people speak the language of Japan's indigenous people, the Ainu.[30] Yūko would like to connect this minority community with Welsh groups, to exchange information on how to keep a native language alive. She even hopes to arrange for Ainu students to visit Wales, so they can see for themselves how a minority language and culture can continue to thrive. 'I think about Welsh stuff all the time, what I can do,' she says, as she heads off to record another radio programme in her silky smooth emcee voice.

With Caernarfon chef Chris Roberts aka Flamebaster

What Do the Japanese and the Welsh Have in Common? 'We share a poetic tradition'

Joe Cairnes: The Welsh and the Japanese have a lot in common, I think. I've never found it difficult to mix so I would guess that comes of having so much in common. We're both island nations – the UK and Japan – split into four, with a big city that dominates the economy. If you're from the countryside, it's kind of similar. The rolling hillscapes. People are down to earth in Wales and I feel like a lot of the folks here in Japan are down to earth as well.

Ursula Bartlett-Imadegawa: To put it bluntly, the Japanese feel very comfortable because the Welsh are about the same height. The land is mountainous like their land. They have this passion for rugby. God only knows why but they are good at it. They like the speed and they like to tackle one another. The Japanese love singing. The Japanese get this communal singing bit. They do. And they're also very clannish. Like the Valleys identity. The Japanese have their company identity with their badge, or they're from the same village. My husband still meets his high school and elementary school classmates: they have reunions every few years. They understand the power of the group working together. The Welsh don't have an aristocracy, so we're all in it together. And the Japanese, what had been their aristocracy was dismantled at the end of the war. They very much keep to themselves, the remaining few. The Welsh as well.

Andy Moore: In terms of our geography, we come from countries that are mountainous and we tend to live around the edge. So a lot of the higher-populated areas tend to be near the sea. I think the geography also creates a kind of isolation. It's just logistically difficult to move around outside of those highly populated areas.

Bet Davies: Ambassador Fujii, who was based in London in the late nineties, I remember him saying he could sense this very close friendship between Wales and Japan which they didn't experience in any other part of the UK to the same extent. Ambassador Fujii's theory was that we share a poetic tradition because we had our court poets' system here as they did in Japan.

Jac Phillips: I do draw a comparison with the Ainu, the indigenous people here in Hokkaidō. In the 1800s, when Russia was bearing down, Japan actually colonised Hokkaidō pretty fast. The Ainu were here and the Japanese culturally assimilated them. And then you're looking at the comparison with how Welsh survived after also being subjugated a lot throughout the years, and it's very similar. Like Welsh was made illegal to speak, Ainu was made illegal to speak. Also the names. Ainu names were taken away and replaced with Japanese names. I think the Ainu died out really fast. It makes me wonder how the Welsh language just fiercely keeps on going.

Abby Hall: One thing that Wales and Japan definitely have in common is a sense of pride in their country. It's not about your country being the best. Other people have this feeling their country is the best country or they are number one, but I find the humble attitude in Wales and Japan is very similar. They understand their place in the world and they don't over exaggerate it for effect. It's just this very calm acceptance of who they are, of where their country is in the world, where they are in the world as people. They love their country, they love the products they produce, they love supporting their local businesses.

I used to work for the British Embassy (in Tōkyō) in the Welsh Government department, and they help with imports from Wales to Japan. It's very interesting because it's the same sort of things that they're communicating: these are high quality ingredients from local farmers. Yes, you're paying extra but you're getting the history and the culture. And it is these things that Japanese people really appreciate. It's not about image, it's always about history. It's about values. It's really interesting when you're promoting products to Japanese people because it's almost exactly the same at home. I think, back home, it's not so much about how a brand looks but it's more about where a brand has been, especially when it comes to food. It almost seems as if these two cultures want the same thing when it comes to purchases and lifestyle, when it comes to what they want to buy or how they want to express themselves with their purchases.

Andrew Beak: Welsh people and Japanese people are very cultural. And they're very defensive about their culture as well. You cannot say anything negative about Japanese culture in Japan because they will aggressively defend it. And I think it's the same in Wales. I mean, they'll take it as a joke but deep down they're not happy. I like that aspect of Japan, the idea of being cultured, liking your culture, telling people about your culture. I think that's a good thing.

Chapter Thirteen

'I Fell into It Entirely': The transient life of travel and culture writer, Lily Crossley-Baxter

Lily Crossley-Baxter

Freelance travel and culture writer Lily Crossley-Baxter is not in Tōkyō. While many of the Welsh interviewees in this book have put down roots – transplantable roots – in Japan, Lily remains fiercely freewheeling. She chases work across Asia, freezing her smartphone contract on departure and reactivating it as soon as she touches back down at Narita Airport. Often out of the country for three or four months at a time, she has no fixed abode and, when I first make contact, is living in a Shibuya share house with fourteen other residents, mostly Japanese renters plus a couple of Chinese and a British friend who is divorcing her Japanese husband. When asked if she feels hiraeth, Lily shrugs and says that she was home in Wales during the summer. And for a month last Christmas. She is a global nomad. But, during the

Covid pandemic, she was stuck in Japan while I was in lockdown in England, so we chatted online and agreed to meet in person once restrictions were lifted. Now that I have arrived in Tōkyō, she is somewhere else. I send out emails to track her down. Eventually, she resurfaces. She's been in France. Now she's in Sheffield. We catch up.

Lily is sharp and sparky, with long black hair and an expressive face. She may be a millennial but no tired snowflake clichés would stick to her. While many long-term Welsh residents of Japan have learned the art of cultural compromise, Lily tells it like it is, unafraid to call out what she views as the country's less than savoury elements. Judgements are instant. Places and situations (Shibuya, earthquakes, gender inequality) are 'mad' and 'insane'. People (the police, doctors, men who grope her on the train) are 'creepy', 'tragic' or 'just plain wrong'. She doesn't hesitate to discuss the issues. 'Don't get me started,' she warns and then launches right in. Her words drip with irony and she illustrates them with images and apps from her phone which she holds up in front of her webcam. Through her eyes, I perceive Japan in a new way: younger, faster and transient.

Born in London in 1990, Lily was eight when her family returned to Wales. At her Penrhyndeudraeth primary school, Lily's English accent was deemed highly suspect. 'Everyone thought I knew the queen,' she says, rolling her eyes. As lessons were conducted entirely in Welsh, Lily had to learn quickly. 'It was "learn Welsh or die"', she recalls. 'So the quicker you learned it, the quicker they stopped disliking you so much.'

At the University of Sheffield, Lily studied English literature, straying into the School of East Asian Studies where she picked up a course in Japanese literature. Her favourite author is feminist noir writer Natsuo Kirino, author of *Out*, in which a downtrodden wife murders her unfaithful husband and her girlfriends help her to cut up and dispose of the body. Lily prefers 'gritty' fiction. 'I don't like it when books get all romantic about Japan,' she asserts. 'Not into that.' But it was a chapter in a Haruki Murakami novel which compelled her to move to the country. In *IQ84*, a girl is confined to a tiny apartment with a schedule and everything she needs to live. Her life is 'super-efficient,' says Lily. 'And for some reason that scene made me want to move to Japan and just have this really simple life.' I ask if she was attracted by the sense of alienation and isolation, a recurring theme in Murakami novels. She considers the question for a moment. 'Isolation seems like a negative term,' she muses. 'But the independence that she has in that novel really appealed to me.'

In 2014, after a brief stint as a social worker, Lily was accepted onto the JET Programme as an ALT. She requested to be sent to Mie prefecture because on a map, it resembled Wales. 'It has mountains and the sea,' she points out. With a long, jagged coastline and numerous forested national parks, Mie is one of the more rural of Japan's forty-seven prefectures, and few of the locals spoke much English. 'You had to learn Japanese to get by,' Lily remembers. 'It's similar to Welsh in that respect.' Posted to the village of Sakura, she taught at two local high schools, one a mixed academic school, the other a boys' sports school where the shaven-headed students attended on scholarships for martial arts, soccer or water polo, and lived in dormitories overseen by the jūdō master and his wife. Their English level was low but the students were well-behaved.

After one year Lily planned to return to social work in the United Kingdom. But on a whim she moved to Tōkyō, picking up full-time teaching work in two junior high schools with evening and weekend stints at an expensive juku (cram school) and a few nights a week at several 'sketchy' bars in the entertainment district of Roppongi. Despite working eighty-five to ninety hours on top of her full-time job, she was still 'crazy broke'. One day she saw an advertisement on Craigslist seeking writers for the online tourism website, *Tokyo Cheapo*. 'They were really chill. They didn't mind if you didn't have experience,' she says. 'You wrote something and if they liked your style, they would take you on.'

Her first published piece was an article about the Ushiku Buddha in Ibaraki prefecture, a 120-metre standing statue with an internal lift. Since then she has written hundreds more articles for *Tokyo Cheapo*, as well as for the *Japan Times*, the BBC, the *Daily Beast*, *The Independent* and many other publications. She became so successful that she was able to give up her other jobs and become a full-time travel and culture writer. Her success surprises her. 'I fell into it entirely,' she admits. 'I never thought I could make money.'

Lily's timing was opportune. After the Tōhoku Earthquake in 2011, not only did the leisure industry collapse but many foreign residents packed up and went home. The Japan National Tourist Board sought to entice them back with travel articles, particularly to rural destinations which needed tourism money. At the same time, editors were keen to move away from parachute journalism, articles written by gap year students and holidaymakers with laptops and an internet connection. They wanted depth and expertise, and Lily soon found herself being invited on press trips. Press trips are all expenses paid tours of destinations made in the company of tourist bureaux representatives who will helpfully point out everything they would like the journalist to write about. In Japan these can be hard work, says Lily, conducted as they are in typical Japanese fashion – at breakneck speed. A standard day will start at 6.30am and finish at around nine or ten at night when she is deposited at some incredible hotel with barely enough time to sleep before she's back on the road. Sometimes Lily will be paired with another foreign writer flown in from Britain or the United States. Used to a more relaxed schedule with ample time for sitting by a hotel pool posting Instagram stories, these other foreign writers find Japan's hectic pace exhausting. 'It's not a holiday,' Lily points out. 'But you do get to do a lot of cool stuff.' Domestic and international tourism does not overlap. 'When I go on these media trips around Japan for promotion tourism, it's always just foreigners,' says Lily. 'We don't go with Japanese writers ever.'

Lily was once taken to Japan's 'most beautiful beach' (she has been to several beaches designated as 'Japan's most beautiful') and told she had seven minutes to enjoy it. She didn't even get to swim.

But she's not a beach person. She prefers forests and hills. Her favourite place is the remote Iya Valley on Shikoku Island, where steep gorges are strung together with jungle vine bridges. 'It's my smartphone wallpaper,' she says, holding her phone screen up to her webcam. 'Is it too much of a stretch to say you prefer the valleys because you're Welsh?' I ask. She concedes there could be something in it, recalling a four-day hike in the Japanese Alps to reach the country's most remote onsen. No one else would go but she jumped at the chance to walk in the mountains. Her journey produced an article for the BBC Travel website.

The Tōkyō megalopolis is viewed as a stylish, progressive destination, and working in journalism brings Lily into the orbit of other foreigners in the creative industries: fashion designers, filmmakers, photographers, models, public relations gurus, cool hunters and advertising agencies. But while they love all that is new and hip, they're less enamoured of Japan's traditional working culture: long but unproductive office hours, endless meetings, and the need for group consensus before a move is made. 'For creatives here, I don't think that old system works at all,' says Lily. Many strike out and establish their own businesses, catering to an international clientele or acting as a bridge between Japanese and overseas markets. 'Everyone who is successful [here] runs their own business,' Lily points out. 'Or works for one of the people who runs their own.' This new generation networks in a more 'chill' way. Contacts are made at parties, in the hottest clubs and online. Not for them the traditional societies such as the Foreign Correspondents' Club which, according to Lily, is 'just a bunch of old men in a room and they just drink and smoke and talk.'

On the subject of 'old men', I ask Lily if her gender has had any impact on her career. There are currently 14,005 British men living long term in Japan but only 5,035 women. Lily says her baffled male editor once asked her why fewer western women remain in Japan long term. 'They just don't see it,' she howls. 'Life is significantly harder if you're female.' Japan is currently 118th out of 146 on the World Economic Forum's Global Gender Gap Index (UK is fourteenth, the United States is forty-third) which measures gender disparities in areas of economy, education, politics and health.[31] Launched in 2013 by the late ex-prime minister Shinzō Abe, 'Womenomics' was supposed to pull Japan out of its economic slump by increasing the number of women in the workplace in well-paid leadership roles including the Diet, Japan's parliament. But when the Japanese government sent Masanobu Ogura, Minister in charge of Women's

Empowerment and Minister of State for Gender Equality, to chair the 2023 G7 summit on gender equality and women's empowerment, it sent a clear message. 'Japan thought it was perfectly acceptable to send a man to talk about women's rights at a women's conference,' Lily wails. 'Any other country would recognise that was a ridiculous thing to do.' The conservative oyaji ('old men') of the ruling Liberal Democratic political party have shown no real commitment to gender equality, preferring, it seems, to keep women at home, raising at least three children to combat the country's plummeting birthrate.[32] Certainly, the number of women in the workplace has increased but women remain confined to low-paying, often part-time, jobs, due partly to a paucity of government-subsidised daycare centres and an age-defined promotion system which penalises them for taking time out to give birth. At the launch of Womenomics, Abe announced his goal to have thirty per cent of women in leadership positions by 2020. Ten years later, the number of women in legislative, senior official and managerial roles stands at less than fifteen per cent, one of the lowest in the world.[33] In Japan's lower house, only ten per cent of its representatives are women; and until last year even their minister for gender equality was a man.

While healthcare for women has been improving, neither contraception, abortion nor the abortion pill (legalised in 2023) are covered by medical insurance and are therefore only available to those with the money to pay for it.[34] Furthermore, Lily points out, the abortion pill is only available after medical consultation ('because God forbid women just go and get things') and costs 100,000 yen (£488) while a partner's consent is generally required before doctors will carry out an abortion (which can cost up to 200,000 yen – £977). 'In the UK, we have really great access to things,' explains Lily. 'We have rights. We're allowed to do what we want with our own bodies. I'd taken that for granted until I came here.' In the face of Japan's strictures, many young people are simply opting out. Marriage rates are low, and consequently so is the birth rate. Japan's population is ageing rapidly, leaving the country with a shortage of workers in roles which women could fill but which Womenomics has failed to bring about.

While #KuToo (Japan's #MeToo movement) has encouraged women's rights activists to raise their collective voice, Lily points out that such groups face a cultural disadvantage. Those who speak out, who voice their dissatisfaction, are disturbing the collective harmony, the 'wa'. If anyone causes ructions in Japan by being unruly, *they* are viewed as the problem. Lily and I are chatting while human rights riots rage in France and climate change protestors are marching throughout the UK. I ask her if we might see women rioting in the streets of Tōkyō anytime soon. 'We might see them but the government won't see them,' cries Lily. 'The women are doing everything right. It's just that the politicians don't care.' Lily is keen to become socially and politically active in Japan and has considered moving into investigative journalism. 'I have enough opinions,' she admits. But Lily lives off Japanese tourism money. She can't bite the hand that feeds her or she risks losing her visa status.[35] 'Once you start publishing things that aren't popular, if they come up with your name....' She leaves the rest hanging.

The fallout from the Covid pandemic proved a watershed for foreign residents in Japan, forcing many – male and female – to rethink their long-term futures in the country. Because, at the height of the pandemic, Japanese citizens were permitted to travel internationally while Japan-based foreigners – even those with permanent residency, Japanese spouses, children, homes and jobs – were not. Perceived as posing a danger to Japanese customers, some foreign residents were also turned away from restaurants or had their hotel reservations cancelled. Foreigners have no recourse against such treatment because Japan has no anti-discrimination laws. While article 14 of the Japanese constitution prohibits discrimination 'in political, economic or social relations because of race, creed, sex, social status or family origin', this only applies to Japanese citizens. A foreigner can't discriminate against a Japanese citizen, but a Japanese citizen can discriminate against a foreigner. Even before the pandemic, landlords could legally refuse to rent apartments to non-Japanese. 'Obviously, this isn't everyone,' says Lily. 'But it's enough that you feel unwelcome.' For many foreigners, Covid brought home to them that however long they lived in Japan, they were never going to be accepted as anything other than guests. Lily is always being asked when she is going home. She shows me a screengrab of a newspaper headline which asks whether the Japanese government intends to ease Japan's worker shortage with 'Women, foreigners or robots'? 'And you know they're going to choose robots every fucking time because women and foreigners are never truly an option.'

Which brings us to the reason why Lily is out of the country. She is not on assignment. She is in the UK. Like many foreign women before her, she's thinking of returning home. Although travel writing is a dream job and earns her a decent salary, Lily wants to make a real difference. She is hoping to return to social work, in a role that supports migrants and refugees. (She once tried to volunteer at a Tōkyō refugee charity but, as Japan admits so few, they already had more volunteers than refugees.[36]) Britain has its own immigration issues but, having been a migrant and understanding the frustrations, Lily is keen to get involved. 'There's so much to do here, whether it's work or volunteering.'

Lily says she'll keep going back to Japan and may even write the occasional article but acknowledges that leisure journalism is moving on. 'Now it's all TikToks,' she says, making a horrified face. And so another talented female worker leaves Japan. Looks like it's down to those robots.

Now based in the UK, Lily remains open to offers of Japan assignments and projects. She can be contacted via her website: lilycrossleybaxter.com and on Instagram @lostandfoundlily

Rainbow Baby 'The Japanese are closer to death, and it's very, very comforting'

Carolyn De Vishlin *took a job with the NOVA eikaiwa in 2002. She later moved to Aichi University in Nagoya where she is now a tenured professor. She met and married her Canadian husband, Dan, in Japan*:

When I was thirty-six, my husband and I were expecting our eldest son. In Japan, there are a lot of maternity clinics rather than hospitals, so a vast majority of Japanese women will go to a clinic and have all of their maternity treatment there and give birth in the clinic. We started out the same way, so I was going back and forth there until six months into the pregnancy. Then the doctor said, 'He's not developing as he should be. You should go to Toyohashi Hospital to find out what's going on.' She wrote a reference letter. The next day, six months' pregnant on a mamachari ('mother's chariot' – a sturdy bicycle popular with Japanese mothers), I went to the hospital and they did scans.

First they said, 'You need to stay in this hospital now for the rest of the pregnancy, on bedrest.'

Then they said, 'It'll be two weeks and then we'll give you a C-section.'

And then it was, 'You're going to have the C-section tomorrow.' This all happened within three hours of consultation. That was intense.

So when I was six and a half months' pregnant, my oldest son, Gryffyn, was born. He was 850 grams – very, very small. They did tests on him and he had a congenital heart condition that wasn't visible on the scans. They kept him in the NICU in Toyohashi for four days and then they transferred him to a specialist children's hospital in Shizuoka, which is like Great Ormond Street in London. The ambulance was enormous. It was like one of those American school buses. And only for him. There were six or seven medical staff in the ambulance with him. My husband Dan and a friend of ours jumped on the Shinkansen and followed him there. I had to stay in hospital in Toyohashi because in Japan, if you have a C-section, you have to stay a minimum of five days. They wouldn't release me until I'd had checks and scans and everything was safe with me. I remember being enormously frustrated. Also I had to fill out a feedback questionnaire about the standard of service I had received at the hospital whilst my child was being ambulanced to Shizuoka. I wanted to get out as fast as I could. There was a nurse at the hospital who spoke very good English and she was very kind. She helped me navigate the system to answer the questions and leave that hospital.

I remember having a little vial of breast milk in an insulated beer bag. I had no way to keep it fresh so I chucked a bunch of cold Coke cans around it and I got on the Shinkansen to Shizuoka by myself, five days after a C-section with this blinkin' bag, and I took a taxi from there to the hospital. I couldn't bloody find where to go because it was all in Japanese. I eventually got sent to the NICU. And then I would imagine it's the same as at home. You have to go through three or four separate doors before you're able to get into the NICU. At each stage, there's a really extreme hand washing, gloves, hair, gown process. Because there are extremely sick babies.

They had family rooms, two-by-two tatami rooms where extremely sick babies' parents could stay. They were ten steps from the NICU entrance. It was very close so that was good. We'd go and be with Gryffyn all the time. The nurses said they were surprised that we came as often as we did because a lot of the babies' parents don't go much. Maybe it's because of work for the man. Paternity leave here is terrible.

The main surgeon wasn't Japanese, he was Korean. His English was flawless. The junior surgeon was writing everything down for us. Her English was flawless too. They explained to us very clearly what was going on so we could understand as much as possible about the rights and the wrongs of the operation and what the risks were. He said the operation had never been done on a baby that small and they weren't sure if it was going to work. We had to be aware of the risks which is why they took pains to talk to us about it. We didn't have a choice. We just said, 'Do whatever you can.'

They operated on him to try to put a stent in his heart. That operation didn't succeed because he was so small. Then they said, 'We'll give him time to recover and we will try again.' The second time they gave him an operation, they opened up his chest and tried to do it that way. But as they were withdrawing, they pierced the heart valve.

The doctor himself came out. I remember him saying it in Japanese. What he said was, 'Let the parents in because it's time.' We came in and one of the medical staff said, 'Stand back, the parents are coming.' All of the operating staff were there: the nurses, the anaesthetist, at least two surgeons plus the junior surgeon and the Korean surgeon plus another surgeon – fifteen or more people. And they all had to stand back with their heads bowed.

Gryffyn was on a big operating table, a tiny baby all covered up in green scrubs. We had to clamber over all this machinery to get to him. Dan and I stroked his head. We could see his heart monitor beeping down. The doctor didn't say, 'He's gone.' He didn't say that, he said, 'His heart has stopped beating.' There was silence for a while. They let us just stay there.

Back in the NICU, they dressed him in white – because the colour of mourning is white – in a traditional Japanese robe, like a little white yukata. They tied it up because he'd had heart surgery. The incubator was now open and there was a little white blanket and pillow. Until he died, we hadn't been able to pick him up because he had all of these wires. All we could do was just put our hands over him.

They gave us the option of having his body with us in the tatami room. At the time, I was horrified at the thought because I had no concept of what that was. Now I know that this is a very lovely thing that people want. In Britain – and I imagine in Japan too but I didn't know at the time – they have a cold bassinet that keeps the baby pink. It gives the parents the opportunity to be with the child for longer and to say goodbye. People can dress the baby and wash the baby for a short period of time. At the time, I did not know this. So when they offered that system, I was absolutely horrified. I said no.

Because he was born in Aichi [prefecture] but died in Shizuoka [prefecture], that made the paperwork challenging. My husband had to fill out all of that paperwork in Japanese. Now he has a bit of a trigger effect about anything to do with paperwork because it was all on him. Because here, unfortunately, they focus only on the mother, and the father has to 'gaman suru' (endure it). They treated me with kid gloves but with him, they were like, 'I'm sorry for your loss but you have to fill out this paperwork.' A friend of ours came and helped Dan to figure that out.

The hospital had a memorial room, like a prayer room. The next day, they said, 'He's in there.' I didn't know what to expect because, shortly after he died, he changed colour and I was terrified of what I might see and what I might remember. So I was unsure about whether I wanted to see him. Now I'm glad I did. The attention to detail was just lovely. They had him in a little open coffin. And they had put makeup on him so that we could see him without being upset.

His colours were normal. It was lovely, and we were emotional, saying our goodbyes.

There was a little knock at the door and almost everyone from the operating room came in to pay their respects: nurses, anaesthetists, tech staff, operating staff. People had come in from their days off. They stood before us formally, put their palms together and bowed. They said wishes and prayers for Gryffyn. They were openly emotional. Some of the nurses were actually crying. We went around and said thank you to everybody. Some of the nurses said, 'Please take care of yourself' and, 'It's awful. I'm so sorry.' Then the funeral directors came in. They didn't put the lid on the coffin, which was important. They took him out and put him in the undertakers' car, then they drove off very slowly. They brought him back to Toyohashi.

A couple of days later we had his crematorium funeral. Here in Japan, it's cremation. There is no other option. At the time, I wasn't sure what I thought about that. I didn't have enough time to give it real thought. It was really short notice because, in Japan, it tends to be quick. It wasn't a chapel. It was a hall, a bit devoid of anything religious. But he was there and there were candles. It was an open casket and at the funeral directors they had this lovely 'option' – for want of a better word – where they put seasonal flowers around the head. This wasn't something we had arranged. We said yes to it because, of course, it worked. So we had a ceremony and some friends came and everyone was able to put little purple irises around Gryffyn's body. And then they sent him into the crematorium.

Everyone had brought refreshments. We sat in a room and we were able to chat and laugh about this and that, just to try and pretend life was normal. We were there for about forty-five minutes and then they asked Dan and I to come to another room where they had my son's ashes and a little bamboo cup. The undertakers said, 'It's your job to put the ashes into the cup.' When someone dies here you use a special tool and you pick out the bones. We did the first couple and then I couldn't do any more.

Now we have Gryffyn with us at home. His ashes are in a little white urn in our bedroom. We had a shelf built in the corner for the urn and two pictures of him when he was alive. In one his eyes are open. At that stage of gestational development babies cannot typically see much of anything, but it's important for us because it showed that he was alive. And also that his eyes were likely blue just like his little brother's. And we have a Buddhist bell. We ding dong ding it in the morning and at nighttime. So he's close. He's at home with us.

In Japan, in my experience, they're very close to death and there's a lot less fear. It's part of Buddhist and Shintō beliefs. That was a side of Japan I'd never seen. And it's not something you want to see very often. But it was a lovely thing. I think we're a lot more distanced. Back home, that fear is almost like something you're born with, like you're born with a fear of snakes. It's inherent. Here it seems to be inherent the other way around. There's very little distance between the death and the dead person and the living people. And I find it very, very comforting. Very comforting.

Gryffyn was born on the twenty-fifth of July and he died on the thirty-first of July, 2014. Sunflowers were blooming at that time. So at his funeral we got a small bouquet of sunflowers, bright and cheery, and Dan and I put it in the coffin with him. And every year we go to the sunflower fields. It's lovely. And every year on Facebook, I'll get lots of people bombarding me with pictures of sunflowers to show that they remember.

Two years later, my second son was born. Rainbow babies, they call them. The baby born after a child has passed away is a rainbow. The rainbow after the storm. He was born in the same hospital. His name is Fynyx. Of course, that's not a real name anywhere but it's 'phoenix', rising from the ashes. And the 'ffyn' part of Gryffyn's name we attached to Fynyx rather than Phoenix. So there's a connection between the two.

Dan and I saw an English-speaking counsellor once. Counselling in Japan is different. It's still a bit taboo. She was a lovely lady but she was a counsellor for people who were living in Japan and having a hard time being an expat. We went to see her once and then we just got on with it ourselves. I got in touch with Sands (stillbirth and neonatal death charity) much later. There's no Sands in Japan, not that I'm aware of. It's an English thing. I said, 'My situation's a little bit unusual. I live in Japan,' and I explained what happened. They recommended certain leaflets and things on the website. My second son knows about his brother and he asks, 'When did Gryffyn die? Why did Gryffyn die? Where's Gryffyn?' And there's a really lovely book called *In the Stars* by Sam Kitson which explains things.

In the Stars by Sam Kitson can be purchased from Sands (the stillbirth and neonatal death society): sands.org.uk

Chapter Fourteen

Puff Puff on Doki Doki Island: Geraint Howells and the Mabinogion world of games localisation

Geraint Howells

I'm playing *Mabinogi*. It's a Korean MMORPG (massively multiplayer online role-playing game) loosely based on the Mabinogion tales of Welsh mythology. Having created my character and selected my race (the choices are human, elf or giant) I am catapulted into a series of fantasy settings in which I will live my best 'Mabinogion' life: killing small animals, shearing sheep and weaving my own cloth.

Meandering around the village of Tir Chonaill, I attempt to make sense of the landscape. The buildings appear Korean in design, square with ornately tiled roofs. Rough paths cut through lush grass while a millwheel turns, grinding wheat and barley from nearby fields. I encounter other players and admire their outfits, predominantly armour, with or without wings. Some are slaughtering racoons with swords. A few are playing lutes to win skill points. Most of us are just standing around in the rain. The aim of the game is to reach Erinn on the continent of Uladh. Is that in Wales?

Mabinogi was launched in 2004 by Nexon Korea. By video game standards this makes it ancient history although, judging by the number of players I encounter buying cloaks, fighting giant spiders and punching wolves, it is still popular. The game has around 741,000 registered players, of whom around seven thousand log in daily.[37] But other than the immediate downpour I encounter on entering the game, I am at a loss to see what is Welsh about it. That is also the view of video game 'localiser', Geraint Howells. As he says himself, 'It's not my place to speculate on what they were thinking, but I would guess they don't know much about Wales.' He didn't work on *Mabinogi*. If he had, there would undoubtedly be more Welsh culture in it.

I have never met Geraint in person, only online, which seems appropriate as this is where he spends his working day. Geraint prepares Japanese games for the English-speaking market. This can include translating dialogue, allocating western names to Japanese characters and flagging up error messages. But adapting Japanese games for overseas sales requires more than just fluency in both languages. It necessitates a thorough knowledge of global gaming culture.

Geraint speaks slowly and deliberately, carefully measuring every word and pausing so often that I can later transcribe our interview in real time. Silences of up to thirty seconds are not uncommon as he considers his answer. I imagine his games are translated extremely precisely. Accuracy is his job. 'Let's commerce!', as I am encouraged to do while pondering the purchase of a pair of spider gloves in the *Mabinogi* town of Dunbarton, would not have made it past Geraint.

Geraint fell into the video game localisation business accidentally. Born in Bangor in 1984, he attended Welsh-language primary and secondary schools, and studied politics and international relations at the University of Manchester. Graduating in 2005, he sought to travel. 'I really wanted to have an adventure, go somewhere far away, live in a foreign country and test myself,' he recalls. Since teaching seemed the easiest way to achieve this, he flew to Japan with Shane English School and taught for two years in Saitama, north of Tōkyō. While there he studied Japanese intensively and passed Level 1 of the JLPT. Before returning to Wales, he applied for jobs at several Japanese companies in Europe. Nintendo sent him to their offices in Frankfurt where he received a thorough grounding in translation, editing and quality assurance testing for the video games market. Since he hadn't actually applied to be a translator, he admits he initially suffered from 'a well-founded imposter syndrome'.

In 2010, he moved to Shloc, a localisation company founded by three co-workers who had decided to pool their expertise. Selling themselves as a freelance community made them more competitive and allowed them to take on more complex jobs which required a team of translators and a wider range of languages. Originally limited to English translation, Shloc soon expanded to include localisers in other European, South American and Asian dialects. It takes on assignments for Sony, Nintendo, Square Enix and other major Japanese games developers. While Shloc is legally forbidden from discussing the games it works on, a quick internet search reveals that Geraint and his colleagues are the localisers behind several instalments of the *Dragon Quest* series, the Level 5/Studio Ghibli collaboration *Ni no Kuni, Pro Evolution Soccer* and most recently, *Death Stranding*.

When Geraint is hired to localise a new game, he begins by playing it. Geraint grew up playing *Mario*

Kart and *Goldeneye* on Nintendo, as well as *Quake* and *Command & Conquer* on his personal computer. 'I have an innate feel for it that comes from having spent a lot of time as a child playing video games,' he says. Playing is essential to good translation. Localisers need to understand the skill level and essence of a game, and the context in which dialogue is spoken.

Japanese is a contextual language. Subjects and pronouns are optional and often omitted, and sentences might only be understood in concert with the phrases around it. 'If you have Japanese without context then it's very, very hard to know what's going on,' explains Geraint. The Japanese dialogue in video games is written for the home market and without any thought to future translation, 'so a lot of the time, without playing it for yourself, you really have no idea what a lot of it is referring to or where it appears,' he adds. Geraint will play the game before he begins translation and then again after his text has been implemented to see whether it fits and is comprehensible.

He will translate both spoken and written Japanese but, he points out, this will not necessarily be word for word. Sometimes he will translate only a context or a situation. For example, in a football video game he might only be given the situation in which a line may appear, such as a player being given a red card in the eightieth minute. Although there is an accompanying Japanese script he would not need to refer to it. It is obvious what English phrases are required in this context, he says. 'It seems self-evident for a football game but it's surprisingly true for a lot of what we do. If you have the visuals and the situation, then the specifics of the text are not the most important thing.' He might even add an English text where there is none in Japanese. 'I mean it *is* translation – but it's translating the context and situation far more than the words.'

Altering or censoring a dialogue or scene may also be required. In the first instalment of *Dragon Quest*, (one of Japan's earliest forays into the video game market in 1985–86), religious themes were edited out for the conservative North American market. The first three games also featured one of the most notorious examples of censoring from Japanese to English. In the Japanese versions, a character is offered 'puff puff', allowing him to rub his face between a female character's breasts. In the English versions, these scenes were rewritten with the character being offered other delights such as a makeup session or having his fortune told. There are now more than ten instalments of the *Dragon Quest* series and 'puff puff' – having become a long-running in-joke in the gaming community – is no longer censored. But issues of gender and race can still be problematic for localisers. Games are products of the society in which they are created, and Japanese games are often culturally and artistically different from their western counterparts. In Japanese games, many female characters have skimpy clothes, disproportionate body shapes and exist solely to act either as mother figures to the hero or to offer sexual favours. 'And I don't think it's going to change at all, to be honest,' admits Geraint ruefully. Cultural editing is therefore another facet of his work.

In an effort to understand Geraint's world, I leave my *Mabinogi* character loitering nervously near some bears, and load the latest version of *Dragon Quest*. Although it was Japan's first major video game, its cultural and artistic impact was so significant that it became the framework for all subsequent Japanese (and some western) game design. For example, in Japanese video game fights, when a character lands a blow, it is common for score numbers to levitate upwards out of the character's body. This originated with the *Dragon Quest* series. 'Now people take it for granted, like that's how it should be,' says Geraint. 'But it's a design decision that was taken in the eighties and has remained in place ever since.' Another convention that has barely changed since the eighties is that Japanese games should be easy to play from the start. A game whose play style is simple and recognisable is always going to find a market. The *Dragon Quest* series has changed very little since 1985, yet it is still popular with players of all ages. The graphics have improved but the basics remain the same. 'And that's not a lack of imagination,' says Geraint. 'That's by design.'

Geraint worked on *Dragon Quest XI: Echoes of an Elusive Age*, so this is the game I load. As it opens, I find myself standing by a turreted castle in a fantasy version of a town in medieval Europe. And it's raining again. Most of the humanoid characters appear to be Caucasian with blue or green eyes and names like Chalky, Amber and Sandy the dog. They express themselves in a variety of American, English and Scottish accents, crying, 'Crikey!' and 'Crumbs!' and offering to help 'Y'all'. Women call the hero 'sweetheart' and 'darling' and the dialogue – some of which must have been localised by Geraint – is sometimes ribald and replete with in-jokes. Puff puff makes its now traditional appearance with our hero closing his eyes in anticipation, then being tied to a bungee cord and pushed off a cliff.

Geraint believes that an experienced player can tell instantly if they are playing a Japanese game. Ten minutes into *Dragon Quest XI*, I have to agree with him. In spite of the Disneyfied European setting, culturally it feels very Japanese. Japan is a group society; its citizens prioritise their obligations to those around them before acting on individual desires. A Japanese economist once told me that this originated out of the country's traditional rice-growing culture. For a successful harvest, fields needed to be flooded by diverting water from a nearby river, a task that took the cooperation of a whole village to ensure everyone's crops received enough water at the right time. It took a group to cultivate 'wet' rice unlike in 'dry' wheat cultivating cultures where all that was required was sufficient rain from the sky. Whether this is true or not, it has to be admitted that the Japanese like to do things in groups. When a Japanese six-year-old begins school they are allocated to their first kumi (group) and are taught to work with their group members, considering their needs and wishes before their own. This continues in Japanese companies, where offices are open plan and employees learn to introduce themselves by their company's name first and their surname second. Although DQXI is a single player game, our hero is soon joined by a group of characters with a variety of fighting skills to help him defeat all the monsters he encounters. In Japan, even in video gaming, no one quests alone.

Another noticeable difference is that Japanese games tend to be cuter and less bloodthirsty than their western counterparts. *Dragon Quest* games have always featured little blue blobs called slimes but even the real monsters look as if they have escaped from a children's cartoon. Kawaii (cute) culture emerged as a movement of rebellion against Japan's workaholic adult society. Now the kawaii aesthetic is all-encompassing. It is present in phenomena from fashion, manga and anime, toy merchandising (such as Hello Kitty), pre-pubescent singing idols (such as AKB48 and Morning Musume), behaviour (speaking in a high-pitched voice and using childish words), and even kawaii handwriting which is big and rounded and bursting with hearts and emoticons. Emojis were invented in Japan, hence their cuteness. In a country where the female ideal is a moe (literally a 'bud', meaning a cute, innocent girl), sexualised figures such as Barbie sell poorly. Many female characters in Japanese video games are moe, which makes their fetishistic outfits, bunny costumes and fishnets, all the more disturbing.

But the lack of bloodlust is also commented upon by several players of *Mabinogi* that I encounter in the game. *Mabinogi* does include battles but also offers less violent ways to 'level up' such as cooking and needlework. Playing festival games with online friends on Doki Doki Island (doki doki is onomatopoeia for a heartbeat in Japanese) is a nice departure from having to constantly tool up and kill things. The most popular western games – *Call of Duty*, *Grand Theft Auto* – are too violent and too criminal to appeal to many Japanese gamers.

Back in the eighties, big Japanese companies dominated the video gaming market, and the Akihabara electronics district in Tōkyō was the global mecca for gamers. But with technological advancements, it has become much easier to create and launch a video game, and smaller companies are now able to compete, especially with games for mobile phones (such as *Fortnite* and *Candy Crush Saga*) which, says Geraint, are increasingly being made outside Japan. 'It's a far more democratic environment than it used to be because now you can make a bestselling game anywhere. You don't need to be working for a big company in Tōkyō anymore.'

Akihabara today is a jumble of collectables outlets and maid cafes, where young men can spend their money on plastic figurines and play games with girls dressed as French maids. A lot of games have moved online. Amazon can deliver the rest. But the Japanese market remains buoyant because, as Geraint points out, unlike in the United States and Europe, everyone in Japan plays video games: children and adults. Many Japanese commute up to four hours a day, often standing, so games for smartphones and tablets have grown in popularity. Japanese trains can be eerily quiet during the morning commute as everyone, from elementary school students to middle-aged office workers, wiggles their thumbs at *Yo-kai Watch* or *Inazuma Eleven*.

Before video games, Japan's favourite pastime was pachinko. Japanese salarymen and professional players could sit for hours in front of their 'lucky' machines, pulling levers and punching dials, attempting to win trays of ball bearings which could be exchanged for small gifts such as cigarettes. Only on days when the pins were realigned would there be any change in playing style. But pachinko parlours have never been popular with women, and school-age children are barred. Yet on days when I queue outside a department store waiting for their 11am opening time, I am surrounded by housewives playing *Pokémon Quest* and *Disney Tsumu Tsumu*. These games remain perennially popular, so developers can just make a new one every couple of years to appeal to the next online generation. 'They don't need to worry about repeating themselves,' says Geraint.

For my final foray into gaming, I log into *Death Stranding,* another Shloc project. This is an example of just how far the gaming industry has crossed over into other media. It features real actors – Norman Reedus, Léa Seydoux and Mads Mikkelsen – in motion capture, and the sweeping landscapes are almost indistinguishable from reality. As in *Dragon Quest*, statistics and data appear on the screen during the game, including details of songs played on the soundtrack. When a new character appears, their character name and, if famous, their real name flashes up.

Having been released in November 2019, *Death Stranding* shows a surprising amount of foresight of the Covid outbreak, at that time no more than a rumour from China. Following a global disaster, our hero is tasked with delivering medical supplies and disposing of bodies in incinerators. Despite its stated location as Washington DC, it's the closest depiction of Wales I have encountered in a video game, with lush green hills, craggy outcrops and stony riverbeds. And the rain is so drenching you can almost feel it on your skin (which is unfortunate as it's lethally poisonous).

Death Stranding takes place on a ruined planet. It has always been my assumption that dystopian landscapes are a common element of Japanese video games because Japanese people tend to be outwardly pessimistic. But Geraint points out they have been a feature of video games worldwide because early technological limitations meant that brown and grey colours were easier to create, and because blocks were easier to construct than, say, trees. (Those of us who played early versions of *Tomb Raider* will recall the blocky jungle levels and Lara Croft's square breasts.) 'So a lot of games took place in bombed-out factories and abandoned cityscapes because they were relatively easy to produce, and that aesthetic survives a lot to this day,' explains Geraint.

Another aesthetic that endures is the Welsh-inspired terrain. This is no accident because, according to Geraint, in the gaming world, Wales and the Welsh language are 'shorthand for fantasy'. *Dragon Quest* was based on early American video games which were in turn inspired by the tabletop roleplaying game devised in 1974 by Gary Gygax and Dave Arneson, *Dungeons & Dragons*. One of their influences was the fantasy world of *The Lord of the Rings* by JRR Tolkien. (George RR Martin has stated that this is also true of the *Game of Thrones* novels and television series.) Scholar and author Tolkien taught medieval Welsh at Leeds University and had an extensive Welsh-language library, including his own annotated copy of the Mabinogion. He admitted that many names, places and words in his works, including *The Lord of the Rings*, were modelled on Welsh language and culture. Consequently, in many Japanese games, although the visual art and playing style is utterly Japanese, the characters and locations are heavily influenced by Wales. Castles, which regularly feature in video games, owe more to the stone turrets of Conwy than to the wood and plaster wedding-cake style of Himeji (or White Heron) Castle with which it is twinned. It also explains the penchant for armour and the almost-Welsh language in certain names and themes in *Mabinogi* (apart from Tir Chonaill which was a kingdom of Gaelic Ireland).

However Japanese games have another, more recent, source for their Welsh influences. In 1984, animator Hayao Miyazaki founded his own studio, Ghibli. Seeking inspiration for the studio's first hand-drawn anime, he travelled to Wales. Arriving during the miners' strike, Miyazaki was deeply impressed by the scenes of struggle that he witnessed, and full of admiration for the men who fought to preserve their livelihoods. Written and directed by Miyazaki, *Laputa: Castle in the Sky* (1986) is about a village mining community fighting an authority which is trying to steal its resources. The castle in the sky is apparently based on those at Caernarfon and Powys, while Welsh terraced houses with chimneys comprise the mining village. There is even a nearby mine and slag heap.

The fight to preserve communities and landscapes set a precedent for Studio Ghibli productions as they often embrace ecological and environmentalist themes. With an anti-war message, a later academy-award nominated animation, *Howl's Moving Castle*, is based on the children's novel of the same name by Welsh author, Diana Wynne Jones. Such is Studio Ghibli's dominance of the anime market that it has encouraged other Japanese filmmakers and games designers to model their own work on Miyazaki's, giving them a Welsh feel. As Geraint points out, 'that's because of *his* work not because anybody else went to the Rhondda.'

Geraint has what is – in many young gamers' eyes – a dream job. He helps to create new video games and he plays them before anybody else. He admits that his entry into the profession was unconventional and that he was 'very, very lucky', (a comment I often hear from clever, hardworking people). Within Japanese business culture, long-term trust and commitment is valued over short-term profit, and Japanese companies are disinclined to work with someone they don't know. Consequently, they do not hold open auditions for every new release and it is difficult to find work without experience and industry contacts. But there are other ways. The conventional career path into game localisation is to start off in quality assurance as a games tester. QA teams work closely with translation teams, so being hired as a QA tester and switching jobs inhouse is common. Skills required to become a linguistic QA tester include a high level of English and an ability to spot spelling mistakes. But an enjoyment of gaming – rather than a high degree of gaming expertise – is also useful because, as Geraint points out, 'it's a pretty joyless way to play a game, systematically trying to find mistakes all the time.' In order to switch to translation, fluency in your chosen language is essential. Geraint knew no Japanese before he arrived in Tōkyō but he achieved the highest level in the JLPT within two years. Growing up bilingual in Welsh and English may have played a part in enabling him to achieve such a high grade in so short a time as, having already learned two languages, he had no intellectual barrier to adding a third. And he was aware how languages can differ.[38] But he also credits his ability to his youth, his total immersion in the language and his interest in the history and etymology of the 2,136 kanji designated by the Ministry of Education, Culture, Sports, Science and Technology

(MEXT) as required for daily life. Learning Japanese, he says laughing, 'was lots of fun'.

Freelancing for localisation companies is another way in. Due to the greater attraction of gaming for boys, the working environment is generally male dominated, although at Shloc the gender split in English to European languages is generally 50/50. Current Japanese–English freelance rates range between 5-30 yen per Japanese moji (character) or English word.

Another way into the industry is to work for a smaller video games company. Geraint suggests approaching the people who create the games you love, making friends with them and offering your services. There may only be low paid or even unpaid work but it will enable you to gain experience and to develop a portfolio to show to the big games or localisation companies when they are seeking new talent. 'Someone whose work can be seen in the wild is always really interesting for a company like ours,' says Geraint.

To work as a localiser these days, you don't even have to live in Japan. For six years Geraint was based at the Shloc offices in Tōkyō. Before the Covid pandemic, Japanese games manufacturers would not permit a new game to leave their premises so Geraint would have to visit them to view forthcoming releases and to talk with the developers in meetings, which sometimes lasted several days. He still flies to Tōkyō periodically but he now works from Anglesey and says it makes little difference. In fact, he finds it advantageous to be based in Europe because the time difference works in his favour. When he lived in Tōkyō, he had to keep the same hours as the developers and they usually worked late. Now, when they're firing off emails in Japan at eleven o'clock at night, it's early afternoon in Wales and Geraint is better placed to answer them. 'Usually when I wake up, a lot has happened in Japan so there's always a bit to catch up on in the morning. But by mid-afternoon, Japan's finished and therefore so am I.' He begins and ends his working days gazing out, not at the wall of the house next door (his view in Tōkyō) but across the steely grey waters of the Menai Strait, towards the mainland. If he cranes his neck, he can even see the limestone towers and steel chains of the Menai suspension bridge.

Back in Tir Chonaill the rain has stopped revealing a sky full of stars. (Night occurs every thirty-six minutes in *Mabinogi.*) Someone rides by on a large dog. Video gaming is a fun way to learn about another culture. Through *Mabinogi*, I can understand the strong influence of Welsh culture on the video game industry. I can also enjoy an amiable group gaming experience. I need some skill points. Where's my lute?

Tattoos Body art and the taboo gang look

Tattoos have traditionally signified membership of Japanese organised crime groups known as the Yakuza. Consequently, foreigners displaying tattoos may encounter problems in daily life.

Abby Hall *has a Japanese fish tattooed on one leg and the lyrics of her favourite Japanese band, The Mad Capsule Markets, tattooed underneath both arms. She also wears a nose ring:*

I finished my undergraduate degree and talked to my course director about joining the JET Programme. He thought I was going to get through with flying colours. I got great results on my degree and my Japanese was good enough. I applied and I got through to the interview stage. After the interview, they sent me an email asking what tattoos I had. And they asked for pictures of my tattoos. I thought it was a bit strange but I sent over pictures with an explanation that, if I were to get on the JET Programme, I could cover them. The next thing I knew, I got an email saying that my application had been rejected. I was absolutely distraught. Later, I heard on the grapevine that it was because of my tattoos.

Gerald Gallivan: I went hiking and I had a T-shirt and shorts on. I thought no one would be able to see me. A week later I got a call from my boss saying a student's grandmother had seen me hiking and she didn't feel comfortable with her child learning from me. I'd been teaching the child already for God knows how many months. Suddenly seeing my tattoo had put her off me.

It's the stigma of having a tattoo, being in a gang – the Yakuza – even though foreigners can't be in the Yakuza. She saw my leg tattoos apparently, not my arm tattoos. My leg's got a picture of the Hokusai wave. It's nothing offensive. It's a picture of a wave. So I don't know what she would have thought. 'Oh, he's got a tattoo. He must be in a gang in his own country.'

To join the gym I signed a disclaimer saying I didn't have any tattoos. I had to. It was on the contract: 'I have no tattoos'. Every gym I went to was like, you can't have tattoos. I can't really go into onsens either with tattoos, unfortunately. The only way I can get into them is if I go to private ones in ryokans (traditional inns), where you rent out a small onsen room for yourself. Or I go to Yakuza-owned onsens where the Yakuza frequently go. Then it's okay. There's one a few towns down on the train. I can go there but it's not really worth the hassle of me going all the way down there for a bath.

I can't swim either (in public swimming pools). There are some beaches where it's restricted as well. Actually, I climbed Mount Bandai on Monday and on the website it said, 'No tattoos allowed'. I went there anyway. No one stopped me. Everybody was nice.

Mike Kettle: In the countryside, right next to British Hills, is a really nice onsen that we used to go to all the time. And I'd been there maybe ten, twenty times and no problems at all. And then one year I went there on New Year's Day. And there were lots of people from Tōkyō and city folk who came up to visit for the holiday. This group of guys from Tōkyō, all about fifty years old, were sitting next to me and one of them was going, 'Oh, you got tattoos.' And then the guy next to him was just going, 'Dame,

dame. Warui ne. Warui yo.' (No, no. That's bad. That's bad.) He was really upset. I was like, 'Oh, I'm sorry. I'll sit on the other side of you.' He left the area. And then about ten minutes later a staff member came up and said, 'I'm so sorry. The customers are upset. Can you leave?' He'd gone and complained about me. Obviously, he didn't think I was a Yakuza. He was probably thinking, this guy's bringing in another culture and diluting ours. Japanese people are very proud of their culture and their history. Sometimes, they'll see another culture as a challenge to that. And it's difficult for some people to accept.

Joanne Tanaka: My Japanese husband has tattoos, which is rare in Japan. He's really into skinhead fashion. He's not into the racism skinheads. He likes the music, the reggae and ska. But he looks a bit intimidating sometimes if he's wearing his braces and Dr Marten boots, and he has tattoos and he shaves his head so he's got the skinhead look. In Japan it's not a typical look.

I was walking through a busy station, and I was pushing my daughter in the pushchair. And this guy – always a guy – was trying to get past me and he kept pushing me and pushing me. But there was nowhere to go. And I kept saying to him, 'Osanaide' (don't push me). And still he kept doing it. I guess he wanted to hurry past. He wanted to get to the elevator. My husband heard me say to this guy, 'Osanaide.' And my husband's like, 'Who's pushing you?' And I pointed to this guy. And the look on this guy's face when he saw my husband. The colour just drained out of his face. And my husband was so angry with him. The guy's like, 'No, I didn't, no I didn't!' And my husband's like, 'Are you saying my wife is lying?' And then the guy's like, 'Oh, I'm sorry. Sumimasen.' The guy obviously didn't know that this foreign lady with a baby was together with a skinhead. If I hadn't had my husband there, this guy wouldn't have thought twice about pushing past me to get to the elevator. But because my husband was there, it taught him a lesson.

Chapter Fifteen

Cutting a 'Mie' for Wales: Ursula Bartlett-Imadegawa fights for national recognition (and supplies her own flag)

Ursula Bartlett-Imadegawa inspects the Welsh flag at the British Embassy

Ursula Bartlett-Imadegawa treats me to lunch at the Foreign Correspondents' Club in the Tōkyō business district of Marunouchi. The FCC was established in 1945 as a press club for foreign journalists but is now also open to diplomats and businesspeople. I say 'people' but our fellow diners are all Japanese and foreign men. And one Japanese woman. As we eat our club sandwiches, I point this out to Ursula, who shrugs. A bright blonde in a sea of pinstripe, she is used to finding herself in a minority group. As long-time president of the St David's Society Japan (SDSJ), she has spent years fighting for recognition for its Welsh members.

Ursula arrived in Tōkyō in the mid-seventies. It was an interest in Japanese arts that brought her here. A native of Llanrumney, in east Cardiff, Ursula was attending a fifth-form class in print making when a teacher showed some examples of ukiyo-e, Japanese prints depicting pastoral landscapes, scenes from folk tales and Katsushika Hokusai's famous 'Great Wave'. Developed from the late seventeenth century, the most popular ukiyo-e featured characters from Tōkyō's pleasure districts, including courtesans, sumō wrestlers and kabuki actors with grimaces and staring eyes. At Cardiff library, Ursula learned more about kabuki, the all-male classical theatre involving colourful costumes, stylised dances and exaggerated performances.

A significant moment in a kabuki performance is indicated when a character stamps his foot, wiggles his head and draws in his chin before striking a pose or 'mie'. As tsuke clappers (two wooden blocks) beat time, he holds the pose for several seconds. A character 'cuts a mie' to show the audience that he has been struck by a realisation or extreme emotion. (The western film equivalent might be an extreme closeup of an actor's face with the chime 'Dan dan daaaaan!') A character crossing his eyes indicates anger, but Ursula thought she would have to be carried out of the theatre laughing. 'I remember that time in the library thinking, "Oh, I've got to go to Japan"', she says. 'And that feeling never left me.' Ursula was in

London studying for a further qualification in art education when she saw a *Times* job advertisement for an art teacher at an international high school in Tōkyō. Despite her tutor's misgivings, she took a leave of absence and flew out. She never went back.

There are fifty international schools in Japan.[39] The oldest were founded in the nineteenth century to teach the children of visiting envoys and missionaries. Ursula was hired by Seishin (also known as the International School of the Sacred Heart), a Catholic girls' school in the expatriate enclave of Hiroo in Tōkyō. At Seishin the students comprised an international blend of Japanese returnees (whose families had lived abroad on company postings) and foreign students. Their fathers were CEOs and diplomats, and their arrivals – and sometimes sudden departures – coincided with their home country's fortunes. Ursula vividly recalls one ambassador and his family being ordered home after the sudden fall of his country's government. The ambassador persuaded Seishin to let his daughter remain at the school where she thrived and graduated. The ambassador disappeared while his wife and younger son were discovered years later in a labour camp.

Economic fortunes too dictated student numbers. In 2003-04, as Japan fell deeper into recession, the American multinational IBM repatriated forty

American families in one week, leaving the playground at the American school deserted. It also impacted local real estate. 'You could hear the air let out of the housing market in Tōkyō, as all the executive apartments just went whoosh!' remembers Ursula. This exodus accelerated after the financial crash in 2008 and the Tōhoku Earthquake and nuclear power plant disaster in 2011 when, Ursula says, 'a lot of families left or the men sent their wives and children away.' After 2011, (and more recently the Covid pandemic) international companies realised they no longer needed to budget for expensive expatriate packages: business class flights, international school fees and rental costs for Homats, the luxury, western-style apartments where families were billeted during their stay. Senior executives could work just as well online from their home countries. 'And if you look at the building that has happened since then there's been a lot more scaled down apartments,' Ursula points out. 'They're making them for the middle management now.' These days foreign multinationals are more likely to send younger executives without family commitments or to promote English-speaking Japanese. Consequently, international schools are struggling to maintain student numbers and places are being filled by ambitious, well-heeled Japanese families keen to raise bilingual children qualified in the International Baccalaureate, a qualification introduced to Japan in the eighties and for which Ursula has been an examiner ever since.

While the expatriates had their luxury Homats, Seishin put Ursula up in an actual palace. The Kuni Palace had been the family home of Princess Nagako of Kuni who, at age fourteen, had been selected as the bride of the future Shōwa emperor, Hirohito. (He had chosen her after observing several contenders from behind a screen.) Following a gynaecologist's assurance that she would give birth to boys, Nagako and the crown prince were married in 1924. After the birth of the fourth girl, the gynaecologist committed suicide. Their fifth child was Akihito, who became the Heisei emperor. The former palace stood in the grounds of the University of the Sacred Heart, and Ursula's friends visited regularly because she lived in such beautiful surroundings.

Ursula was also privileged in other ways. Japan in the seventies was a country in transition, steadily rebuilding and modernising after its destruction during the Second World War. But foreigners remained few in number, and single foreign women were a rarity. Ursula found herself invited to dinner parties by the wives of CEOs to make up numbers.

In front of a decorated fusuma panel at the Kuni Palace

Well-heeled expatriates shopped at National Azabu, an import supermarket conveniently located in the midst of the foreign embassies. But Ursula and three American friends preferred to eat cheaply at Japanese restaurants. They adored sushi, soba, tempura and tonkatsu washed down with umeshu, plum liqueur. Until they learned enough Japanese, they would point randomly at menus and eat whatever arrived no matter how bizarre. Japan's first McDonalds had opened in 1971 in Ginza's Mitsukoshi department store. When Ursula followed her excited American friends there, 'I hadn't a clue what McDonalds was,' she recalls, adding, 'I was not very impressed. And I've never been since.' Ursula and her friends socialised in Roppongi, now a district of nightclubs and hostess bars but back then the playground of a cool, much-envied western elite. When the first disco opened in nearby Akasaka, Ursula and her friends were waved straight in.

In the holidays, they went travelling. On trains, they were stared at by Japanese passengers, and – at local ryokan – the staff accompanied them to the ofuro (communal bath) to make sure they didn't put soap in the water. As an art lover, Ursula dragged her friends to pottery and paper-making villages, and even to Katsura Imperial Villa where they were given a special tour. 'We actually went into the building which you can't do now,' she points out. They also enjoyed skiing and, on one trip, Ursula was persuaded by a Tōkyō University law student to attempt the highest slope. When she injured her knee, Yukihiro Imadegawa (accompanied by his sister) called the next day to check on her recovery. (She'd gone to the kabuki.) He soon found himself driver and translator on her art research trips.

Ursula had no plans to remain in Japan and, when her contract ended, she moved to Münich to

With kabuki onnagata (male actors who play female roles)

teach at a school there. But when Yukihiro flew over, they decided to marry, which they did in 1980. A Japanese wedding does not only represent a personal milestone. It also signals a professional commitment. (A man with a wife at home is ready to dedicate all his time to his company.) Because Yukihiro was a newly qualified lawyer, it was important to have the wedding in Japan and to invite his colleagues. Ursula wore western wedding dress for both the Catholic wedding and the Japanese reception at the Meiji Kinenkan (a traditional hall at Meiji Jingu shrine in Tōkyō). 'I foolishly opted not to wear a kimono but I wish I had now,' she admits. Ursula returned to teach at Seishin and the couple moved into a small apartment in Yokohoma, close to where Yukihiro was in training at the law courts. A son, Owain Yoshihiro (now a lawyer like his father), and daughter, Rhyannon Hiroko (now a journalist for the *Nikkei* newspaper in London), were born after their return to central Tōkyō.

In 1981, Ursula and Yukihiro (and two long-departed expatriates: Madoc Batcup and Adrian Jenkyn) decided to establish a Welsh society. When the news reached Catharine Huws Nagashima, she organised their inaugural meeting at a restaurant down in Zushi. Also present was Catharine's friend, Doris Gertrude 'Rose' Iwata.

I first met Rose online. Born in 1937, she is the youngest of four sisters from Cydweli in south Wales. Having trained as a religious studies teacher, in 1960 she had been en route to a school in Australia when she was offered a job at Seisen primary school in Tōkyō. 'I didn't want to come to Japan,' she said, in a faint voice on a Zoom call. 'I wanted to go to India because I wanted to see the Taj Mahal.' Rose is not Catholic. She suspected the nuns offered her the job because she had auburn hair, which was a rare sight in Japan. After marrying her Japanese husband, Masa, in 1963, they established a despatch agency, supplying English language teachers to Japanese schools. In the early sixties, Tōkyō was a city under construction, feverishly preparing for the 1964 Tōkyō Olympics, the event that would symbolise Japan's postwar recovery. Rose didn't appreciate the continual noise but, from the window of her Yoyogi apartment, she did see Emperor Hirohito as he passed by on his way to the opening ceremony. Rose and Masa are remembered by the society for bringing the first Welsh flag (which they bought on Swansea market) to Japan.

The founders of the St David's Society Japan agreed that their primary aim was to provide a home for Welsh members to meet, speak their national language and have fun. And in the years of Japan's bubble economy, there was plenty of money around to do just that. As many of the early members were high-powered businessmen, the society could afford to hire entire beer halls for gatherings and hold parties in members' palatial Homats. As club historian, Catharine arranged historical trips while Ursula organised visits to pottery villages, art museums and to the Kabukiza, Tōkyō's most famous kabuki theatre, where she had helped to establish English audio commentaries.

The SDSJ was not the only British club in town. When Ursula first arrived in Japan, the St George's Society was the largest organisation with the most clout. Its president was like a 'mini ambassador', she remembers, and its members were overwhelmingly expatriates of a certain class. Teachers were not welcomed. 'They didn't want anything to do with us,' Ursula recalls through pursed lips although, as a representative of the SDSJ, she was once invited to their St George's Ball, a grand occasion with five hundred guests. When the recession bit and the elite expatriates departed, Ursula suggested to the society that they open up their membership to a wider section of British residents in Japan. 'Oh no, they're not the right kind of people,' was the response. 'I was a bit put out by that,' Ursula admits. She pauses dramatically (and possibly wiggles her head). 'Not only do they not have their balls anymore, they no longer exist!'

The St David's Society has not been immune to Japan's changing fortunes. 'Japan is no longer the extravagant country it was,' says Ursula, sadly. But, unlike the St George's, it endures. With around seventy active members, it is adapting to cater for a younger, single, middle-management crowd who are more likely to view the society as a place to network. And although there isn't as much money around as there used to be, they continue to hold small events: pub nights, picnics in the park and Welsh film screenings. 'We had to reorient ourselves to being a smaller society and limit expensive events to once a year,' says Ursula. The 'once a year' event is the St David's Society annual dinner which I have flown to Japan to attend.

Although some members had reservations, the SDSJ has also opened memberships to non-Welsh

At the 2019 Rugby World Cup

who are interested in learning more about Wales, including Japanese who have spent time there either for study or for work. Explains Ursula, 'The main thrust of the society was for Welsh people to have fun together but at the same time I felt very passionate about promoting Wales in Japan because I was fed up with being mistaken for an American.' The society agreed that their second objective was to inform people about Wales. Some of the people they wished to inform worked at the British embassy.

For several years, the SDSJ had to push to be recognised by British diplomats. When other societies were invited to embassy events, they were forgotten. When they were summoned to a gathering, Ursula recalls the British ambassador talking about the impact of all the other expatriate societies in Japan but failing to mention the Welsh. 'And I made myself very unpleasant afterwards,' she assures me, drawing in her chin. The embassy has a Welsh Development Office although until recently (and this was pointed out to me by several interviewees) their representative has never been Welsh.[40] (Ursula thinks that recent appointees have been better than an early representative – who I will not name – who used to 'just sit at the bar of the American Club and wait for Japanese people to tap him on the shoulder'.) Ursula and other club members often support the Welsh Office (as unpaid volunteers) and are enthusiastic about the good work they are currently doing. But it has not always been the case. Back in the nineties, Ursula was asked to represent Wales at a trade fair by taking to the stage waving a Union Jack. 'I said, "I'm *not* going on with a British flag." If I was representing Britain I would have been proud to wave the flag but I was supposed to be representing Wales, so I refused.' A speedy telephone call to the embassy confirmed that they didn't even own a Welsh flag, so Ursula phoned Rose and Masa who immediately couriered over the Red Dragon they had bought on Swansea market. 'And the next day I walked on with our Welsh flag,' says Ursula. 'Because the embassy DID. NOT. HAVE. ONE.' If this was kabuki, Ursula would now stamp her foot and cross her eyes.

Ursula and the society stepped up their efforts to be recognised by the embassy, refusing to take no for an answer. When Ursula worked with the Japanese company Dentsu to bring over a Welsh male voice choir, she telephoned the then ambassador, Sir John Whitehead, and said, 'Wouldn't it be lovely if the embassy invited them to a reception?' After a long pause he replied, 'I don't even do that for the Royal Shakespeare Company.' 'And where I got it from I'll never know,' says Ursula. 'I said, "This is for WALES!"' The reception went ahead and ended with everyone, including the ambassador, singing late into the evening.

To remind the embassy of their continued existence, the society sends the ambassador thirty-six daffodils every first of March. For the last few years, the embassy has responded by running the Red Dragon up the embassy flagpole. Ursula has even taught the embassy's chef how to make Welsh cakes and bara brith. 'He makes them beautifully,' says Ursula proudly. She is now regularly invited to embassy events as the society's representative. 'Who knows when it could change but certainly the Welsh society is *known*,' she assures me. The vigour of the St David's Society Japan has even been a topic of conversation at the mission's central Tōkyō compound. An ambassador once asked Ursula, 'Why is the Welsh society thriving and the other societies aren't?' She could have told him what she told me, that she had actively waged a campaign to get the embassy's attention. 'I was strategic,' she says, before reconsidering. 'Don't put that down.' What she actually said to the ambassador was, 'We're just very enthusiastic, supportive and interesting.'[41]

'I'm not at all an aggressive person and I'm not pushy,' Ursula says, as we pull on our coats. 'But I feel I have to [be], for Wales.' In kabuki, when a character 'cuts a mie', the audience is allowed to shout encouragement from the stalls. And, as Ursula hurries away to make final arrangements for the St David's Day dinner, I feel like cheering after her. To survive, every expatriate society needs an organiser, a chivvier, a sweet talker, and if necessary, a fighter. For the St David's Society Japan, that person is Ursula.

Natsukashii, Hiraeth 'I miss the craic… and Heinz baked beans'

Yūko Nakauchi: Japanese people love that Welsh word, hiraeth. Many people understand that feeling. We often use natsukashii. It's all good memories in the past. Good days. Sort of like sweet and bitter. That makes me emotional.

Andy Moore: When I first came to Japan in 1998 I brought with me a Tom Jones cassette and a cassette by a guy named John Edwards – he writes books on Wenglish. I like where he's talking about how the Welsh use English. It's very humorous. And I've got a tea towel which is the Welsh flag. Those things I brought with me because I wanted to have some connection to home. And these items keep me connected. I don't really feel homesick but I do feel a connection. When I talk to my son, sometimes I'll call him boyo. I'll do a bit of Windsor Davies, 'my lovely boy', things like that, things that my father said to me. Again it kind of keeps a connection there. My son has got a Wales polo shirt and a Welsh rugby shirt that was issued for the last World Cup. He still wears those.

Mike Kettle: I miss the warmth of my small town where I grew up and where everyone knows everybody else. There is such a beautiful community feeling to it. Also, my dad being a minister, he has a pastoral role and he's operating as the town counsellor a lot of the time. When people lose someone, they'll come to the house and he'll sit them down and have a cup of tea. My dad is an expert at reassuring and comforting people. I've never seen anyone better, to be honest. And he's just such a warm character, he brings a lot of people in. I miss that aspect of it. I'd like to bring that to Japan, to my community. I try to recreate it as much as I can.

Simon Whalley: I miss the craic. I miss going to the pub. Going to the pub and listening to stories. It's just not the same in Japan. Even if you go to an izakaya, people don't talk to other people. They're all in their little crowds. Whereas if you go to a pub in Swansea, it's just good times. Everyone's friendly. You can go and talk to people. Strangers talk to each other. In

Japan it's not taboo but it's not something that people do a lot of, talking to strangers. I miss that.

John Llywelyn: The things I'm really missing here are a full English breakfast because you can't get black puddings here, can't get a proper sausage, and a normal tin of Heinz baked beans is 350 yen (£1.70) a tin. So it's a bit of a luxury item. It's not like the four-pence tins of beans Asda were doing.

Eddy Jones: As soon as you become an expat, there's something that makes you a little bit different. For our [international school] students, we use the phrase 'third culture kids'. But I think for the adult generation, we've become a kind of TCK as well. Because there's a lengthening distance between here and home. And feeling that kind of strangeness about which is home. Home is where I am at the moment. But as soon as I'm in one place, I'm homesick for the other.

Pred Evans: When I used to go back with work to London and then pop down to Wales, it was incredible. It was so different from Tōkyō, or Bangkok where I am now. It was like I was in some kind of movie. It was almost surreal, the beauty. I would get excited with [wife] Asami walking around seeing a horse in the field. And that's not just because I've been living in big cities for so long. It's also because it really is genuinely a stunning location, where my parents live. There are no houses. The nearest house is a hundred metres away. The nearest village is three miles away. And I was brought up in a very healthy environment. Now I appreciate it more than before.

Joe Cairnes: I miss the countryside, for sure. I miss friends. I miss the views from the top of the hill overlooking Aberystwyth. I miss hiking. I miss the landscape.

Tim Pelham Williams: I miss mountains and sky. Honestly, hiraeth, I'm down with that.

Afterword

The Welsh in Japan: Embedded, Assimilated and Adaptable

It is the evening of the St David's Society's annual dinner. It's being held at the Foreign Correspondents' Club in Marunouchi Nijūbashi, a building which covers an entire block and requires multiple elevator lobbies, only one of which connects to the FCC on the fifth floor. Despite having been here before, I take the wrong elevator twice, arriving a few minutes late, only to join a queue of guests waiting to check in. At the head of the line is Ursula, bustling and organising and telling a flustered woman with a guest list to admit everyone quickly. Guests are assigned to tables according to career or affiliation. In the confusion, I am sent to the wrong one.

In the dining room, taster bars offering complimentary Welsh whisky prompt guests to mingle before finding their seats. There are small Welsh flags dotted around the room, and I notice a large one hanging on the wall. It is the one Rose and Masa Iwata brought to Japan, the Red Dragon they had to courier to Ursula because the British embassy didn't have one and she wouldn't take the stage without it.

As one of the society's founding members, Rose, now confined to a wheelchair, is being honoured this evening. So too, is Catharine Huws Nagashima, whose life story inspired this book. Wearing her distinctive knitted cap, Catharine is easy to spot. Since I visited her in Zushi, she has lost her husband but, when I ask her how she fills her days she replies, 'I'm still teaching, of course.'

Ursula appears at my elbow and informs me that it is a very good turnout this year: sixty-nine attendees comprising society members, honoured guests and a few wandering Welsh who like a party. Although it marks St David, Ursula has moved the event from the first to the ninth of March to coincide with FOODEX Japan, an international food and beverage exhibition taking place nearby. She points to two of the tables which are occupied by visiting Welsh food exporters looking wide-eyed and well refreshed. Or maybe it's just the light-headedness that hits you on your first visit to Japan when you can't get over how clean and safe it is, how the trains run on time, and how polite the people are.

Another FOODEX guest, Jimmy Williams, executive chef at Signatures in Conwy, is seated at a table with the British Consul and various government officials, both local and visiting. At the same table is Ursula's 'superstar'. According to her, young Lord Gregory Mostyn (seventh Baron Mostyn) is keen to promote Japanese tourism in north Wales, 'because he owns most of it'. This includes Llandudno, which is one stop on the 'Roads of Castles in Wonderland in north Wales', a tour devised by North Wales Tourism with the Japanese in mind. Japanese tourists generally arrive in Wales via one of two routes: from Manchester in the north or from Bristol and Bath in the south. Unless they stay to play golf in Newport, they spend no more than a day in the country. Last year Greg (as he introduces himself) opened his home, fifteenth-century Mostyn Hall, to bespoke tours, which he conducts in Japanese. On a previous visit to Tōkyō, Ursula asked him to speak to her art group. When it became known that he was single, several Japanese mothers raised their hands and offered their daughters. 'It was embarrassing,' recalls Ursula with glee. Greg won't be drawn on the reason for his latest trip to Tōkyō, except that it's to do with real estate.

Ursula and the British Consul, Martin O'Neill, present gifts to Kōji Tokumasu, Tadayuki Itō and Kasumi Ohigashi

Ursula now appears behind a podium at the front of the room. Before dinner, there are speeches to be made and guests to be honoured. She thanks a Scotsman in a kilt at the 'Celtic societies' table, while a man in a cravat (musical impresario Suguru Minamide, who introduces himself as 'the Andrew Lloyd Webber of Japan') gets a mention. He is sat among a group of actors and musicians at the 'creatives' table.

Seated next to public relations consultant Abby Hall and several tough-looking Japanese men, I wonder what assignation my table has been given. Then Ursula calls the men up to the podium and I

Tadayuki Itō, Mike Galbraith (sports writer), Kasumi Ohigashi, Abby Hall and Lord Gregory Mostyn

realise I have been seated at the 'rugby union' table. The first man is Kōji Tokumasu, who brought the Rugby World Cup to Japan in 2019. To Japanese rugby fans, his life story is legend. As a twenty-four-year-old rugby fan, he arrived in Cardiff in 1977 with no money and no job. Finding work as a cleaner, he stayed for two years, attending a local college and playing rugby for the college team. When he returned to Japan, he coached rugby and later joined the Japan Rugby Football Union where, through his job in international relations, he lobbied to have Japan awarded the World Cup. Standing next to

Tokumasu is Tadayuki Itō, who scored Japan's first ever try against Wales at Cardiff Arms Park in 1973. He is accompanied by Kasumi Ohigashi, a fellow tour team member. We watch a video of Itō scoring the try. Later, I excitedly have my photograph taken with them, and realise we are all the same height, five foot two. I remember what Ursula told me about a conversation she'd had at a press club event with the Japanese coach just before the Rugby World Cup in 2019. He'd said he trained his players to look at their opponents' knees but no higher in case they fell over backwards. Instead they would exploit their natural abilities: low tackles, swift manoeuvring and speed. Japan made the quarter finals, Wales the semis.

Dinner is, of course, lamb. A few guests complain that it is undercooked. 'They've done it the American way!' wails Ursula, mortally offended. It is nevertheless delicious, served with potatoes and peas. The bara brith, too, fails Ursula's taste test ('very dry'), but I help myself to several pieces.

Back at my table, I meet Llion Jones from Abergynolwyn in mid Wales, now working as a software engineer for Google Japan. He is something to do with ChatGPT. 'I'm the T part,' he says.[42] Not yet a society member, he came this evening because he wanted to connect with his homeland. He's amused that, despite being six thousand miles away, the society has still managed to decorate the room in a way that reminds him of his village hall back home. Llion misses speaking his first language and wonders aloud if there are any other Welsh speakers in the room. Ursula instantly appears and hurries him away to meet Catharine. He later tells me that he also bumped into Takeshi Koike and found hearing fluent Welsh coming out of the mouth of a Japanese person 'a strange experience'.

Another non-member, Zachary Fox, is an associate producer for the BBC drama, *Tokyo Vice*, currently filming a new series in the city. The BBC are putting him up in an executive apartment complex but he is missing Wales and, when he found the dinner advertised on the internet, he signed up. He is delighted to see his tiny village represented at the taster bar in the form of Penderyn whisky. In a metropolis of nearly twelve million people, he finds this comforting because, when he gets off the train at Shinjuku, he knows the same number of people use the station daily as the entire population of Wales.

As I sit with my glass of Penderyn and a fourth slice of bara brith, I look around the room and wonder what I can conclude about the Welsh community in Japan. The Patagonian Welsh settlement Y Wladfa was established in response to an observation by its founder[43] that, unlike other nations, the migrant Welsh tended to assimilate into their host culture, losing their national identity in the process. On my journey around Japan I have encountered many Welsh migrants who seem to have blended so seamlessly into the landscape as to almost disappear. On Ōsakikamijima, Simon Whalley is firmly embedded on his vegan farm: planting, harvesting and trying to keep the wild boar out. Ski instructor Jac Phillips has blissfully lost himself in his Hokkaidō wilderness. Even translator Geraint M told me that he felt so at ease around the other expatriates of the Tokyo American Club that he did not feel the need to 'go and be with my people'. Compared to the British or the Americans I have encountered in Japan, the Welsh appear more adaptable to their host culture and, dare I say it, often quicker at picking up the Japanese language.

Having quizzed several of the interviewees about why this could be, I have concluded that it stems from the fact that the Welsh are raised to navigate two cultures – Welsh and British – both inside and outside Wales. Wales' soft border results in easy and regular movement throughout Britain. Quite a few of the interviewees went to university in England or Scotland, and several had left Wales in search of work before moving to Japan. Additionally, not all the interviewees have two Welsh-language parents, meaning that, when growing up, they sometimes spoke English at home and Welsh at school (or vice versa). That most of the interviewees are to some extent bilingual in Welsh and English suggests they mastered linguistic adaptability at an early age. Because of the recent resurgence of Welsh-language teaching in schools, younger interviewees, especially, were comfortable living in two languages, and saw no mental or intellectual barrier to adding a third.

But at the same time, a close Welsh community in Japan does exist, if you want it. Here at the St David's Society dinner, I can see it operating to its full effect. In one corner of the room, deep in conversation, are Catharine, Rose and Ursula, whose mutual lifelong friendship has been sustained by their decision long ago to form a group where Welsh members can find a home, speak their national language and have fun. In another corner, the younger crowd – Abby and Zack and Llion and Greg – are creating a new Welsh network, friending each other on their smartphones.

Wherever and however they choose to live, Welsh migrants in Japan still share commonalities. Whether out of economic necessity, a sense of adventure or for love, they have all left Wales. In doing so they have discovered opportunities and new ways of living: the ability to purchase their own land, the chance to set up their own businesses, to make movies, appear on television, pursue a love of Japanese art or to write. Whether for a short time or a lifetime, Japan has offered them something they could not find at home. Their decision to take on the challenge of moving overseas and start again makes them different. It gives them mental and emotional strength.

This is not to say they don't miss Wales. Everyone I have interviewed admits to feeling some measure of hiraeth, if not instantly then as time goes on and Wales becomes a memory. For some, that feeling will lead them back home. A couple of people interviewed for this book have already left, either to return to the UK (if not Wales) or to migrate to a third country. Others will probably never leave. Jac Phillips admitted that he was 'terrified' of going back. Andrew Beak told his parents that if he did return home, 'it means I've failed'. And there are those who discover aspects of Wales within Japan. Eddy Jones finds it in Afan no Mori, the late CW Nicol's forest. John Llywelyn and Jac Phillips see a better Wales in Hokkaidō. But the next time the Welsh rugby (or some other Welsh sporting) team tours Japan, every one of the interviewees will be out there in their red shirts, waving y Ddraig Goch. After all, there is no better Welshman than an exile. Gorau Cymro, Cymro oddi cartref.

Llion Jones, Abby Hall and Zachary Fox with daffodils

Staying On or Moving On 'I was very free in Japan but being treated as a foreigner is wearying'

John Llywelyn: I don't see myself moving from here. I really like the country. It's got everything I want. I see Hokkaidō as the best island in the world. It's got amazing snow in the winter. The summers are really nice. The terrain reminds me of north Wales. It's got the mountains and the rivers and the lakes and the beaches and you can surf, you can kayak and go hiking and climbing. But the seasons are more extreme. So they're a bit better. I'll have a better summer here than I would back home.

Gareth Jenkins: Despite being a passionate Welshman and loving Wales, I don't think I could move back, to be honest. Basically, all my skills gained through university are Japanese ability and business studies, but to get a good job in the UK I'd probably have to live in London, realistically, and I don't like London. And I'm settled in Japan. Considering the fact that my wife doesn't speak English that well, I don't think I'll move back to Wales to live. So I'll probably die in Japan. Which is fine by me.

Andy Moore: There is part of me that imagines going back home. Daydreaming. I have this idea of moving back home with my family and what it would be like if my son was in school in Wales. These ideas cross my mind. I don't really have any plans to do that. I think the actual practicality of it may be a lot more difficult. My son would be okay for a visa but it would be much harder for my wife to get one under the current government rules and regulations.

Jac Phillips: I'm a lifer at this moment in time. I'm terrified of going back to the UK. I don't know what I'd do. I never saw a future in Wales, or saw myself doing anything in Wales. But I love it. I miss socialising and speaking Welsh but I don't get fulfilment. I'd go back home and see the parents but then I'd feel at a loose end, not working or not doing something. I don't know what I would do back home.

Clive Davies: Every now and again it's nice to go back [to Wales]. It's like a reset button. And then you've had enough after a week. Then you're glad to come back [to Japan]. I think it's a bit like living in a bubble. Japan doesn't feel like the real world. It's not reality here. You have a slightly privileged position as a foreigner in Japan because you benefit from the country – it's still one of the safest places and it's convenient – but you are never expected to put in the hard-working hours that the locals do. There's something about the short, sharp shock of reality when you go anywhere else.

Carolyn De Vishlin: I don't think I've ever consciously considered myself a lifer in all of the time I've been here. I've been here consecutively, all the way through from 2002 until now, and this length of time was not intentional at all. But the fact that my husband's from Canada and I'm from Wales – when we were first together, it was always with the intention of going back to one or the other country at some point. The longer you stay, the more difficult it is to get back. I don't consider Japan my permanent home and I don't think I ever will, even if it continues to be my permanent home. I don't think I'll ever consider it the place I'll end up retiring, even if I do end up retiring here. I think mentally I'll be outside.

Geraint Howells: It's hard to leave and easy to stay in Japan. I think everyone knows. I felt like it was time, and if I left it much longer then it might be too late. Also I'd met my partner and we both wanted to move together. It was just nice timing. I could have stayed on but I didn't have a particular reason to, which is not to say I had a particular reason to come back [to Wales]. But it felt like enough. I was starting to get fed up of it. And I felt like a change as well.

Of course, looking back now, it is all rose tinted but I think being a foreigner and being treated as a foreigner is wearying. Of course, there's loads of things I like about it. I think I felt very free there, I mean, I *was* very free there. Some aspects of life there are very easy. I think the reason I stayed for so long was not because I love Japan but because it's harder to leave, and I don't think those are the same things.

Pred Evans: It was painful. I mean, I was excited. I was still young enough. If that happened, now, I wouldn't be able to leave. But I was ambitious enough or stupid enough to just take that plunge. And my wife Asami was very excited about the prospect of doing something completely different. But I remember going to see a concert – it was Coldplay in Tōkyō – and I found it emotional. I'm not a huge fan of Coldplay but while listening to their songs and looking around at the entire 99.9 per cent Japanese audience, I felt really emotional thinking this country has given me so much. So much. So many deep, rich experiences and so many opportunities and so much kindness. And here I am, willingly leaving.

Endnotes

1 Reference to a 'Welchman' is from Richard Cocks' letter to Sir Thomas Smythe and the East India Company in London, dated 10 March, 1620, in volume 1 of *The English Factory in Japan 1613–1623* by Anthony Farrington (British Library, 1991), p785.

2 The antics of Thomas Jones and Christopher Evans are noted in Farrington volume 2 which contains extracts from John Saris' journal of the voyage to Japan in 1613, p995-6, and in *Samurai William: The Adventurer who Unlocked Japan* by Giles Milton (Sceptre, 2005 edition), p180.

3 Figures are from June 2023 and taken from 'Statistics on Foreigners Resident' on E-Stat, the portal site of official statistics of Japan which can be accessed at: e-stat.go.jp

4 The current UK population is approximately 67.5 million and Welsh, 3.1 million, meaning that the Welsh constitute 4.5 per cent of the UK population.

Figures taken from the Office for National Statistics at: ons.gov.uk

5 I am grateful to Bet Davies, formerly of the Wales Tourist Board and the Welsh Development Agency for explaining the economic and cultural links forged between Wales and Japan during this period, many of which were established by Bet herself.

6 Figures on Japanese companies in Wales taken from the website: tradeandinvest.wales

7 In 2023, digital mapping technology revealed that the Japanese archipelago is made up of twice as many islands as previously thought. See: theguardian.com/world/2023/feb/16/japan-sees-its-number-of-islands-double-after-recount

8 The issue of Japan's concreted rivers is discussed in *Dogs and Demons: The Fall of Modern Japan* by Alex Kerr (Penguin, 2001).

9 Figures taken from the 'Family Database' of the Organisation for Economic Cooperation and Development, and the *Japan Statistical Yearbook 2024* available online at: stat.go.jp

10 Figures on child suicides in 2023 are taken from the *Asahi Shimbun* newspaper (asahi.com/ajw/articles/15215106?msockid=391135ba1310682e3ad63a1217106a57). See also 'Japan's Child Suicide Crisis' at NHK World-Japan website (nhk.or.jp).

11 JET statistics taken from the programme website at: jetprogramme.org. See 'participating countries'.

12 Just before this book was submitted, Andrew informed me that Berlitz teachers are again considering strike action.

13 Percentage taken from 'English Schools Face Huge Insurance Probe' by Barry Brophy in the *Japan Times* (12 April, 2005).

14 Monbukagakushō (previously Monbushō) is the Japanese Ministry of Education, Culture, Sports, Science and Technology (MEXT). It manages a fully funded scholarship programme for suitably qualified candidates to study at universities in Japan.

15 Paul's professor, Masahiro Chatani (1934–2008), was the inventor of pop-up origami architecture.

16 Quotation taken from Bruno Taut's *The Rediscovery of Japanese Beauty* (Iwanami Shinsho, 1936).

17 Such clubs were the forerunners of the infamous and controversial Juliana's Tōkyō (in operation from 1991–1994), where sexily clad women were admitted for free to dance on platforms while being ogled by salarymen in suits. Paul put his head around the door once or twice. 'It was wild,' he recalls.

18 Bush-hammered concrete is created when dried concrete is hammered or drilled to give it a rough, weathered texture.

19 *Angry White Pyjamas: An Oxford Poet Trains with the Tokyo Riot Police* by Robert Twigger (Indigo Press, 1997).

20 *Variety* quotation taken from 12 July, 2001 review, available online at: https://variety.com/2001/film/reviews/firefly-dreams-1200469153/

21 *Screen International* quotation taken from 19 July, 2001 review, available online at: screendaily.com/firefly-dreams/406344.article

22 Award data is taken from the movie's entry on the IMDB website at: imdb.com

23 The Hiroshige Utagawa ukiyo-e woodblock print is called 'Sudden Shower Over Shin-Ōhashi Bridge and Atake'.

24 Cherry blossoms traditionally symbolise the beauty and fragility of life. For the few days each year when cherry trees produce their fragile blooms, Japanese enjoy hanami (blossom viewing) parties under the trees, drinking alcohol and singing karaoke. Ōka (cherry blossom) was also the name given to the human-guided flying bombers which were utilised by the Japanese navy towards the end of the Pacific War in 1945. Pilots were sealed into the bombs on one-way kamikaze missions.

25 Sydney Film Festival review quotation. Available here: montecristoentertainment.com/filmreviews.aspx

26 www.japanwritersconference.org

27 *Wales wo shirutame no 60 sho* (*Sixty Chapters to Get to Know Wales*) by Norio Yoshiga (Akashi, 2019).

28 *Basics of the Welsh Language,* (*Walesgo no kihon* in Japanese) by Yoshifumi Nagata and Takeshi Koike (Sanshusha, 2011).

29 This was an intensive study programme known as an Wlpan course, derived from the Hebrew word for 'studio', Ulpan.

30 According to Dr Takeshi Koike, the number has dropped to around ten.

31 Figures taken from the World Economic Forum's annual Global Gender Gap Report for 2024. Available online at: webforum.org/publications/global-gender-gap-report-2024/digest/

32 In 2019, Liberal Democratic Party politician, Yoshitaka Sakurada, gave a speech urging the (presumably older) audience to tell their children and grandchildren to give birth to at least three children in order to combat the nation's shrinking population.

33 Figure taken from WEF's Global Gender Gap Report 2024. See note 31.

34 The abortion pill was legalised in France in 1988, in the United Kingdom in 1991, and in the United States in 2000.

35 The Japanese Constitution allows foreign residents

the right to political activism except where it is deemed inappropriate, such as those actions which have an influence on political decision-making.

36 Since 1982, over 100,000 people have applied for refugee status in Japan. Of these, less than one per cent have been accepted. In 2023, 13,823 people applied for refugee status, with 303 accepted. Figures taken from the Japan Association for Refugees at: refugee.or.jp

37 Estimates taken from the MMO Populations website available at: mmo-population.com

38 This opinion was also expressed by CW Nicol. Interviewed for the BBC television show, *Japanese Language and People*, he said that the Welsh are used to speaking two languages so he had 'no prejudice against learning another'.

39 Figures taken from international-schools-database.com

40 During the writing of this book, a new representative was appointed. Richard Koizumi is half Welsh and half Japanese, and Ursula has high hopes he will do a lot for Welsh–Japanese relations.

41 Just before going to press, Ursula told me that, at the embassy reception for King Charles' official birthday party, the new Welsh representative informed her he had instructed staff to put Red Dragon flags on all

Welsh products being displayed at the event, 'which was most satisfying,' she said.

42 As ChatGPT had only recently been launched, I had little idea what he was talking about. But on googling Llion, I discovered he is a software engineer and artificial intelligence researcher, and one of the eight creators of ChatGPT – the T part stands for Transformer. I later received an email from Llion informing me that he was leaving Google to cofound a startup, Sakana AI. His departure from Google made headlines in the *Washington Post*, the *Financial Times* and numerous other news outlets.

43 Y Wladfa was founded by nonconformist preacher, Michael D Jones.

List of Interviewees

>>**Nery Rees Asai** (from Cwrtnewydd, Ceredigion) studied sociology at the former University of Glamorgan (now the University of South Wales) before joining the JET Programme as an ALT in 2001. Posted to Maebashi in Gunma prefecture, she remained on the programme for three years before moving to work in kindergartens and international schools. She later obtained a master's degree in TESOL from the University of Birmingham, a doctorate in education through the University of Bath, and is currently an assistant professor at Meiji Gakuin University in Tōkyō. She met her Japanese husband on a Hokkaidō to Kagoshima bicycle ride, and they have one son who she is raising to be trilingual in Welsh, Japanese and English.

>>**Ursula Bartlett-Imadegawa** (from Llanrumney) travelled to Japan in the mid-seventies to work as an art teacher at Seishin International School, before moving to another international school, Seisen, later in her career. She married her lawyer husband, Yukihiro, in 1980, and they have two children. Ursula is a cofounder of the St David's Society Japan, and its long-time president. She enjoys kabuki performances and helped to establish audio commentaries in English at the Kabukiza, Tōkyō's most famous kabuki theatre.

>>Architect **Paul Baxter** (from Cricieth) graduated from the University of Cambridge and, in 1984, travelled to Tōkyō as a Monbushō (now Monbukagakushō, the department of Education, Culture, Sports, Science and Technology or MEXT) scholar. During the economically vibrant years of the eighties and early nineties, he worked for world-famous architect Takahiko Yanagisawa at his company TAK, helping to meld western influence with Japanese design. In 1998, he returned to London with his wife, Kumi, and their three children. He later became a partner at Nicholas Hare Architects.

>>Born in Swansea and raised in Cardiff, **Andrew Beak** eschewed an undergraduate degree in

astrophysics for the Japanese language, following it up with a master's degree in Chinese studies, both at the University of Leeds. At Leeds he met his first Japanese wife and moved with her to Yokohama but they divorced after he relocated to Kōbe city. He now lives in Takarazuka near Ōsaka, and works as a private English language teacher. He has recently started his own teaching business and subscription YouTube channel: BEK English @bekeikaiwa

>>Writer **Dan Bradley** (from Port Talbot) studied English at the University of Cambridge before joining the JET Programme in 2006. In Miyagi prefecture, he taught English for three years as an ALT before returning to the UK to work as a Japanese to English translator. His writing grew out of this love of language learning and translation, and his short fiction, essays, memoir and translations have appeared in *Ambit*, *Granta*, *New Welsh Review* and *The Guardian*.

>>**Joe Cairnes** (from Aberystwyth) graduated with a degree in biochemistry from the University of Liverpool and was sent to Shibata in Niigata prefecture as an ALT on the JET Programme in 2002. After three years, he moved to work in a laboratory, editing scientific reports for a contract drug research

company in Kagoshima, Kyūshū. After completing a distance-learning master's degree in environmental policy and design, he moved to Tōkyō to work in the carbon trading department of a Japanese bank. Taking ten months away to complete a master's degree in business administration at HKUST in Hong Kong, he returned to Tōkyō to work for Deutsche Bank. Now married, he has two children, Dylan and Rhiannon, and is building a house in Naka-Meguro in Tōkyō.

>>Raised in Penrhyndeudraeth, **Lily Crossley-Baxter** studied English literature at Sheffield University. In 2014, she moved to the village of Sakura in Mie prefecture to spend a year as an ALT on the JET Programme. Relocating to Tōkyō and seeking extra work, she became a freelance travel and culture writer. She has written for *BBC Travel*, *Time Out* (US), *The Telegraph*, the *Daily Beast*, the *Japan Times* and many other publications. Lily's uncle is architect Paul Baxter.

>>In 2018, with a degree in Japanese from the University of Edinburgh, **Bethany Jo Cummings** (from Porthcawl) 'escaped' to Japan on the JET Programme, working as CIR at the Ōta city ward office in Tōkyō. In 2019, she appeared on the Tōkyō

Broadcasting System's variety show, *Made in Japan,* in which she and a camera crew visited her family in Porthcawl. She now works for ByteDance as a content quality assurance analyst for TikTok.

>>Born in Manchester but raised in north Wales, **Bet Davies** graduated with a master's degree in Welsh literature and language from the University of Wales, Aberystwyth (now Aberystwyth University). In 1973, she joined the Welsh Tourist Board, rising to become head of public relations. She was later headhunted by the now defunct Welsh Development Agency, an organisation tasked with attracting business development and investment to a Wales in economic strife. For her work promoting bilateral ties between Wales and Japan, Bet received the Japan Foreign Minister's Special Commendation in 2002. Bet supplied me with a lot of information on Japanese businesses in Wales.

>>**Clive Davies** (from Llangadog) met his Japanese wife at a gig in London and followed her back to Japan in 1999. He works as a gaitare, a foreign talent, appearing in small roles and as an extra in Japanese commercials, television shows and movies. A cult movie buff since childhood he is also the author of

Spinegrinder: The Movies Most Critics Won't Write About (Head Press). He discusses cult movies on his YouTube channel: davies clive @ychyfis

>>**Carolyn De Vishlin** (from Newport) has an undergraduate degree in English literature and religious studies from the University of Wales, Newport, a master's degree in politics and international relations from the University of Wales, Trinity Saint David, an MSC in research methods and a doctorate – via distance learning – in policy sciences from Nottingham Trent. Carolyn had always dreamed of working for the diplomatic service but, when told she lacked experience and a unique language, she decided to study Japanese and, in 2002, moved to Japan to work for the NOVA English conversation school. In 2007 she moved to Aichi University where she is now a tenured assistant professor. She met and married her Canadian husband in Japan. Their first child, Gryffyn, died shortly after birth. Their second, Fynyx, was born in 2016.

>>**Peredur (Pred) Evans** (from Llandysul) studied French at the University of Oxford before moving to Japan as an ALT on the JET Programme in 1997. He

was posted to the northern city of Sendai and taught in junior high schools for three years. After a brief spell studying Japanese at Kyōto University of Foreign Studies, he began working for the British Council in Tōkyō, developing links between Japanese and British schools. In 2006, Pred (and his Japanese wife, Asami) moved with the British Council to Trinidad and Tobago, and then to the Bangkok office as Director of Programmes in 2008. He is now a lecturer at Thammasat University and is studying for his doctorate.

>>**Gerald Gallivan** (from Cardiff) loves to travel. After realising that his undergraduate degree in archaeology from Lampeter (now the University of Wales Trinity St David) was going to lead to a lifetime of low pay and volunteer work, he did a postgraduate diploma in English with TEFL. In 2014, he moved to Japan to work for the Peppy Kids Club English conversation school. Four years later, he moved to the Cambridge English school in Sendai, Miyagi prefecture. On weekends, he covers up his extensive tattoos and goes hiking.

>>**Eluned Gramich** (from Haverfordwest) has always wanted to be a writer. Following an undergraduate degree in English literature from the University of

Oxford and a master's degree in creative writing from the University of East Anglia, she was accepted as a Daiwa scholar in 2012 and spent two years studying Japanese in Tōkyō. Her account of a homestay in Hokkaidō, *Woman Who Brings the Rain* (New Welsh Rarebyte, 2015 [eBook], 2016 [print]), won the New Welsh Writing Awards 2015 WWF Cymru Prize for Writing on Nature and the Environment and was shortlisted for the Wales Book of the Year in 2016. Now with a doctorate from Aberystwyth University, Eluned works as a librarian at the National Library of Wales and has published two further books, *Sleep Training* (The Ghastling, 2020) and *Windstill* (Honno, 2022).

>>A love for the Japanese band, The Mad Capsule Markets, and an interest in the Japanese language led Skewen native **Abby Hall** to study for a two-year business degree at the University of Glamorgan (now the University of South Wales) followed by a four-year degree in business studies and Japanese from Cardiff University. Gutted to be turned down for the JET Programme (which she believes was because of her tattoos), Abby stayed on at Cardiff to do a master's degree in Japanese translation before moving to Japan in 2017 to work for the WinBe English language

conversation school, where she remained for one year. An internship at the British Embassy led to a move into social media for the 2019 Rugby World Cup and later for the Tōkyō 2020 Olympics and Paralympics Organising Committee. She now works as a freelance public relations consultant with clients including the Panasonic Wild Knights rugby team, Japan national rugby teams and World Rugby. Abby is on Twitter and Instagram @wasabihall

>>In 1990, **Chikako Hirono** spent six months teaching Japanese language and culture at St Nicholas Church in Wales School, Cardiff. Returning to Ōsaka and to her career as an advertising copywriter, she later cofounded the Kansai branch of the St David's Society Japan which runs cultural festivals, language classes, quizzes, movie nights and bake sales. She is a co-author of the Japanese-language book, *Sixty Chatpers to Get to Know Wales*. The Kansai St David's Society can be contacted at: kansaistdavidsocietyjapan.jimdofree.com or via Facebook.

In 2005, with a degree in politics and international relations from the University of Manchester, **Geraint Howells** (from Bangor) sought adventure and moved to Japan to work for Shane English School in Saitama.

Two years later, he returned home fluent in Japanese and was hired by Nintendo in Frankfurt where he trained as a video game localiser, translating and adapting Japanese games for the English-speaking market. After joining Shloc, a community of freelance localisers, he now works from home in Anglesey.

>>**Catharine Huws Nagashima** (from Anglesey) studied geography at the University of Wales, Aberystwyth, before moving to Greece to work for the father of ekistics, Constantinos A Doxiadis. She met her Japanese husband, Kōichi, there at the Center of Ekistics. They moved to Japan in 1965 and settled in the seaside city of Zushi in an old family bessō (summer house), where they raised six children. Catharine is one of the cofounders of the St David's Society Japan and is the club's historian.

>>Born in 1937 in Cydweli, **Doris Gertrude 'Rose' Iwata** (née Allen) trained as a religious studies teacher before deciding to accompany her friend to a school in Australia in 1960. When they stopped off in Japan, Rose was recruited as a primary school teacher by Seisen International School. She married Masahiko in 1963 and they had three children. The couple established a despatch temping agency, supplying

English language teachers to Japanese schools. Rose and Masa are two of the founder members of the St David's Society Japan, and are credited with bringing the first Welsh flag to the country. Rose died in 2024.

>>**Gareth Jenkins** began learning Japanese at his Aberystwyth secondary school when Ceredigion county employed a Japanese teacher. At sixteen, he did a two-week homestay in the Japanese town of Kaya, funded by the Aberystwyth–Kaya Friendship Association, a group started with the support of Frank Evans, who had been a prisoner of war in Japan during the Second World War. Gareth went on to study business studies with Japanese at Cardiff University before joining the JET Programme in 2001, firstly as an ALT, and then as a CIR. While on the programme, he married his Japanese wife. They have two children and live in Ōmuta, Fukuoka prefecture on the island of Kyūshū, where Gareth works as a medical interpreter at a local hospital.

>>With a degree in botany and zoology from the University of Bristol, and a PGCE in primary education from Swansea University, **Eddy Jones** (from Cardiff) moved to Japan to work at the British School in Tōkyō in 1986. After returning to the UK to

study for a master's degree in advanced Japanese from Sheffield University, he moved back to Japan as a CIR on the JET Programme and was posted to Nagano prefecture where he became close friends with CW Nicol. He later returned to the international school system where he has worked ever since, most recently in Nagoya.

>>**Mike Kettle** (from Cilycwm) studied psychology and philosophy at Swansea University. After completing a one-month TEFL course in Prague, in 2007 he moved to Japan with the NOVA English conversation school for six months until they went bankrupt. Returning to Wales, he completed a master's degree in marketing and management, again from Swansea, after which he taught in an English private school, worked in a homeless shelter, completed two stints teaching in Saudi Arabia, and two more in Japan before taking a job at British Hills in Fukushima. He now works as a course coordinator for sophomore English at Kanda University of International Studies in Tōkyō.

>>**Takeshi Koike** knew nothing about Wales before his university, Ōbirin, sent him to Lampeter on a one-year study abroad programme in 1992. But he

enjoyed learning Welsh, particularly Welsh songs and poetry. With a master's degree and a doctorate in English linguistics from Dokkyō University, he now teaches Welsh at Daitō Bunka University in Tōkyō. He is a co-author of several Japanese-language books on Wales including *Basics of the Welsh Language*, and he hopes to write a Welsh–Japanese dictionary and grammar book before he retires.

>>**John Llywelyn** learned to ski on the dry ski slopes of Llandudno. After five years in the merchant navy, he became a ski instructor and moved to Niseko, Hokkaidō in 2019. He and his Japanese wife are refurbishing an akiya across the road from Jac Phillips, with whom he often works. In the summer, he takes tourists white water rafting.

>>**Geraint M** (from the Rhondda Valley) studied French and Spanish at the University of the West of England before working in publishing and television in London, Paris and New York. Having married in the USA, he moved to Tōkyō in 2016, when his Japanese husband relocated to his firm's Tōkyō office. As Japan does not recognise same-sex marriage for Japanese citizens, Geraint could only enter Japan on a study visa and had to attend a Japanese language school

for two years. He now works as an English language copywriter at the same company as his husband.

>>**Andy Moore** (from Newport) studied biological sciences at Lancaster University. He moved to Japan in 1998 as an ALT on the JET Programme and stayed for two years in Wakayama before coming back to the UK and working at a travel agency. He returned to Japan in 2006 to work for one of the major chain English schools. He now lives in Tōkyō and works as a corporate trainer for Japanese companies.

>>Six feet tall and eighteen stone, **Jaime Morrish** is an ex-bouncer and jiu jitsu instructor from Aberdare. With an undergraduate degree in applied linguistics and TEFL from Swansea University, in 2008 Jaime moved to Gifu prefecture as an ALT on the JET Programme. An exponent of martial arts since the age of two, he added jūdō, aikidō and karate to his skill set. In 2012, he returned briefly to Swansea to complete a master's degree in TEFL and a Certificate in English Language Teaching to Adults (CELTA). He is now an associate professor at Sugiyama Jogakuen University and runs a class in jiu jitsu in the city of Nagoya. Married with one daughter, he is currently completing his doctorate (on the efficacy of the JET Programme).

>>**Richard Mort** studied French and German at the University of Manchester and worked for nearly two decades in Tōkyō as a freelance translator before moving his family to Germany in 2020, in order to find better services for one of his two sons, who has special needs. In 2006, **Neil and Annie Mort**, Richard's father and stepmother, visited his son in Japan and were given a tour of Afan no Mori forest by the environmentalist, CW Nicol.

>>A fan of British movies, Tōkyō-native **Yūko Nakauchi** first learned about Wales when she saw the film *Un Nos Ola' Leuad*. Dropping out of her Japanese university, she moved to Lampeter to study for a Welsh-medium degree in Welsh theatre and television studies from Aberystwyth University. After graduation, she returned to Tōkyō and became a disc jockey for InterFM but, following the Tōhoku Earthquake of 2011, she and her Swedish husband relocated to his home country. She now works with the Kansai branch of the St David's Society Japan, emceeing cultural events and, through her website (www.boredakikaku.com), provides a bridge between Wales and Japan. This includes a Japanese-language podcast in which she discusses everyday Welsh culture, kotsu kotsu (step by step).

>>With an undergraduate degree in politics and anthropology from the University of Manchester, **Richard O'Shea** (from Neath) moved to China for a year in 2007, then to Japan for a brief, three-month job for Westgate (a teacher despatch company) during which time he met his future wife. They married in 2012, own a house in Arakawa in downtown Tōkyō, and have three children. After studying for a master's degree in TESOL by distance learning from the University of Derby, Richard moved to Nihon University School of Medicine where he teaches in the same faculty as Tim Pelham Williams. A fan of all sports, he plays second row for the Tōkyō Gaijin rugby team.

>>**Jac Phillips** (from Llanharan) is a qualified backcountry skiing guide, wilderness first responder and expert in avalanche risk management. He spent several years working as a ski instructor in Europe and New Zealand before he and wife, Makenzie, set up a bespoke ski and backcountry exploration company, Summit, in Hokkaidō in 2020. They live and work in the town of Furano where they are refurbishing an akiya. They can be contacted at: www.summitski.jp

>>**Joanne Tanaka** (née Davies) has an economics degree from the Open University but had always

wanted to learn a language. She chose Japanese because it looked cool. During a three-week holiday in Japan in April 2011, she met her husband, Yoshi. (They'd previously chatted online.) She moved back to Japan in 2013 on a working visa and they married a year later. They have one daughter and live in Saitama. Joanne works at an English-environment nursery preschool in Saitama prefecture just outside Tōkyō.

>>In 2000, after graduating with a degree in tourism management and business from the University of Gloucestershire, **Simon Whalley** (from Aberdare) backpacked around Asia before arriving in Japan in 2003 and opening a bar on the northern island of Hokkaidō. Seeking warmth and a new career, he gained a master's degree in Teaching English to Speakers of Other Languages (TESOL) from Sheffield Hallam University and now works for the Hiroshima Global Academy on the island of Ōsakikamijima in the Seto Inland Sea. Having purchased land and an akiya, he, wife Kaori and son Indy are developing it as a vegan farm and hoping to attract tourism to the island.

>>**John Williams** (from Llantrisant) is an award-winning film writer, director and producer. A graduate

of Trinity College, Cambridge, John moved to Japan in 1988 to teach English at an English conversation school in Nagoya, and became involved in the city's vibrant 8mm film culture. As writer/director, his Japanese-language films include *Firefly Dreams* (2001), *Starfish Hotel* (2006), *Sado Tempest* (2013) and *The Trail* (2018). He teaches film production and translation at Sophia University in Tōkyō, and has just completed a feature film and documentary, both shot on Sado Island.

>>**Tim Pelham Williams** (from Brecon) studied philosophy at University College London before moving to Malaysia in 1993 and working in English-language publishing for a decade. After returning to the UK and taking a TEFL course, he moved to Japan in 2002 and taught at Shane English School. Liking language, he returned once again to the UK in 2007 and did a master's degree in applied linguistics and TESOL at Anglia Ruskin University. After teaching at Temple University in Tōkyō, he moved to Nihon University School of Medicine in 2018 where he teaches in the same faculty as Richard O'Shea.

Notes on Interviews, Japanese Spellings and Statistics

My interviews have been lightly edited, cutting out the 'umms', 'errs' and 'you knows', with some small additional stylistic changes made during the publication process. I have made grammatical changes where transcription from spoken to written English would have rendered the sentence incomprehensible. As they reminisced, many of the speakers talked a lot in the present tense, even when recalling the past. Where necessary, I have put past events back in the past. Sometimes, speakers digressed or changed subject, or else we moved to another topic and returned to it later in a subsequent interview. Where this has occurred, I have moved sentences or paragraphs to improve the flow of the story. All excerpts have been factchecked by the interviewees.

Japanese words have been translated into rōmaji

(the roman alphabet) according to the Hepburn system. Macrons represent the long vowel sounds ō and ū, as in jūdō and Tōkyō, except where it comprises part of an English language name, such as the Tokyo American Club.

In Japan, personal names are generally spelled with the surnames first, followed by given names. To correspond with the Welsh names in this book, I have written them with the surnames last.

I have used the latest statistics available. In some case these are for the year 2020, which may be atypical due to lockdowns and other effects of the Covid pandemic.

Yen to Sterling exchange rates are correct as of July 2024.

Glossary and Abbreviations

abunai	dangerous, risky
Ainu	Japan's indigenous population whose native lands include Hokkaidō and surrounding islands
akiya	literally 'empty house': abandoned home, often rundown and left unoccupied for several years
amado	traditional sliding wooden shutters pulled across windows to protect a house against storms
ame	hard-boiled sugar candy which in its liquid state is moulded into various colourful shapes. As far back as the ninth century, ame was eaten at the emperor's court as medicine. Ame sweets became

	a children's favourite from the Edo Period (1603–1868).
anko	sweet red azuki bean paste eaten as a filling in buns and rice cakes, and as a topping on desserts
arubaito	from the German 'arbeit', arubaito is part-time work, usually done by a younger person. Older part-time workers do 'pāto'.
bessō	second home, sometimes a countryside retreat or seaside villa
bakufu	The Tokugawa bakufu (or shogunate) was the military government of Japan in power from 1603 to 1868. The head of the bakufu held the title of shōgun.
biwa	Japanese short-necked lute with a pear-shaped base, the biwa arrived from China in the seventh century
budōkan	martial arts training hall. The most famous of these is the Nippon Budōkan in Tōkyō which was built for the 1964 Tōkyō Olympics and has hosted many sports events

	and music concerts. The Beatles played there in 1964.
butō	style of dance theatre which emerged after the Second World War, incorporating elements of the grotesque and absurd
dai-fan	super fan or extreme enthusiast
daimyō	feudal warlords who held regional power under the shōgun
dan	ranks or levels attained by black belt martial arts practitioners
danran	literally 'sitting together in a group', danran evokes the warmth of a happy family get-together
dasai	tacky, lame, uncool
dō	'the path' or 'the way', it generally refers to the journey a student must follow to master their craft through discipline and continual practice
dōjō	place of learning such as a martial arts training hall where students can study dō'
doki doki	Japanese onomatopoeia for a beating heart due to fear, love or nervousness

eikaiwa	English language conversation school
eikyū-shūshoku	women's 'eternal employment', meaning marriage and children
furusato	one's hometown, generally the place from which your family originated, even if that was several generations ago
fusuma	opaque sliding panels, often highly decorated, which are used to divide rooms
gaijin	shortened form of 'gaikokujin' meaning 'foreign country person' or foreigner
gaitare	foreign talent or support artist. Generally refers to foreigners who work as television and movie extras.
gaman suru	to endure, be patient or show restraint
ganbaru/ganbatte	to persevere, do one's best, try one's hardest
ganko	stubborn or pig-headed
genkan	porch where shoes are removed before stepping up into the main house
genki	happy, upbeat, in good health

genmai	unpolished brown rice
gentō	'magic lanterns': shows incorporating colourful slide projections were popular before movies were introduced in the late nineteenth century
gi	(full form, dōgi), hard-wearing training uniform worn when practising martial arts, consisting of drawstring trousers and wrapover jacket tied with a belt; otherwise known as 'angry white pyjamas' in Robert Twigger's book of the same name
goemonburo	literally 'cauldron bath': metal bathtub heated from beneath by an open fire
hāfu	literally 'half', refers to people with one Japanese and one foreign parent
haigamai	semi-polished rice with bran removed but germ remaining
haiku	short seventeen syllable poem in a five, seven, five pattern
haikyo	literally 'ruins', haikyo enthusiasts are urban exploration ('urbex')

	fans who visit and photograph abandoned places, of which there are many in Japan
haka	family grave of stone or marble; the dead are cremated and placed on the family butsudan (shrine) at home, before their ashes are interred in the haka
hakama	traditional unisex culotte-style trousers often worn by martial artists
hanami	flower viewing: in spring, blossom-viewing parties are held under cherry trees; alcohol and karaoke are often involved
hanko	seal or stamp used in place of a signature, also known as 'inkan'
haragei	literally 'belly talk/art': encompasses ways of communicating (including facial expressions and silence) without direct speech
hassaku	Japanese citrus which looks like an orange, is the size of a grapefruit and tastes like a blend of the two

Hinamatsuri	Dolls' Day (or Girls' Day) is a traditional Shintō festival held in March. It is celebrated with a display of dolls of the imperial family.
homat	this brand of spacious luxury apartment appeared in the sixties specifically to attract foreign expatriates in Tōkyō. Built primarily in the upscale neighbourhoods of Hiroo, Azabu and Roppongi, they were designed for western families and included room for big American appliances and at least two bathrooms. Although the era of the homats ended with Japan's fall into recession, they remain popular with wealthy buyers.
hon	book
honban	the real take in the filming of a television or movie scene
horigotatsu	low table with a heater underneath. Japanese homes are generally poorly insulated and do not have central heating. Table

	heaters and hot carpets are used to heat the body but not the room.
igirisu	Britain/the UK: from 'inglês', a word learned from the Portuguese who arrived in Japan before the English. Although there is a word for Wales (ウェールズ or ue-ruzu), igirisu generally refers to anyone from the UK
ijime	bullying
ikebana	flower arranging
ishin-denshin	literally mind to mind communication: communicating through a passive form of mutual understanding
izakaya	pub or bar, emphasising good food to pair with alcohol
Japow	Japanese powder snow
jidaigeki	historical dramas generally set in the Edo period (1603–1868), before the arrival of western foreigners
jin	(or nin): means 'person'
jinbei	cool cotton loungewear worn in the summer mostly by men and

	children (women wear yukata), comprising loose wrapover top and shorts
jitsuka	practitioner of jiu jitsu
jiu jitsu	literally the 'gentle art': originally a fighting discipline practised by the samurai class, modern jiu jitsu is understood to be the Brazilian style
jizō	small stone statues of guardian deities found at temples, graveyards and the side of roads, said to protect travellers and children, including the souls of aborted foetuses and children who have died young. They can often be seen wearing knitted bibs and hats, in red to ward off evil.
JLPT	the Japanese Language Proficiency Test is administered by the Japan Foundation and offered in Levels N5 (beginner) to N1 (advanced). N2 is generally required for Japanese university entrance or for working in Japanese companies.
jōyō kanji	kanji for regular use, as designated

	by the Ministry of Education, Culture, Sports, Science and Technology (MEXT); they currently number 2,136
jūminhyō	residence record or certificate, legally required to access services such as a bank account or national health insurance
juku	cram school offering private lessons, often in preparation for school or university entrance examinations. Students attend juku after the regular school day or at weekends.
kabuki	classical theatre known for its use of glittering costumes, bright expressive stage makeup and exaggerated movements. The most famous theatre for kabuki is the Kabukiza in Tōkyō.
kaijū	monster such as Godzilla or Mothra
kakkoii	cool, stylish, good-looking
kanji	alphabet of ideograms of Chinese origin, one of the three writing systems used in Japan

kanji kentei	twelve-level kanji aptitude test, usually for school-age students
karōshi	literally 'overwork death'
kawaii	cute
kenchō	prefectural office where local government staff are based
kissaten	traditional café
kōban	small neighbourhood police office
koinobori	giant carp windsocks flown outside Japanese homes to celebrate the public holiday Children's Day (formerly Boys' Day) in May; carp represent strength and courage
kominka	(also, minka): wooden, often thatched, house built using traditional techniques
kone	from 'connections', kone are vital to obtaining job offers and advancement
kotatsu	low table with heater underneath to warm the legs
kumi	group
kuyashii	regrettable or frustrating
kyū	rank or level attained by martial

	arts practitioners below the level of black belt
ma	negative space
machizukuri	town planning
mamachari	sturdy bicycle used by mothers to ferry their children around
matsuri	summer festival which often ends with evening fireworks
'Meshi! Furo! Neru!'	'Food! Bath! Bed!'
mie	a stylised pose and facial expression in kabuki, signifying a key moment in the drama
mikan	satsuma or clementine orange
minshuku	traditional family-owned bed and breakfast-style guest house
mochi	glutinous rice cake
moe	literally a 'bud', meaning a cute, innocent girl
moji	single character from one of the three alphabets
MEXT	(also, Monbukagakushō, previously Monbushō): Ministry of Education, Culture, Sports, Science and Technology
mono no aware	the impermanence of all things
natsukashii	bitter-sweet feeling of nostalgia

	(the Welsh hiraeth is the closest word)
nattō	fermented bean curd, healthy but pungent
nemawashi	preparing the ground by informally lobbying or eliciting feedback
nengajō	New Year's greeting card
nepo (baby)	(English word), short for nepotism: job or role obtained through family connections
nigedasu	to escape or run away
nomunication	communicating through after-hours drinking, often with clients or co-workers
nori	dried seaweed
obi	wide sash or belt worn with traditional clothing and martial arts wear
ofuro	bathtub
okazu	side dishes of meat, fish, tōfu or vegetables which accompany rice
okonomiyaki	similar to pizza: mixture of vegetables and meat fried on a table hotplate
okusan	wife, literally 'Mrs Interior'

omiyage	souvenir: it is customary to bring back gifts from holidays and business trips for family, friends and office colleagues
onsen	natural hot springs
ōsōji	big clean-up which takes place every new year in Japanese homes
otaku	anorak or nerd
oyaji	father or old man
pasa pasa	dry, lacking in moisture
pika pika	polished, shiny, glistening
pinku	erotic, soft porn movies
pork barrel money	(English word) government spending on local projects in order to gain political favour
ryokan	traditional inn or hotel
ryū	style, form or system
saigen	variety shows in which news events are reenacted
sakoku	period between 1639 and 1853 when Japan was closed to most of the outside world, particularly westerners, except the Dutch
sensei	suffix attached to the names of teachers and other experts in their field

Setsubun	bean-throwing ceremony held the day before the beginning of spring
Shichigosan	'Seven, Five, Three' festival in which children of those ages are dressed up and taken to their local shrine
shima (or jima)	island
Shintō	the 'Way of the Gods': national belief system
shōganai	it can't be helped, it is what it is
shōgun	military ruler and head of the bakufu or military government
shōchū	traditional liquor
shōji	sliding screen with wooden lattice frames and paper panels. Unlike fusuma, shōji are translucent and therefore used at windows or in rooms which require natural light.
shōjin ryōri	traditional Buddhist 'devotion' cuisine which is mostly vegetarian or vegan
soroban	abacus
sunameri	finless porpoise
sugoi	'Wow! Amazing!' Or alternatively, 'Horrible! Terrible!' It depends on the context.

sukiya	(or sukiya-zukuri), single-storey structure of thick beams and solid columns supporting an ornately tiled roof, based on traditional teahouse design
tabehōdai	all you can eat
tarento	television personality who may – or may not – have acting and singing skills
tatami	rectangle of rush matting, measuring 0.9 by 1.8 metres (three feet by six feet) which equals one jō. Rooms are often measured by the number of mats they can fit.
tokonoma	alcove in which a hanging scroll or flower arrangement is displayed
tonkatsu	deep-fried breaded pork cutlet
tsubo	unit of measurement. 1 tsubo = 3.3 square metres. It is twice the size of a jō which is the measurement of one tatami mat. One square kilometre = 30.25 tsubo.
ukiyo-e	literally, 'pictures of the floating world', depicting characters and scenes of daily life – and nightlife

umeshu	plum liqueur
wa	combining the concepts of harmony, unity and conformity, generally within a social group or society
Yakuza	gangsters, members of organised crime syndicates
yukata	light summer kimono
'Yūyake Koyake'	literally 'sunrise, sunset': song that is heard across Japan in the evenings, as it is played daily as a test of the Japan emergency tannoy system (see Chapter Two for the words).

Acknowledgements

'The Transplantable Roots of Catharine Huws Nagashima' was originally published by New Welsh Review/Reader (NWR 124, autumn 2020), following its being awarded first prize in the New Welsh Writing Awards 2020 Rheidol Prize for Prose with a Welsh Theme or Setting, judged by Gwen Davies. 'Powder to the People!' was previewed in *New Welsh Review* 136 (winter 2024). The author kindly acknowledges the generous support of the Daiwa Anglo-Japanese Foundation in funding her subsequent journey to Japan after the pandemic, enabling her to complete this book. Thanks also to all the interviewees.

Praise

'Fantastic group portrait of people and place' Nick Bradley, author of *The Cat and the City*

'This is a pitch-perfect series of dispatches from Japan, each chapter an invitation into a different life – not to mention the fascinating interludes that intersperse each of the interviews. Enlightening and engaging at every turn.' Andrew Kenrick, founding- and co-editor, *Hinterland*

Special Thanks

Special thanks are due from the publishers to Richard Powell, our philanthropic sponsor in the New Welsh Writing Awards manuscript prize, which was set up by *New Welsh Review* in 2015, and has greatly benefitted from ongoing generous annual support since 2019, making possible publication of this book and titles by Jasmine Donahaye, Peter Goulding, Eluned Gramich and many others.

PARTHIAN A CARNIVAL OF VOICES